FEDERAL SUITABILITY
AND
SECURITY CLEARANCES

ISSUE MITIGATION HANDBOOK

William H. Henderson

Last Post Publishing
Pacific Grove, California

2

Published by
Last Post Publishing
1120 Forest Avenue, PMB 274
Pacific Grove, CA 93950
editor@LastPostPublishing.com
http://LastPostPublishing.com

Printed in the United States of America

ISBN: 978-0-9793466-3-7
LCCN: 2011902983
Library of Congress subject heading:
Security clearances—United States—Handbooks, manuals, etc.
Includes bibliographical references and index.

LACK OF TRANSPARENCY

"Most agencies make little effort to disseminate any information regarding the personnel security process to applicants, contractors, and employees subject to investigation or reinvestigation. These individuals thus remain largely uninformed with respect to basic, unclassified information concerning the overall process, the length of time it takes, the standards applied, and their own status. . . . In addition, those subjected to the clearance process often do not understand it. Some assume, for example, that they will be denied a clearance for reasons that are not actually grounds for rejection."

Report of the Commission on Protecting and Reducing Government Secrecy (Washington, DC: Government Printing Office, 1997)

ABOUT THE AUTHOR

William Henderson is a retired federal investigator who worked as a field agent and supervisor for the Defense Investigative Service (DIS) and its successor organizations (Defense Security Service—DSS and Federal Investigative Services Division of the Office of Personnel Management—OPM) for over 20 years. He was previously an Army Counterintelligence Agent and a security manager at the Satellite Control Facilities Operation of Ford Aerospace & Communications Corporation.

He wrote his first personnel security investigation report in 1970 for the U.S. Army. His assignments included CI Special Operations in Japan and Korea, Source Administration in Vietnam, CI field office duty in Chicago, tactical CI operations in Colorado Springs, and a position on the J2 staff at CINCLANT.

While with DIS, DSS and OPM, he held assignments as a Special Agent, Senior Resident Agent, and Assistant Special Agent-in-Charge. His duty station was in Monterey, California where he conducted numerous security investigations of former Soviet Bloc émigrés teaching at the Defense Language Institute. He conducted background investigations in major metropolitan areas throughout the United States.

In June 2007 he wrote and published, *Security Clearance Manual*, the first book of its kind to explain the security clearance process and show applicants how to avoid the detours and roadblocks that normally delay a clearance application from a speedy and successfully conclusion. Since then he has published numerous articles on federal personnel security issues and processing. He has been interviewed and quoted in newspapers and radio programs. He also provides consulting services to individual and corporate clients.

CONTENTS

6

PART I

FEDERAL CLEARANCE

PROCESSING

CHAPTER 1

INTRODUCTION TO PART I

The three most commonly asked questions about federal clearances are:

1. *How do I get a clearance?*
2. *What is my chance of getting a clearance?*
3. *How long will it take?*

The most commonly unasked question is:

What can I do to overcome potentially disqualifying information and avoid the normal delays associated with clearance processing?

To apply for a federal clearance you must be sponsored by a federal agency or a federal contractor for a position that requires a clearance. In order to be sponsored you must be employed by or have an employment relationship with the federal agency or contractor. Most employment relationships are established by a "Conditional Offer of Employment—COE." Basically the COE is a written commitment for employment by the prospective employer indicating that employment shall commence after the clearance is granted. The employment relationship is established when the applicant accepts the offer in writing.

The second two questions are tied together for applicants whose cases contain unfavorable security or suitability information. Only about 1% of applicants are formally denied a security clearance.[1] A

---

[1] There are no statistical data available on the denial rates for federal employment suitability, fitness, or credentialing determinations.

much larger percentage of applicants fail to receive a security clearance, because they drop out of the process before a final clearance determination is made. The most common reasons this occurs are:

1. The COE was contingent on receiving an interim clearance and an interim clearance was not granted due to unfavorable information in the applicant's clearance application form.

2. The COE or actual employment was contingent on receiving a final clearance, but the process took longer than the prospective employer or applicant was willing to wait, resulting in the withdrawal of the clearance request.

In both cases the process terminates without a final clearance determination. Failure to receive an interim clearance is the more prevalent of the two situations. In recent years the Defense Industrial Security Clearance Office (DISCO), which is a Central Clearance Facility and part of the Defense Security Service (DSS), declined to grant interim security clearances to 20 to 30% of applicants. So, for many people who apply for a clearance the more important questions are:

• How do I improve my chance of receiving an interim clearance?

• How long will it take for me to receive a final clearance?

• What can I do to reduce the time it takes, so that I can remain a candidate until a final decision is made?

This book was written for prospective clearance applicants whose personal histories contain unfavorable security or suitability information. It shows how security and suitability issues are mitigated at the earliest possible stage of the clearance process thereby improving the chance of receiving a clearance before clearance sponsorship is withdrawn. The book addresses the 3 major Federal Personnel Security Programs:

• National Security Clearances

• Federal Employment Suitability and Fitness Determinations

• Homeland Security Presidential Directive 12 (HSPD-12) Credentialing

All 3 programs have similar eligibility criteria and processes, but there are differences. This book covers issues and issue mitigation[2] of standard eligibility criteria for all 3 programs. Eligibility criteria for national security clearances[3] are the most comprehensive, so security clearance processing procedures and data are used to explain basic concepts and their relationship to receiving a clearance. Over 90% of all credentialing, suitability, fitness, and security clearance investigations for the federal government are conducted by the Federal Investigative Services Division (FISD) of the Office of Personnel Management (OPM); however, these investigations are adjudicated by the federal agencies that request the investigations from OPM. Approximately 21 federal agencies conduct their own investigations, but they all adhere to the same investigative standards used by OPM.

DISCO processes the vast majority of security clearances for federal contractor personnel.[4] Administratively the security clearance adjudication process at DISCO is slightly different from other federal adjudicative facilities, but case outcomes are statistically similar at all facilities.

DISCO receives completed security clearance investigations from OPM. DISCO reviews the investigations, but they can only grant security clearances; they are not authorized to deny or revoke security clearances. If derogatory information in a case reaches a certain threshold, it must be referred from DISCO to the Defense Office of Hearings and Appeals (DOHA) for adjudication. The table on the next page shows the progression of completed investigations once they are received at DISCO and work their way through the adjudicative process. Cases containing the most serious derogatory information, typically go through 4 levels of adjudicative review (not including the appeal process) before a final decision is made to deny or revoke a clearance, but the granting of a clearance can occur at the 1st level or at any of the subsequent review levels.

---

[2] Throughout this book the term, "mitigation," is used to encompass information that mitigates, rebuts, extenuates, or explains potentially disqualifying security or suitability issues.

[3] Throughout this book the term, "security clearance," is used to mean "national security clearance;" the type of clearance required for access to classified national security information.

[4] DISCO processes more than 150,000 security clearances each year for Department of Defense contractors and contractors of 23 other federal agencies. These are referred to as industrial cases.

Typical Distribution of DISCO/DOHA Case Outcomes

Completed investigations received by DISCO	150,000
Clearances granted by DISCO	142,000
Cases referred from DISCO to DOHA	8,000
Clearances granted by DOHA staff adjudicators	5,800
Statement of Reasons (SOR)[5] issued by DOHA	2,200
Clearances denied or revoked due to no response to SOR	500
SOR responses received by DOHA	1,700
Clearances granted by DOHA after review of SOR response	400
Cases referred to DOHA Administrative Judges	1,300
Clearances granted by DOHA Administrative Judges	450
Clearances denied or revoked by DOHA Administrative Judges	850

Source: April 2010 Defense Industrial Security Clearance Office response to a Freedom of Information Act request.

Like other adjudicative facilities only about 1% (roughly 1,350 cases—the sum of 500 + 850) of the approximately 150,000 completed investigations received by DISCO each year result in security clearance denials or revocations.

While 99% may seem like a very large percentage of security clearance approvals, it overstates the true percentage of people who

---

[5] An SOR is a written notification of why a preliminary determination to deny or revoke a security clearance was made.

are likely to be eligible for a security clearance. An unknown number of people choose not to apply for positions that require a clearance, because they believe there are factors in their life that would inevitably result in a clearance denial. Some potential applicants fail to receive sponsorship because they are screened out of the process by prospective employers. And as explained earlier, many are not hired because they fail to receive an interim clearance required for the job by the prospective employer due to derogatory information. And others drop out of the process because major derogatory information causes the process to continue for an unacceptable period of time. Anecdotal information suggests that approval rates for suitability, fitness, and credentialing determinations are lower than for security clearances.

For applicants whose cases contain no derogatory information or only minor derogatory information, interim clearances can be granted a few days after the clearance application is submitted. In the past most final clearance delays were due to investigative backlog. Today the length of time it takes to get a final security clearance decision usually depends more on the level of adjudicative review at which the decision is made. Applicants who receive interim security clearances usually receive their final security clearances in less than the overall average time of 86 days (about 133 days for employment suitability). This is because their clearances are usually granted by the first-level adjudicator.

For applicants whose cases contain moderate to major derogatory information, the earlier they are able to effectively articulate all the mitigating factors directly related to the issues present in their cases (and in some cases the positive whole-person factors), the greater the probability that they will be granted a clearance at one of the earlier stages of adjudication. Cases containing very serious/complex issues and those than can only be mitigated by positive "whole person" factors are usually decided by third- or fourth-level adjudicators and take the longest amount of time. Average processing times do not apply to applicants with moderate to major security/suitability issues. They should look at other factors presented in this book, as well as the total range of processing times, which can be as little as 1 month to more than a year. (See Chapter 3 for more information on clearance processing times.)

CHAPTER 2

FEDERAL PERSONNEL SECURITY PROGRAMS

People often use the generic term, "security clearance," when referring to any government determination regarding an individual's eligibility for access to protected information, facilities, or computer systems, as well as suitability or fitness for federal employment. There are 3 major federal personnel security programs and each has its own distinct process. All 3 programs have provisions for an interim eligibility authorization pending the completion of a background investigation and a final eligibility determination. All 3 programs require:

- sponsorship by a federal agency or federal contractor,
- submission of application forms and fingerprints,
- investigation of the applicant's background, and
- favorable adjudication of the investigation.

The government is in the process of aligning these 3 programs under a single unified structure (see Executive Order 13467), but each program currently has its own standards and processes that are separate and distinct from each other. These programs are for:

- National Security Clearances,
- Employment Suitability or Fitness, and
- Homeland Security Presidential Directive 12 (HSPD-12) Credentialing.

It is possible to be subject to any combination of these 3 programs. Depending on the timing and sequence in which the programs are encountered, an applicant could submit 3 different application forms with fingerprints, undergo 3 different background investigations, and have each of the 3 investigations adjudicated separately under different standards.

National Security Clearances are governed by Executive Order 12968 and exist for the purpose of safeguarding classified national security information. Under this program federal employee and federal contractor positions are designated as "non-sensitive," "non-critical sensitive," "critical sensitive," and "special sensitive." Generally position sensitivity designations are directly related to the level of classified national security information for which access is needed (none, Confidential[6]/Secret, Top Secret, or Sensitive Compartmented Information and certain other Special Access Programs). Some positions may be designated as non-critical sensitive or critical sensitive, even though actual access to classified national security information is not required. Applicants must submit a Standard Form 86—SF86 (Questionnaire for National Security Positions) and undergo one of the following types of background investigations for an initial clearance:

- National Agency Check[7] with Law and Credit Checks (NACLC) for military and contractor Confidential and Secret clearances, as well as contractor Department of Energy (DOE) "L" access authorizations.

- Access National Agency Check with Inquiries (ANACI) for federal employee Confidential clearances, Secret clearances, and DOE "L" access authorizations.

---

[6] As a practical matter Confidential clearances are rarely issued anymore. This is because the investigative requirements for Confidential clearances are exactly the same as Secret clearances. It is much more practical to issue Secret clearances to people who general only require access to Confidential information, but who may occasionally require access to Secret information. Properly applied need-to-know restrictions are relied upon to limit a person's access to only the classified information that is required to do his/her job.

[7] A National Agency Check (NAC) is a standard component of all federal background investigations. A complete description of an NAC is provided at Chapter 4—Investigations.

- Single Scope Background Investigation (SSBI) for Top Secret clearances and DOE "Q" access authorizations, as well as access eligibility for Sensitive Compartmented Information (SCI) and certain other Special Access Programs (SAP).

Some SCI and SAPs have an additional requirement of a polygraph examination. The granting or denying of a security clearance is based on the criteria contained in the *"Adjudicative Guidelines for Determining Eligibility for Access to Classified Information."* SCI eligibility has additional standards listed in Intelligence Community Directive Number 704. There may be program-specific requirements for other SAP eligibility. E.O. 12968 requires agencies to provide individuals review and appeal rights for security clearance denials and revocations, but these rights do not apply to interim clearances. After the granting of a security clearance, reinvestigations are required at periodic intervals (5 years for Top Secret, 10 years for Secret, and 15 years for Confidential). Federal agencies are conditionally required to reciprocally accept security clearances granted by other federal agencies.

Employment Suitability is governed by Executive Order 10450 and Title 5, Code of Federal Regulations, Part 731 (5 CFR Part 731) and was established to insure that the selection and retention of federal employees are clearly consistent with the interests of the national security and to maintain the integrity or efficiency of federal service. The term, *Employment Suitability*, and the provisions of 5 CFR Part 731 apply primarily to federal "competitive service" appointments. These positions are required to be designated as low, moderate, or high risk, depending on the position's potential for adverse impact to the efficiency or integrity of federal service. *"Positions at the high or moderate risk levels would normally be designated as 'Public Trust' positions. Such positions may involve policy making, major program responsibility, public safety and health, law enforcement duties, fiduciary responsibilities or other duties demanding a significant degree of public trust, and positions involving access to or operation or control of financial records, with a significant risk for causing damage or realizing personal gain."* Applicants are required to submit either a Standard Form 85—SF85 (Questionnaire for Non-Sensitive Positions) or Standard Form 85P—SF85P (Questionnaire for Public Trust Positions). They may also be required to submit a Standard Form 85PS—SF85PS (Supplement Questionnaire for Selected

Positions) and/or an Optional Form 306 (Declaration for Federal Employment). These forms are used to conduct one of the following background investigations:

- National Agency Check with Inquiries (NACI) for Low Risk positions;

- Moderate Risk Background Investigation (MBI)[8] for Moderate Risk positions;

- Background Investigation (BI) for High Risk positions.

The criteria for making employment suitability determinations are contained in 5 CFR Part 731, §731.202 (5 CFR 731.202). Competitive Service applicants and employees are entitled review and appeals rights for any adverse suitability determination. Executive Order 13488 created a requirement that all personnel occupying Public Trust positions be subject to period reinvestigations and gave OPM authority to establish standards for such reinvestigations; however, OPM has not yet established the standards. The only current requirements for reinvestigations of personnel occupying Public Trust positions are those established by individual agencies pursuant to the Federal Information Security Management Act of 2002 (Title III of E-Government Act) and the White House Office of Management and Budget (OMB) Circular No. A–130. Federal agencies are conditionally required to reciprocally accept favorable employment suitability determinations made by other federal agencies.

Additionally, agencies may require job candidates to successfully pass a drug screening test, medical exam, psychological exam, and/or polygraph exam.

Employment Fitness is a term used for making hiring or retention decisions for federal "excepted service" and temporary positions at all risk levels and Public Trust determinations for contractor positions. Although, 5 CFR Part 731 applies primarily to "competitive service" positions; federal agencies are encourage to apply its provisions to excepted service[9], temporary, and contractor positions. Federal agencies are also authorized to establish additional job-specific fitness criteria based on the nature of these positions. There must be a nexus

---

[8] Prior to October 2010, the MBI was known as a Minimum Background Investigation.
[9] Excepted Service appointments are governed by 5 CFR 302.203.

between the additional criteria, the agency's mission, and the position duties. Federal agencies generally follow the investigative requirements and adjudicative standards of 5 CFR Part 731 for employment fitness determinations; however, they rarely provide any review or appeal procedures for excepted service, temporary, or contractor personnel found to be unfit. Reinvestigation requirements are currently the same as for "competitive service" positions, and conditional reciprocity of fitness determinations is permitted under OPM "Guidance on Implementing Executive Order 13488."

Additionally, agencies may require a job candidate for an excepted service position to successfully pass a drug screening test, medical exam, psychological exam, and/or polygraph exam.

Homeland Security Presidential Directive 12 (HSPD-12), *"Policies for a Common Identification Standard for Federal Employees and Contractors,"* was issued in August 2004. It requires that personnel granted physical access to federally controlled facilities or logical access to federally controlled computer systems be issued standardized Personal Identity Verification (PIV) cards (also referred to as credentials). The purpose of HSPD-12 is to enhance security, increase government efficiency, reduce identity fraud, and eliminate potential for terrorist attacks. It was estimated that HSPD-12 compliant cards will be issued to 4.3 million federal employees and 1.2 million contractors. According to OMB as of March 2010 only 64% of PIV cards have been issued. Within the Department of Defense (DoD) PIV cards are known as "Common Access Cards" (CAC).

For most federal employees and some contractor employees HSPD-12 credentialing requirements and processing are nearly invisible, because the issuance of HSPD-12 PIV cards occurs almost automatically when there is a favorable security clearance, employment suitability, or employment fitness determination. For many contractor employees HSPD-12 is the only federal personnel security program they will encounter.

A National Agency Check with Inquiries (NACI) investigation is conducted based on the submission of either an SF85 or SF85P. The completed investigation is adjudicated using OPM's *"Final Credentialing Standards for Issuing Personal Identity Verification Cards under HSPD-12."* OMB Memorandum M-05-24 allows for the reciprocal acceptance of favorably adjudicated NACI and NACLC investigations (or better) previously conducted for HSPD-12 Credentialing, Employment Suitability, Employment Fitness, or National Security Clearance determinations as the basis for granting a PIV card without any further investigation or adjudication. This applies regardless of how long ago the last investigation took place, provided there has not been a break-in-service of more than 2 years since the last background investigation.

An applicant can be issued an interim PIV card as soon as favorable advance results from the FBI National Criminal History (fingerprint) Check portion of the NACI are received. Issuance of a final PIV card takes place after the favorable adjudication of the completed NACI investigation. Adjudication can be done by either the personnel or security office of the requesting government agency using OPM's *Final Credentialing Standards*. PIV cards are valid for no more than 5 years and must be surrendered or cancelled when access is no longer officially required. Currently there is no requirement for reinvestigations for the reissuance of PIV cards.

Federal Information Processing Standards Publication 201-1 created a requirement that agencies maintain appeal procedures for those who are denied PIV cards or whose PIV cards are revoked. OPM's *Final Credentialing Standards* provides additional information regarding the requirements for appeal procedures and reciprocity.

Individuals who require PIV cards and are also applying for employment with a federal agency or a federal contractor for jobs that are subject to employment suitability/fitness and/or national security clearance determinations are first processed in accordance with the procedures for those programs. A favorable determination under either program can then be used as the basis for issuing a PIV card without any further investigation or adjudication. An unfavorable determination under either program can also be used as the basis for denying a PIV card. Under these circumstances no appeal procedures are required for PIV card denial or revocation.

Appendix G is a "Clearance & Investigation Chart" that summarizes the different position risk levels, sensitivity levels, clearances, investigations, reinvestigations, and forms.

ACCESS TO CLASSIFIED INFORMATION VERSUS SECURITY CLEARANCE

Within all federal agencies, except the Department of Energy (DOE), there are only three levels of classified material and three security clearances—Confidential, Secret, and Top Secret. The Department of Energy (DOE) has the same 3 levels of classified material, but some of their classified material is further designated "Restricted

Data" (RD or "Formerly Restricted Data" (FRD). DOE basically has only two levels of security clearances—"L" access authorizations and "Q" access authorizations.[10] DOE "L" access authorizations are comparable to Secret clearances, and "Q" access authorizations are comparable to Top Secret clearances.[11] Within DOE access to Restricted Data at the Secret and Top Secret levels requires a "Q" access authorization.

All access to classified information is based on having the appropriate security clearance and a "need to know." Need-to-know can be either a formal or informal determination. Generally all classified information exists within one of these two "need-to-know" realms. Information that falls into the realm of informal need-to-know determinations is often referred to as "Collateral Classified" information. Information that falls into the realm requiring formal access authorizations (another term for need-to-know) is controlled within **Special Access Programs** (SAP), including Sensitive Compartmented Information (SCI). Access to SCI is regulated by the Director of National Intelligence under Intelligence Community Directive (ICD) Number 704, "Personnel Security."

Acronyms such as SAP, SCI, CNWDI (Critical Nuclear Weapons Design Information), SIOP-ESI (Single Integrated Operations Plan—Exceptionally Sensitive Information), RD, FRD, ATOMAL (NATO Atomic Material), COSMIC Top Secret, SPECAT, CRYPTO, COMSEC, etc., are not clearances. They refer to categories of classified information, some of which involve extra need-to-know restrictions or special access authorizations. For instance, the term COSMIC stands for "Control Of Secret Material in an International Command." COSMIC Top Secret is merely the term used for NATO Top Secret information. There are many caveats stamped or printed on classified documents with exotic sounding words, but most are only acronyms or short titles for special administrative handling procedures.

---

[10] DOE uses the term "access authorization" instead of "security clearance." Within DoD "access authorization" has a different meaning than "security clearance." Among federal personnel security specialists the term "access eligibility" or "eligibility for access" has replaced both "security clearance" and "access authorization." Within this book "security clearance" means "eligibility for access."

[11] DOE also has QX and LX clearances that are granted to individuals employed by a DOE access permittee. QX is for access to Secret and/or Confidential Restricted Data, and LX is for Confidential Restricted Data. Information regarding the DOE access permit program is found in 10 CFR 725.

Note: Throughout the rest of this book anything stated about Secret security clearances will apply equally to DOE "L" access authorizations and anything stated about Top Secret clearances will apply equally to DOE "Q" access authorizations, unless specific differences are noted.

SPECIAL ACCESS PROGRAMS

Executive Order 12958 defines SAP as "A program established for a specific class of classified information that imposes safeguarding and access requirements that exceed those normally required for information at the same classification level." SAPs are established only when the program is required by statute or upon the specific finding that the vulnerability of, or threat to, specific information is exceptional; *and* the normal criteria for determining access to information classified at the same level are not sufficient. The purpose of establishing a SAP is to:

1. enforce need-to-know,

2. keep accesses to a minimum,

3. enhance other security measures as needed, and

4. identify who has had access.

SAPs can be approved by the Secretaries of State, Energy, Defense, and Homeland Security, as well as the Director of National Intelligence. SAPs are categorized as 1) Intelligence, 2) Acquisition, and 3) Operations/Support. SAPs are further categorized by their Protection Levels:

Acknowledged – SAP whose existence is publicly acknowledged.

Unacknowledged – SAP with protective controls which ensures the existence of the Program is not acknowledged, affirmed, or made known to any person not authorized for such information. All aspects are handled in an unacknowledged manner.

Waived – SAP that the approval authority has determined the existence of which should not be included in annual reports to Congress, because such reporting would adversely affect national security. These SAPs are reported to the chairman and ranking minority member of each of the congressional defense committees.

The most commonly known Special Access Program (SAP) is Sensitive Compartmented Information (SCI). SCI, as the name implies, is made up of compartments. Each compartment involves a different category of intelligence information. These compartments are organized into 3 sensitivity levels that have different investigative requirements:

1. SSBI without polygraph

2. SSBI with Counterintelligence Scope polygraph[12]

3. SSBI with Full Scope polygraph[13]

Certain other designated SAPs require an SSBI regardless of the level of classified information involved and may also require a polygraph exam. Secret and Top Secret "Restricted Data" is controlled as a SAP.

INTERIM VERSUS FINAL CLEARANCES

Interim security clearance, suitability, fitness, and credentialing determinations are based on the completion of partial investigative requirements and are granted on a temporary basis, pending the completion of the full investigative requirements and a final eligibility determination.

The importance of interim clearances cannot be over emphasized. In many cases interim clearances can be granted in a few days, whereas final clearances can take months. Not all federal agencies consider interim clearances for all positions, but interim clearances have become widely used because of the excessive length of time it took to complete clearance investigations in the recent past. Many employers need to fill vacant positions immediately and cannot wait for an applicant to receive a final clearance. Often job candidates receive "Conditional Offers of Employment—COE" contingent on obtaining an interim clearance. If the interim clearance is declined, the COE is withdrawn, and another candidate who either already has a clearance or who receives an interim clearance is hired. As previously stated the

---

[12] Question topics covered in a DoD Counterintelligence Scope polygraph exam are listed at Appendix 2 to DoD Regulation 5210.48-R, Polygraph Program, January 1985.
[13] Full Scope polygraph exams (also known as Extended Scope exams) are a combination of a Counterintelligence Scope exam and a Lifestyle exam.

denial rate for final security clearances is only about 1%; whereas, the declination rate for interim security clearances has been between 20% to 30%. For applicants with moderate to major unfavorable issue information in their personal histories, it is necessary to mitigate this information at the earliest stage of the clearance process in order to receive an interim clearance.

Interim clearances can be declined when any potentially disqualifying issue exists. Sometimes it's not possible to fully mitigate a potentially disqualifying issue without the information obtained through a clearance investigation, but often it is possible to receive an interim clearance, if the applicant provides information on the clearance application form (or in an attachment to the form, if permitted) that fully mitigates the potentially disqualifying information. This is because interim clearance decisions are made before the clearance investigation is completed. If a drug-related issue occurred several years ago, it can sometimes be mitigated by merely listing the type, frequency, circumstances, and dates of drug use as required by the application form. But some questions on the clearance application form do not specifically ask for any mitigating information, and failing to provide more mitigating information than required by the form is a mistake. Applicants should always include additional mitigating information in the "Continuation Space" at the end of the paper version of the application forms or in the "Optional Comment" field following the appropriate question on the Electronic Questionnaire for Investigations Processing (e-QIP) version of the forms.

Once granted, an interim clearance can be withdrawn any time previously undisclosed adverse information surfaces during the background investigation. There is no right to rebut or appeal the declination or withdrawal of an interim clearance. Government agencies are not required to give any reason for either action.

There are scores of federal adjudication facilities employing several hundred trained professional adjudicators who are authorized to make interim and final clearance decisions. There is a much greater number of personnel security specialists, assigned to a multitude of military and government security offices that initiate or process security clearance requests, who are also authorized to make interim clearance decisions. Among this latter group the level of training and experience vary greatly. Consequently there is much less consistency in interim clearance decisions than in final clearance decisions. Success in obtaining an interim clearance may depend more on the experience, training, and mindset of the decision maker than on the persuasiveness of the mitigating information submitted.

In the vast majority of cases where an applicant successfully mitigates a security issue with information included in or submitted with an SF86 and receives an interim clearance, they also later receive a final clearance.

Final security clearance, suitability, fitness, and credentialing determinations are made based on the following completed investigations:

Clearance/Determination	Investigation
Low Risk (contractor)	None
Low Risk (federal employee)	NACI
Moderate Risk	MBI
High Risk	BI
Confidential/Secret/"L"	NACLC or ANACI
Top Secret/"Q"	SSBI
HSPD-12 Credential	NACI or better

An Interim Confidential or Secret clearance can be granted on the basis of a favorable review of the applicant's SF86, a review of appropriate federal clearance databases, and the submission of a request for a NACLC or ANACI. An Interim Top Secret (TS) clearance can be granted on the basis of a favorable review of the applicant's SF-86; a favorable NAC; a favorable credit report; and the submission of a request for an SSBI. A decision regarding an interim Secret clearance can be made within a few days, and a decision regarding an interim TS clearance can be made in a few weeks. DISCO considers all applicants for an interim Secret clearance. DISCO considers all applicants for TS clearances for both an interim Secret clearance and later for an interim TS clearance. Some federal agencies do not grant interim clearances, and some only consider granting interim clearances to applicants for designated positions.

There is no government-wide rule regarding interim employment suitability or fitness determinations. According to 5 CFR 731.104, "There is no time limit . . . to conduct the required investigation of an applicant. . . . Investigations should be initiated before appointment but no later than 14 calendar days after placement in the position."

Consequently many federal agencies make interim suitability and fitness determinations, so that applicants can be placed in jobs without having to wait until the full investigation is completed and a final determination is made. This is done to minimize situations where employees and contractors must be fired due to unfavorable final determinations. Typically interim suitability and fitness determinations are based on a review of the applicant's SF85, SF85P, and/or OF306; a check of federal clearance databases, and a credit check.

Interim HSPD-12 credentials can be issued based on favorable advance results from the FBI National Criminal History (fingerprint) Check portion of the NACI.

CHAPTER 3

CLEARANCE PROCESSING TIMES AND ISSUES

CLEARANCE PROCESSING TIMES

There's been a lot of improvement in case processing time over the past few years. Most of the improvement is directly related to the reduction in the backlog of investigations. Since October 2006, OPM, which conducts the vast majority of all federal clearance investigations, has reduced the number of pending initial investigations that are more than 180 days old from about 99,000 to 1,500. They did this primarily by increasing their investigative staff. OPM currently has a combined federal and contractor investigative staff of about 8,500 personnel—about 6,500 of whom are field investigators. Ten years ago OPM and DSS together had half that many investigators. Seven intelligence agencies and 14 other federal agencies conduct their own clearance investigations. The following chart shows the average processing time for the fastest 90% of initial security clearances by agency for the 1st quarter of Fiscal Year 2010 (October to December 2009):

Fastest 90% of Initial Security Clearances

AGENCIES	% OF WORK LOAD	INITIATION TIME (DAYS)	INVESTIGA- TION TIME (DAYS)	ADJUDICA- TION TIME (DAYS)	TOTAL DAYS END- TO-END
All Agencies	100%	11	46	14	71
DoD (Total)	88.8%	11	42	15	68
Army	37.4%	6	42	10	58
Navy	17.4%	16	43	12	71
Air Force	13.2%	12	40	28	80
DISCO	19.6%	14	44	20	78
DHS	2.3%	29	48	48	125
DOE	0.9%	9	47	11	67
DOJ	0.7%	12	60	42	114
NRC	0.3%	23	55	49	127

DOT	0.3%	15	39	11	65
Treasury	0.2%	18	54	54	126
HHS	0.3%	27	52	13	92
OPM	0.1%	6	70	10	86
Interior	0.1%	18	55	47	120
Commerce	0.1%	9	42	9	60
VA	0.0%	23	54	31	108
IC (Total)	4.5%	7	61	22	90
CIA			78	49	127
DIA		41	55	9	105
FBI		35	76	6	117
NGA		7	25	31	63
NRO		3	27	31	61
NSA		7	70	10	87
State			43	11	54
Other (Total)	1.2%	13	50	19	82
USCG	0.8%	11	42	12	65
CBP	0.0%	30	233	31	294
ICE	0.0%	8	36	131	175
USAID	0.1%	24	45	20	89
BBG	0.0%	29	264	14	307
USSS	0.0%	14	104	18	136
ATF	0.0%	23	54	26	103
AF OSI	0.0%	1	71	20	92
DHS HQ	0.0%	8	40	7	55
Peace Corps	0.0%	11	33	4	48
TVA	0.0%	2	30	1	33
BEP	0.0%	8	24	2	34
BPD	0.0%	10	16	1	27
Postal Insp.	0.0%	9	43	2	54

Notes: The first 15 agencies in the chart receive investigative services from OPM and account for a combined total of 94.3% of the total workload.

The next 7 starting with the CIA are Intelligence Community (IC) agencies that conduct their own investigations and account for a combined total of 4.5% of the total workload.[14]

The remaining 14 "other" agencies also conduct their own investigations and account for a combined total of 1.2% of the total workload.

DHS HQ 1st quarter FY2010 data unavailable; data shown for 4th quarter FY2009.

Source: Security and Suitability Process Reform—Strategic Framework, February 2010, A joint report by OMB, DoD, OPM, and ODNI

The differences in investigation time for agencies whose investigations are conducted by OPM are attributable to the types of background investigations being conducted. Clearance investigations for Army, Navy, Air Force, DOT, and Commerce have a higher percentage of NACLCs and ANACIs, which involve much less work than SSBIs. In

---

[14] In addition to conducting its own investigations, the FBI conducts a very limited number of investigations for DOE "Q" access authorization positions designated as a "Position of a High Degree of Importance or Sensitivity."

the chart "Initiation Time" is the time in days from the date of submission by the applicant to the receipt date of all information and forms required to conduct an investigation by the investigative service provider. Time is listed in calendar days.

If current staffing at OPM and the adjudicative facilities remains the same, there should be little change in average case processing times for this year and the next 2 years. However, during FY2010 the number of pending adjudications at DISCO increased dramatically from 2,037 to 17,936. This was due to staffing problems caused by their scheduled relocation from Columbus, OH to Fort Meade, MD. Many DISCO adjudicators have quit their jobs in anticipation of the scheduled move to Fort Meade, and many others are expected to leave DISCO before the move occurs in September 2011. This same problem may affect many of the 9 other DoD CAFs. All DoD CAFs will be colocated at Fort Meade by September 2011. There should be some further reduction in average investigative time once new investigative standards are established and implemented. Currently the Joint Security and Suitability Reform Team is finalizing new investigative standards and plans to fully implement them by December 2013.

Compared to a few years ago, 78 days is a vast improvement for initial DoD industrial security clearances (cases processed by DISCO). But 78 days is an average for the fastest 90%, and an average is just a mathematical calculation. Here's a better approximate representation of how it looked for the entire DISCO applicant population in FY2009.

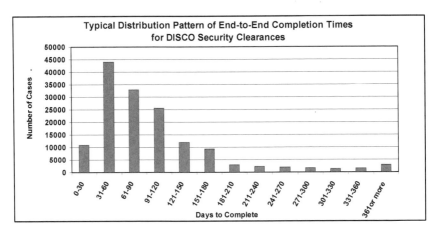

The fastest 90% include those cases taking up to 180 days. Most cases taking longer than 180 days are those that involve major derogatory information and those that require investigative activity in over-seas locations. The Government Accountability Office (GAO) made a similar analysis of DoD security clearances cases completed in 2008 and determined that 33% of decisions for Confidential and Secret clearances and 61% of decisions for initial Top Secret clearances took more than 120 days to complete.[15]

There are 3 situations where time spent on case processing is not include in computing average case completion times. Approximately 13.6% of DISCO cases were rejected by either DISCO or OPM due to errors on the SF86 or because of fingerprint cards. These cases must be resubmitted as new investigative requests. DoD-wide in FY2009 about 20% of all investigations were returned to OPM, because the investigations were incomplete. Probably more than half of these cases were sent back to OPM, when a Subject Interview was required and the Subject of the investigation, who had been in Iraq or Afghanistan, returned to the U.S. The other cases were returned to OPM due to deficiencies in investigative scope, period of coverage, or case expansion to properly resolve and/or corroborate unfavorable information. When cases are returned to OPM, they are reopened as new investigations and the elapse times for the cases are reset to zero. Cases sent from DISCO to other CAFs for adjudication are also excluded from the averages. Each year DISCO sends 5% to 10% of its cases to DOHA for adjudication. These are the cases where DISCO is unable to grant a clearance due to the presence of major derogatory information. Additionally in FY210 DISCO sent 48,186 initial investigations and 6,078 periodic reinvestigations to other CAFs for SCI eligibility determinations. The average adjudication time for the fastest 90% of initial clearance for these cases was 125 days in FY2010.

A new SF86 was approved by OMB in March 2010. Phased implementation of this new SF86 began at the end of February 2011, and it is expected to take a few months before all federal agencies are using the new form. It is significantly more complex than the previous SF86 and will probably increase the rejection rate. More than ever applicants with complicated personal histories will need help in filling out the SF86 properly. On the positive side, as more requesters begin to use SWFT, the Secure Web Fingerprint Transmission system, it should help lower rejection rates. Currently most fingerprints for DISCO cases

---

[15] GAO Report 09-400, "DOD PERSONNEL CLEARANCES: Comprehensive Timeliness Reporting, Complete Clearance Documentation, and Quality Measures Are Needed to Further Improve the Clearance Process," May 2009.

are mailed to OPM. The mailed fingerprint cards sit in a bin at OPM until they are matched with the SF86. If fingerprint cards are not matched to an SF86 within 14 days, the SF86 is rejected, returned to DISCO, and the request for investigation must be resubmitted. SWFT will enable a more efficient matching of SF86s to fingerprint cards and eliminate the time OPM spends scanning paper fingerprint cards before they can be forwarded to the FBI.

DISCO interim Secret clearance decisions take about 3 working days. These decisions are based solely on a review of the SF86 and a review of online federal investigative and security clearance databases. In recent years DISCO has granted interim clearances in only 70% to 80% of its cases. When compared the 1% denial rate for final clearances, the 20% to 30% declination rate for interim clearances clearly shows the importance of providing as much issue mitigation as possible in the SF86, so that adjudicators have that information available when making interim clearance decisions.

The following chart shows the average processing time for the fastest 90% of Employment Suitability Determinations made based on investigations conducted by OPM during 1st quarter of Fiscal Year 2010 (October to December 2009).

Fastest 90% of Suitability Determinations
(OPM Conducted Investigations only)

AGENCIES	% OF WORK LOAD	INITIATION TIME (DAYS)	INVESTIGA-TION TIME (DAYS)	ADJUDICA-TION TIME (DAYS)	TOTAL DAYS END-TO-END
All Agencies	100%	27	43	40	110
DoD (Total)	37.0%	28	40	30	98
Army	11.4%	28	41	28	97
Navy	7.9%	28	40	32	100
Air Force	9.0%	24	40	40	104
Industry	0.1%	38	38	16	92
DHS	12.8%	36	45	76	157
DOE	0.8%	14	39	28	81
DOJ	5.1%	29	56	112	197
DOT	2.7%	15	39	11	65
HHS	3.8%	30	50	175	255
NRC	0.0%	50	47	57	154
OPM	0.3%	11	59	6	76
Treasury	6.5%	17	52	40	109
Interior	4.4%	28	42	42	112
Commerce	3.7%	20	46	75	141
VA	22.8%	23	40	24	87

Source: Security and Suitability Process Reform—Strategic Framework, February 2010, A joint report by OMB, DoD, OPM, and ODNI

As with security clearance investigations, since all suitability investigations shown in the chart were conduct by OPM, the differences in investigative time are probably attributable to the type of background investigations being conducted. For instance the investigations for DoD, DOE, DOT, etc. may have a higher percentage of NACIs and MBIs for low-risk and moderate-risk positions, which involve much less work than LBIs and BIs for high-risk positions.

CLEARANCE ISSUES

During FY2008 DOHA Administrative Judges decided about 1,300 security clearance cases. These were cases where applicants received and responded to an SOR that specified why DOHA felt that the applicant should not be granted a clearance, and the cases were ultimately decided by a DOHA Administrative Judge.

The *Adjudicative Guidelines* defines 13 issues that can be listed in an SOR. Twelve of the 13 issues are listed below and ranked according to the frequency they appeared in the case synopses followed by the total number of times they were listed.

Fiscal Year 2008 DOHA Cases

Issues Cited	Number
Financial Considerations	681
Personal Conduct	497
Foreign Preference	272
Criminal Conduct	252
Foreign Influence	155
Drug Involvement	134
Alcohol Consumption	108
Sexual Behavior	17
Use of IT Systems	14
Handling Protected Information	11
Outside Activities	5
Psychological Conditions	3

DOHA posts clearance decisions at their website, where it is possible to skim over a synopsis of each case or read complete case decisions. The information presented here is based on security issues listed in the case synopses, which should also be the same as the issues listed in the SORs for these cases. One issue, *Allegiance to the United States*, was not cited in any of the cases.[16] Except for Financial Considerations, which increased slightly, more recent DOHA cases reflect generally the same distribution of issues.

Although, there were about 1,300 DOHA cases that were adjudicated by DOHA Administrative Judges in FY2008; many cases had multiple issues. The number of separate issues present in each case ranged from 1 to 4. For example 3 delinquent debts would all be covered under the one issue of *Financial Considerations*; whereas, 3 delinquent debts plus 2 petty theft convictions would result in 2 issues—*Financial Considerations* and *Criminal Conduct*.

Financial Considerations was by far the most prevalent issue and appeared in over 50% of the cases. Although *Personal Conduct* was the second most frequently cited issue and appeared in 38% of the cases; it was often cited due to falsification of information related to one of the other issues. *Foreign Preference*, cited in 21% of the cases, and *Foreign Influence*, cited in 12%, frequently appeared together. The vast majority of *Foreign Preference* issues were based on the possession of a foreign passport and dual-citizenship; whereas, *Foreign Influence* was usually based on close relationships with foreign nationals who present a "heightened risk" of foreign exploitation. *Criminal Conduct* ranked fourth, but its ranking was slightly inflated by the use of this issue to cover the criminal aspect of falsification, illegal drug use, and alcohol-related arrests already covered by the *Personal Conduct, Drug Involvement*, and *Alcohol Consumption* issues. *Drug Involvement* was cited in 10% of the cases and Alcohol Consumption was cited in 8%. The remaining issues were cited in 1% or less of the cases. About 63% of all these cases resulted in a clearance denial or revocation.

Historically the most prevalent suitability/security issues have been *Criminal Conduct, Drug Involvement, Alcohol Consumption*, and *Financial Considerations*. *Personal Conduct* has also been a leading issue, but as previously indicated, it is regularly cited when

---

[16] *Allegiance to the United States* has rarely been an issue in security clearance adjudications, because background investigations that develop credible information concerning this issue are almost always closed before completion and transferred to a federal criminal investigative agency.

applicants list false information on their security forms regarding arrests, drugs, alcohol, or finances. Over the years the number of cases involving *Financial Considerations* has gone up or down in response to changes in the economy, particularly unemployment. In FY1998 it was only the 5th most prevalent issue.

In the past 10 years the number of clearance investigations processed at DISCO has increased about 50%, but the number of cases with significant derogatory information has increased by more than 500%. In FY1998 DOHA Administrative Judges reviewed about 250 cases, compared to 1,315 in FY2008. Some of this is attributable to the dramatic increase in the number cases citing *Foreign Preference* and *Foreign Influence* as issues. In FY1998 these two issues were cited in DOHA cases a total of 15 times, compared to a total of 427 times in FY2008.

Issue distribution in DOHA cases differs significantly from cases at other major DoD Central Adjudication Facilities (CAF). Eighty-one percent of the clearances denied or revoked by the Department of Navy CAF in FY2008 were due to *Financial Considerations*. The number of *Foreign Preference* and *Foreign Influence* issues in DOHA cases is currently greater than at other major DoD CAFs.

There is no statistical information available on the distribution of issues present in Employment Suitability, Fitness, or HSPD-12 Credentialing determinations. Anecdotal information about these types of cases suggests that the distribution is similar to security clearance cases with the exception of Foreign Preference and Foreign Influence. This is because Foreign Preference and Foreign Influence are not included in the standard eligibility criteria for these types of determinations. Foreign Influence is sometimes added as a job-specific employment fitness criteria for certain positions.

CHAPTER 4

INVESTIGATIONS

BASIC COMPONENTS OF INVESTIGATIONS

There are many types of Personnel Security Investigations (PSI) conduct by OPM and the 21 other federal agencies authorized to conduct PSIs. All PSIs include some or all of the following basic components:

Review of Clearance Application Form & Check of Clearance/Investigations Databases—All PSIs include a review of the clearance application for completeness and for the existence of potentially disqualifying conditions and a check of online federal clearance/investigations databases. For security clearances this is done by the personnel security office of the federal agency authorized to grant interim clearances. For employment suitability, fitness and HSPD-12 determinations this is generally done by the federal agency's Human Resources office.

NAC (National Agency Check)—The NAC is a standard part of all investigations and reinvestigations. All NACs include record checks at:

- FBI-HQ (name check)
- FBI-ID (fingerprint check)
- CVS (OPM's Central Verification System)[17]
- SII (OPM's Security and Investigations Index)

---

[17] CVS is checked using an online computer program and provides linkage to SII and JPAS.

- JPAS (DoD's Joint Personnel Adjudication System)
- DCII (Defense Central Index of Investigations)

Other federal agencies are checked as appropriate and can include records of the:

- Citizenship and Immigration Services (formerly Immigration and Naturalization Service)
- State Department
- Central Intelligence Agency
- Military Personnel Record Centers
- Treasury Department
- National Guard Bureau
- U.S. National Central Bureau (USNCB)[18]

Credit Search—A credit search (or credit check) is a verification of Subject's financial status through a search of all three major credit bureaus covering all locations where the subject has resided, been employed, and/or attended school for six months or more during the past seven years. It is a standard component of all PSIs, except the NACI.[19]

Enhanced Subject Interview (ESI)—In October 2010 OPM re-named the Personal Subject Interview (PRSI) and now calls it an Enhanced Subject Interview. It is a standard component of all OPM PSIs, except the NACI, NACLC, and ANACI. An ESI can be added to the NACLC and ANACI when required by case expansion criteria based on listed or developed derogatory information that exceeds certain thresholds. Other agencies continue to use the PRSI. The ESI and the PRSI are essentially the same. Throughout this book the term ESI is used to refer to both the PRSI and the ESI. Both are in-depth interviews of the Subject of an investigation conducted by a federal

---

[18] As of 1 March 2005 (as part of a NAC) OPM requests USNCB to conduct a records check at the International Criminal Police Organization (INTERPOL) when, for six months or more, the Subject of an investigation: (1) had a non-military foreign residence; (2) had non-military employment overseas; (3) was engaged in academic activities abroad; or (4) when the Subject admits to, or there is developed, criminal activity overseas within the investigative coverage period.

[19] All DoD NACIs include a credit check.

investigator (Special Agent) or a federal contract investigator (Special Investigator) that cover all information in the clearance application form plus certain other information not included in the application form. ESI procedures vary slightly from agency to agency, but most agencies follow the same basic format and cover the same topical areas. Subject Interviews generally and the ESI are addressed in greater detail later in this chapter.

SPIN (Special Interview)—A SPIN is a type of Subject Interview used to obtain details regarding specific unfavorable information (including significant discrepancies on an SF85, SF85P, or SF86) from the Subject of an investigation and afford him/her the opportunity to explain the situation and provide mitigating information. A SPIN can be added to any standard investigation. The SPIN focuses only on unfavorable information or major discrepancies on the application form or developed from other sources during the investigation. However, there are some changes being implemented that could result in the SPIN being replaced in many cases by an ESI. In late 2010 OPM began using the ESI in place of a SPIN for NACLCs and ANACIs when discrepant or unfavorable information triggered a Subject Interview under case expansion criteria. It is unclear whether OPM will continue to made the SPIN available as an option within a Reimbursable Suitability/security Investigation (RSI) or whether other investigative agencies will replace the SPIN with an ESI. General information about Subject Interviews is provided in greater detail later in this chapter.

RSI (Reimbursable Suitability/Security Investigations)—An RSI is a focused investigation used by OPM to address issues that were left unresolved by a completed standard investigation or issues that arise after a clearance is granted. An RSI is a customized investigation that permits requestors to select specific investigative actions, such as a Subject Interview or other specific interviews and record checks needed to resolve issues.

Polygraph—Polygraph screening examinations are administered when eligibility for access to some SCI programs and certain other SAPs is required in addition to a collateral security clearance. Polygraph exams are not used when only a collateral security clearance, employment suitability/fitness, or HSPD-12 credentialing determination is required; however, they can be required for suitability/fitness determinations for certain federal law enforcement positions. In rare instances issue-oriented polygraph exams are offered to applicants to resolve serious credible derogatory information or when requested by applicants for exculpatory purposes in connection with a security clearance investigation. OPM does not conduct polygraph examinations. Polygraph screening examinations are conducted by Intelligence Community (IC) agencies that adjudicate SCI and/or SAP access eligibility. They can also be conducted by federal law enforcement agencies for employment suitability and fitness screening and by other federal agencies when needed to resolve security issues that cannot be resolved through other investigative methods. Polygraph is addressed in greater detail at the end of this chapter.

STANDARD INVESTIGATIONS

The following paragraphs describe the components of standard investigations used by federal agencies as the basis for credentialing, suitability, fitness, and security clearance determinations. All investigations can be expanded beyond their basic scope to resolve credible security or suitability issues. Some agencies have their investigation service provider expand investigations based on written expansion criteria for common issues and may also request additional investigation based on an adjudicator's review of the completed investigation. Other agencies decide whether to return an investigation to the investigation service provider for expanded coverage only after an adjudicator's review of completed case.

NACI (National Agency Check with Inquiries)—An NACI is the basic investigation for federal employment in Low Risk/Non-Sensitive positions and for HSPD-12 Credentialing. It is usually based on an SF85, but an SF85P is authorized for HSPD-12 Credentialing. It consists of a NAC plus written inquiries and record searches covering:

- Employment and employment supervisors, 5 years
- Education, 5 years and verification of highest degree
- Residence, 3 years
- Listed references
- Law enforcement agencies, 5 years

Written inquiries are sent to current and past employers and supervisors, schools attended, and references. Local law enforcement authorities can also be sent letter inquires, but many of these checks are done electronically using the National Law Enforcement Telecommunications System (NLETS). (Note: By special agreement with OPM all NACIs requested by DoD agencies include a credit search.)

NACIC (National Agency Check with Inquiries and Credit)— An NACIC can be used for contractor Moderate Risk Public Trust positions and is based on an SF85P. It is a NACI plus a credit search.

NACLC (National Agency Check with Law and Credit checks)[20]—An NACLC is used for Non-critical Sensitive positions, Confidential clearances, and Secret clearances for military and contractor personnel. It also satisfies the investigative requirement for DOE "L" access authorizations for contractor personnel. An NACLC can be used for a federal employee requiring any of these same clearances, if they previously had a favorably adjudicated NACI. The NACLC is based on an SF86. It consists of an NAC plus credit search and checks of local law enforcement records where the subject has lived, worked, and/or attended school within the last 5 years, and if applicable, of the appropriate criminal justice agencies for any identified arrests. The NACLC is also the required reinvestigation for federal employees, military personnel, and contractor personnel for continued access at these same clearance levels.

ANACI (Access National Agency Check with Inquiries)—An ANACI is a combination of an NACI and an NACLC. It is used for Non-critical Sensitive positions, Confidential clearances, Secret clearances, and DOE "L" access authorizations for federal employment applicants. It is based on an SF86 and consists of a NACLC plus written inquiries covering employment and employment supervisors (past 5 years), schools (past 5 years and verification of highest degree), residences (past 3 years), and all listed references.

MBI (Moderate Risk Background Investigation)—An MBI is used for Moderate Risk Public Trust positions and is based on an SF85P. An MBI consists of an NACI, credit search, and ESI. When

---

[20] An NACLC is sometimes referred to as a National Agency Check with Local Agency Checks and Credit Checks.

based on an SF86, it also satisfies the investigative requirements for all Non-critical Sensitive positions, Confidential clearances, Secret clearances, and DOE "L" access authorizations.

LBI (Limited Background Investigation)—As of 1 October 2010 this investigation was no longer offered by OPM; however, other agencies may continue to use it until new national investigative standards are fully implemented. When based on an SF85P, the LBI is use for Moderate Risk or High Risk Public Trust positions. An LBI consists of an NACLC and an ESI plus interviews and record checks covering employment/schools (past 3 years and verification of highest degree) and residences (past 1 year), and review of any court actions for past 3 years. When based on an SF86, it also satisfies the requirement for all Non-critical Sensitive positions, Confidential clearances, Secret clearances, and DOE "L" access authorizations.

BI (Background Investigation)—The BI is used for High Risk Public Trust positions and is based on an SF85P. A BI consists of an NACLC and an ESI plus interviews and record checks covering employment (past 5 years), schools (past 5 years) and residences (past 3 years), and review of any court actions for past 5 years. When based on an SF86, a BI also satisfies the requirement for all Non-critical Sensitive positions, Confidential clearances, Secret clearances, and DOE "L" access authorizations.

SSBI (Single Scope Background Investigation)—The SSBI is used for all Critical Sensitive and Special Sensitive positions, Top Secret clearances, DOE "Q" Access Authorizations, SCI, and most other SAPs. It consists of:

- NAC on the Subject of the investigation
- Credit search
- ESI
- NAC on Subject's current spouse or cohabitant
- Verification of all employment activities for past 7 years, including corroboration of all periods of unemployment of 2 months or more,
- Interviews of 2 references at each employment of 6 months or more for past 7 years

- Verification of all prior federal and military service
- Interviews of 2 references at each school covering the past 3 years
- Interviews of 2 references at each residence covering the past 3 years
- Review of any court actions covering the past 10 years
- Interview of any former spouse divorced within the past 10 years
- Interview of 4 social references who collectively cover at least the past 7 years (at least 2 of whom are not listed on the SF86)
- Record checks at local law enforcement agencies where the Subject lived, worked, and/or attended school within the last 10 years, and at the appropriate agency for any identified arrests.
- Verification of citizenship or legal status of all foreign-born immediate family members and foreign-born cohabitant

SSBI-PR (SSBI Period Reinvestigation)—An SSBI-PR (also known as an SBPR) is based on an SF86. It is used as a reinvestigation for anyone whose initial investigation was an SSBI. The SSBI-PR consists of:

- NACLC
- ESI
- NAC on new spouse or cohabitant
- Verification of all employment since last investigation
- Interview of 2 employment reference at each employment of 6 months or more since last investigation
- Interview of 2 social references (at least 1 of whom is not listed on the SF86) covering past 5 years
- Interview of 2 neighbors at most recent residence of 6 months or more (verification of current residence regardless of length)
- Review of any court actions covering the past 5 years

- Check of the Department of Treasury's Financial Crimes Enforcement Network (FinCEN) database

PPR (Phased Period Reinvestigation)—The PPR is based on an SF86. It can be used as a reinvestigation for anyone whose initial investigation was an SSBI when the individual's SF86 contains no security or suitability issues. The PPR consists of the same components as the SSBI-PR, but without interviews of social references or neighbors.

PRI (Periodic Reinvestigation)—The PRI is used as a periodic reinvestigation for Public Trust positions and is based on an SF85P. It consists of an NAC, credit search, and ESI plus written inquiries to listed references and record checks at law enforcement agencies covering the past 5 years.

PRI-R (Periodic Reinvestigation-Residence)—The PRI-R was used as a periodic reinvestigation for Public Trust positions. It was based on an SF85P. OPM stopped offering this type of reinvestigation in October 2010. It consisted of a PRI plus interviews and record checks covering residences for the past 3 years.

SUBJECT INTERVIEWS

A Subject Interview is a standard component of certain investigations and can be an added component to any investigation. They take two forms—the Special Interview (SPIN) and the Enhanced Subject Interview (ESI). Both ESIs and SPINs are conducted by federal investigators (Special Agents) and federal contract investigators (Special Investigators).

Usually there is only one investigator, but occasionally a second investigator may be present. An applicant has the right to have a personal representative or attorney present during the interview, but this is rarely necessary or beneficial. You should:

- Arrive promptly for the interview and silence your cell phone.

- Don't bring any weapons with you into the interview room, even if you are authorized to have them.

- Bring a government-issued photo ID, such as a driver's license or military ID card.

- Bring a personal address book or anything that contains contact information on your associates and family members.

- Bring a copy of your SF85, SF85P, or SF86.

- If your case involves some security or suitability issues, bring any relevant documents with you to the interview, such as birth/citizenship certificates, passports, financial documents, court records, etc.

- Ask the investigator for a business card.

After identifying himself with his badge and credentials and examining your identification, the investigator usually begins by explaining the purpose of the interview, the provisions of the Privacy Act, and the criminal penalties for false statements. You will also be reminded that your participation in the interview is voluntary. It's your choice to answer some, all, or none of the questions. However, refusal to answer any legitimate question can result in a clearance denial. Only when the investigator asks a question that is obviously beyond the scope of an investigation, can you refuse to answer and not risk a clearance denial. Such questions usually relate to religious beliefs; opinions regarding racial matters, political or union affiliations; and lawful sexual conduct that would not make you susceptible to blackmail. OPM federal investigators have the applicant answer questions under oath or affirmation. OPM contract investigators have the applicant make an unsworn declaration. Both procedures carry equal weight under the law. You may be asked to sign a specific release for information concerning financial matters, mental health counseling, and/or substance abuse counseling. Refusal to sign a release, even if you know that the information being sought does not exist, can result in having your clearance denied. Under certain circumstances investigators may request a signed, written statement (affidavit) from you covering security or suitability issues discussed during the interview.

The investigator will ask for details about potential security or suitability issue information listed on your application form or received from other sources. The investigator will also try to discover unfavorable information that is not listed on the form. Answer the investigator's questions as precisely, truthfully and completely. It's the investigator's responsibility to ask questions that will elicit the details regarding anything that might be considered a security/suitability issue. These questions will cover who, what, when, where, how, why, and who else knows. Additionally investigators are trained to determine and report the following factors:

- nature, extent, and seriousness of the conduct;
- circumstances surrounding the conduct, to include knowledgeable participation;
- frequency and recency of the conduct;
- individual's age and maturity at the time of the conduct;
- extent to which participation is voluntary;
- presence or absence of rehabilitation and other permanent behavioral changes;
- motivation for the conduct;
- potential for pressure, coercion, exploitation, or duress; and
- likelihood of continuation or recurrence.

These factors[21] are taken from the *Adjudicative Guidelines* and known as the "general criteria." However, each of the 13 guidelines for security clearance adjudication has its own set of mitigating conditions, many of which are not specifically cover by the general criteria. Unfortunately background investigators receive little training on the unique mitigating conditions listed under each of the 13 guidelines. Therefore, you should be prepared to volunteer mitigating information that is not elicited by the investigator's questions.

If you and the investigator prepare properly for your Subject Interview, the interview should be completed in one session. Occasionally at some point after the interview, there may be a need for a follow-up contact with the investigator. This usually occurs when you were unable to provide some information at the time, the need for a written release arises later, some minor matter requires further clarification, or you later remember some pertinent information.

The ESI is a required part of all investigations and periodic reinvestigations for Moderate Risk and High Risk Public Trust positions and for Top Secret clearances. OPM is now using an ESI in place of a SPIN on NACLCs and ANACIs when required for case expansion purposes. ESI procedures vary slightly from agency to agency, but most agencies

---

[21] Most of these factors are also listed at 5 CFR 731.202.

follow the same basic format and cover the same topical areas. The ESI should take about an hour for the average person who has completed the clearance application form accurately and only has a few residences, jobs, and schools listed on the form. If you have had extensive foreign travel, foreign contacts, or problems involving such things as alcohol, drugs, finances, or criminal conduct, the interview could take much longer.

The investigator will essentially cover every question on your clearance application form to confirm the accuracy and completeness of the information you provided, plus some questions that are not on the form. For security clearances, questions on the SF86 cover most of the security issues listed in the *Adjudicative Guidelines*. But a few of the 13 guidelines are either not addressed or only partially addressed in the SF86. In one manner or another, questions covering all 13 guidelines will be asked during the interview. The same applies to the SF85P and the employment suitability criteria at 5 CFR 731.202 and any job-specific employment fitness criteria established by various federal agencies.

Like the clearance application forms,[22] ESI questions are based on certain time periods. Some questions pertain to your entire life. Others pertain only to the last 7 or 10 years (or back to your 16th or 18th birthday depending on your age). For the purpose of the interview questions, the seven- or ten-year time frame is based on the date you completed the clearance application form. If you completed the form on March 1, 2011, ten years includes everything between March 1, 2001 and the date of your interview. Under certain circumstances investigators are authorized to ask about relevant information regardless of how long ago it occurred.

Many investigators follow the sequence of the questions on the application form, so you can follow along on your copy of the form. As each question is asked, you should volunteer any information that mitigates, clarifies, explains, extenuates or otherwise decreases the possible negative effect of unfavorable information you listed on your form. If the investigator fails to ask you about any unfavorable information listed on your clearance application form, mention the information yourself. If you don't, it will have to be addressed during a

---

[22] The new March 2010 version of the SF86 changed the time period for many questions. Questions regarding residence, education, and employment now cover 10 years for all levels of security clearances. Other questions that previously required 10 years of information were reduced to 7 years.

follow-up interview and will delay your clearance. If you have been involved in serious misconduct, had significant financial problems, or have extensive foreign connections, it would be wise to make a written explanation of the situation(s), including all applicable mitigating conditions. Give a copy of the written explanation to the investigator.

If a major discrepancy or security issue surfaces through one of the other components of the security investigation, it usually necessitates a separate SPIN to resolve the matter.

POLYGRAPH

DoD Regulation 5210.48-R, "Polygraph Program," January 1985, states:

"Polygraph examinations are conducted as a supplement to, not as a substitute for, other forms of investigation that may be required under the circumstances. Applicants for employment, assignment, or detail to positions requiring access to specifically designated information in SAPs . . . who refuse to take a polygraph examination will not be selected or assigned. Persons who refuse to take a polygraph examination in connection with determining their continued eligibility for access to specifically designated information in SAPs, to include incumbents of positions subsequently determined to require such access, may be denied access to the classified information in question.

When deception is indicated by the examiner's interpretation of polygraph charts . . . an in depth interview of the subject will be undertaken by the examiner immediately following the running of the chart, to resolve any indication of deception. If the indication of deception cannot be resolved through such means, the subject will be so advised and the results of the examination forwarded to the requesting Agency. If, after reviewing the polygraph examination results, the requesting Agency determines that they raise significant question relevant to the subject's clearance or access status, the subject shall be given an opportunity to undergo additional examination by the examining Agency, using the same or a different examiner. If such additional examination is not sufficient to resolve the matter, a comprehensive investigation of the subject shall be undertaken, utilizing the results of the polygraph examination as an investigative lead. If such investigation develops no derogatory information upon which an unfavorable administrative action to the subject may be independently based, no such action shall be permitted, unless [personally approved by one of the Secretaries of the Military Departments or the Director, NSA, for their respective Components, or the Secretary or Deputy Secretary of Defense for other DoD Components] . . . in specific cases based upon his or her written finding that the information in question is of such extreme sensitivity that access under the circumstances poses an unacceptable risk to the national security. In such cases:

The determining authority shall notify the subject, in writing, that, although the investigation that followed the indication of deception during the polygraph examination did not in and of itself provide an independent basis for denial of access, a determination to deny such access to the subject had been made, based upon the finding of the determining authority that access under the circumstances poses an unacceptable risk to the national security. The subject shall also be advised, in the case of a determination made by a Component authority, that the determination may be appealed to the Secretary of Defense. Determinations by the Secretary of Defense are conclusive.

Additionally the 1997 *Report of the Commission on Protecting and Reducing Government Secrecy* stated:

*The polygraph examination is [often] conducted before the background investigation, saving additional resources should the applicant be rejected as a result of polygraph admissions. According to a May 1993 NSA letter to the White House, "**over 95% of the information the NSA develops on individuals who do not meet federal security clearance guidelines is derived via [voluntary admissions from] the polygraph process.**"* (emphasis added)

These paragraphs seem contradictory in that they indicate polygraph exams are not a substitute for background investigations, but also indicate that applicants can be rejected based solely on the results of polygraph exams. One explanation is that some applicants can be rejected based on employment suitability or fitness standards at any stage of the processing. Some positions requiring SCI eligibility also require favorable employment suitability or fitness determinations. Adverse employment suitability or fitness determinations in such cases can be made before the field portion of a background investigation is initiated. (See the topic on "Employment Suitability Versus Security Clearance" in the next chapter.)

Within DoD the most commonly used exam is the CI Scope polygraph exam. However, DoD personnel detailed to the National Security Agency and the Central Intelligence Agency are subject to Full Scope exams.

In October 2006 DOE changed its polygraph policy. The policy change eliminated most routine counterintelligence (CI) scope polygraph exams for clearance screening purposes and created a new program of random CI exams of designated personnel, as well as issue-oriented exams based on CI information. Mandatory screening exams are limited to DOE intelligence and counterintelligence personnel, personnel with SCI or other SAP access, personnel with regular and routine access to Top Secret information, and selected personnel based on risk assessment. The policy change did not affect the use of poly-graph for interim "Q" access authorizations under the DOE Accelerat-ed Access Authorization Program.

Regardless of the frequent challenges to the accuracy of polygraph examinations, its usefulness in the security vetting process is undenia-ble. As indicated in the 1997 *Report of the Commission on Protecting and Reducing Government Secrecy* quoted above, the utility of the polygraph is the ability it gives to the polygrapher to obtain voluntary admissions of previously undisclosed misconduct from applicants. Once an admission of disqualifying conduct is made, the actual poly-graph test results (if there was one) are unnecessary.

CHAPTER 5

ADJUDICATION & APPEALS

With a few exceptions the 3 federal personnel security programs have generally the same potentially disqualifying conditions. Employment suitability, fitness, and HSPD-12 credentialing do not have disqualifying conditions for "Foreign Preference," "Foreign Influence," or "Outside Activities." And they do not have specific disqualifying conditions for "Psychological Conditions," "Handling Protected Information," and "Use of Information Technology Systems," but some aspects of these issues are covered under other criteria.

All 3 programs rely on general mitigating factors to determine whether a potentially disqualifying condition has been alleviated. These general mitigating factors are listed at subparagraph c of 5 CFR 731.202, at paragraph 2 of the *Adjudicative Guidelines,* and at pages 70 and 76 of this book. The *Adjudicative Guidelines* also lists additional specific mitigating factors for each of its 13 adjudicative criteria. For security clearance determinations *"The adjudication process is the careful weighing of a number of variables known as the **whole-person** concept. Available, reliable information about the person, past and present, favorable and unfavorable, should be considered in reaching a determination."* Unfortunately the "whole-person" concept is not mentioned in HSPD-12 credentialing, federal employment suitability, or fitness standards.

HSPD-12 Credentialing—HSPD-12 credentialing determinations are governed by OPM's "Final Credentialing Standards for Issuing Personal Identity Verification Cards under HSPD-12."[23] This docu-

---

[23] A copy of OPM Memorandum, July 2008, Subject: Final Credentialing Standards for Issuing Personal Identity Verification Cards under HSPD-12" is at Appendix B.

ment establishes 6 disqualifying standards and 7 supplemental disqualifying standards. Most of the disqualifying standards begin and/or end with the same words:

"There is a reasonable basis to believe . . . that issuance of a PIV card poses an unacceptable risk."

The *Final Credentialing Standards* explains that:

"A reasonable basis to believe occurs when a disinterested observer, with knowledge of the same facts and circumstances, would reasonably reach the same conclusion."

"[A]n "unacceptable risk" refers to an unacceptable risk to the life, safety, or health of employees, contractors, vendors, or visitors; to the Government's physical assets or information systems; to personal property; to records, including classified, privileged, proprietary, financial, or medical records; or to the privacy of data subjects."

Although the *Final Credentialing Standards* does not list mitigating factors; federal agencies generally use the same mitigating factors used for employment suitability determinations. Federal Information Processing Standard 201-1 requires that each federal agency (or department) establish its own appeal (reconsideration) process to review requests by persons who have been denied a PIV card or have had their PIV cards revoked. For example the Department of Interior has established the following procedure for appealing a PIV card denial:[24]

(1) Appeal Rights for Federal Service Applicants
When the PIV-I Adjudicator determines that a PIV-I Applicant has not provided his or her true identity during the registration process or is otherwise found unsuitable, and the determination results in a decision by the agency to withdraw an employment offer, or remove the employee from the federal service, the procedures and appeals rights of either 5 CFR Part 731, Subparts D and E (Suitability), 5 CFR Part 315, Subpart H (Probationary Employees), or 5 CFR Part 752, Subparts D through F (Adverse Actions) will be followed, depending on the employment status of the federal service applicant, appointee, or employee. Employees who are removed from federal service are entitled to dispute this action using applicable grievance, appeal, or complaint

---

[24] Appendix E to U.S. Department of the Interior Personal Identity Verification (PIV) Policy and Guide for Federal Employees and Contractors, December 2005.

procedures available under Federal regulations, Departmental directives, or collective bargaining agreement (if the employee is covered).

(2)　Appeal Rights for Contract Applicants and Agency Affiliates
Notice of Proposed Action - When the PIV-I Adjudicator determines that a PIV-I Applicant has not provided his or her true identity or is otherwise not suitable to be employed in the current or applied for position, e.g. an unsuccessful adjudication, the PIV-I Adjudicator shall provide the individual reasonable notice of the determination including the reason (s) the individual has been determined to not have provided his or her true identity or is otherwise unsuitable. The notice shall state the specific reasons for the determination, and that the individual has the right to answer the notice in writing. The notice shall inform the individual of the time limits for response, as well as the address to which such response should be made.

Answer - The individual may respond to the determination in writing and furnish documentation that addresses the validity, truthfulness, and/or completeness of the specific reasons for the determination in support of the response.

Decision - After consideration of the determination and any documentation submitted by the PIV-I Applicant for reconsideration of the initial determination, the Agency Head/Staff Office Director or his/her designee will issue a written decision, which informs the PIV-I Applicant/Respondent of the reasons for the decision. The reconsideration decision will be final.

DoD, which issues the largest number of PIV cards (called Common Access Cards—CAC within DoD), has proposed[25] using the procedures established for security clearances for appealing CAC denials.

Federal Employment Suitability—Federal employment suitability determinations (including those for Public Trust positions) are based on *"Specific factors"* listed at 5 CFR 731.202(b) and *"Additional considerations"* listed at 5 CFR 731.202(c). Adjudicating these Specific factors and Additional considerations involves a process in which suitability issues are divided into 14 categories and assigned seriousness levels of A, B, C, or D. Issue seriousness level can then be upgraded or downgraded based on frequency and recency of occurrence. An explanation of the *Additional Considerations*, as well as OPM's Issue Characterization Chart and issue upgrading/downgrading process is provided at Appendix D. Procedures for adverse suitability actions are prescribed at 5 CFR Part 731, Subpart D and procedures for appealing adverse decisions are prescribed in Subpart E:

---

[25] Federal Register /Vol. 75, No. 151 / Friday, August 6, 2010 / Proposed Rules.

Subpart D—Agency Suitability Action Procedures

§731.401   Scope.
This subpart covers agency-initiated suitability actions against an applicant or appointee.

§731.402   Notice of proposed action.
(a) The agency must notify the applicant or appointee (hereinafter, the "respondent") in writing of the proposed action, the charges against the respondent, and the availability for review, upon request, of the materials relied upon. The notice must set forth the specific reasons for the proposed action and state that the respondent has the right to answer the notice in writing. The notice must further inform the respondent of the time limit for the answer as well as the address to which such answer must be delivered.

(b) The notice must inform the respondent that he or she may be represented by a representative of the respondent's choice and that if the respondent wishes to have such a representative, the respondent must designate the representative in writing.

(c) The agency must serve the notice of proposed action upon the respondent by mail or hand delivery no less than 30 days prior to the effective date of the proposed action to the respondent's last known residence or duty station.

(d) If the respondent is employed in a position covered by this part on the date the notice is served, the respondent is entitled to be retained in a pay status during the notice period.

§731.403   Answer.
A respondent may answer the charges in writing and furnish documentation and/or affidavits in support of the answer. To be timely, a written answer must be submitted no more than 30 days after the date of the notice of proposed action.

§731.404   Decision.
The decision regarding the final action must be in writing, be dated, and inform the respondent of the reasons for the decision and that an unfavorable decision may be appealed in accordance with subpart E of this part. If the decision requires removal, the employing agency must remove the appointee from the rolls within 5 work days of the agency's decision.

Subpart E—Appeal to the Merit Systems Protection Board

§731.501   Appeal to the Merit Systems Protection Board.
(a) Appeal to the Merit Systems Protection Board. When OPM or an agency acting under delegated authority under this part takes a suitability action against a person, that person may appeal the action to the Merit Systems Protection Board (hereinafter "Board").

(b) Decisions by the Merit Systems Protection Board.
(1) If the Board finds that one or more of the charges brought by OPM or an agency against the person is supported by a preponderance of the evidence, regardless of whether all specifications are sustained, it must affirm the suitability determination. The Board must consider the record as a whole and make a finding on each charge and specification in making its decision.
(2) If the Board sustains fewer than all the charges, the Board must remand the case to OPM or the agency to determine whether the suitability action taken is appropriate based on the sustained charge(s). However, the agency must hold in abeyance a decision on remand until the person has exhausted all rights to seek review of the Board's decision, including court review.
(3) Once review is final, OPM or an agency will determine whether the action taken is appropriate based on the sustained charges and this determination will be final without any further appeal to the Board.

(c) Appeal procedures. The procedures for filing an appeal with the Board are found at part 1201 of this title.

Federal Employment Fitness and Contractor Fitness—Except for the limited examples of disqualifying factors listed at 5 CFR 302.203, there are no government-wide standards for federal employment fitness or federal contractor fitness determinations. Agencies are only encouraged to follow the adjudicative criteria established at 5 CFR 731.202 and any job-specific eligibility criteria they have established. Agencies are not required to provide any appeal process for unfavorable fitness determinations and seldom do. Unlike other agencies, DoD's policy for contractor fitness (trustworthiness) determinations requires the use of the Adjudicative Guidelines with rebuttal and appeal rights that are the same as for security clearances.[26]

Security Clearances

"The 2005 federal adjudicative guidelines state that each security clearance case is to be judged on its own merits and a final decision to grant, deny, or revoke access to classified information is the responsibility of the specific department or agency. Any doubt about whether a clearance for access to classified information is consistent with national security is to be resolved in favor of national security. Executive Order 12968, which authorized the federal guidelines, makes it clear that a determination to grant clearance eligibility is a discretionary decision based on judgments by appropriately trained adjudicative staff. The guidelines, therefore, are not to be considered

---

[26] Deputy Under Secretary of Defense, Memorandum for Director, Defense Office of Hearings and Appeals (DOHA), Subject: Adjudication of Trustworthiness Cases, November 19, 2004.

a simple checklist. Adjudicators are to consider available, reliable information about the person—past and present, favorable and unfavorable—in reaching an 'overall common sense' clearance eligibility determination, a process known as the 'whole person' concept.

"In making determinations of eligibility for security clearances, the federal guidelines require adjudicators to consider (1) guidelines covering 13 specific areas, (2) adverse conditions or conduct that could raise a security concern and factors that might mitigate (alleviate) the condition for each guideline, and (3) general factors related to the whole person."[27]

Although adverse information concerning conduct or conditions covered by 1 of the 13 guidelines may not be sufficient for an unfavorable determination; the applicant can be disqualified, when the information indicates a recent or recurring pattern of irresponsibility, questionable judgment, or emotionally unstable behavior.

Security clearances are adjudicated using the *Adjudicative Guidelines*. Adjudication to determine eligibility for access to Sensitive Compartmented Information (SCI) uses the *Adjudicative Guidelines* plus the eligibility standards in Director of National Intelligence (DNI) Intelligence Community Directive (ICD) Number 704, which imposes stricter standards for "Foreign Influence."

The *Adjudicative Guidelines* are currently being revised, but it unknown when the revisions will be completed, approved, and implemented. It is anticipated that the number of criteria will be reduced through consolidation (e.g. Sexual Behavior) and other redundancies removed. Possible other changes that may occur include addressing the use of "medical marijuana" and reconciling the difference that exists with the "Foreign Preference" criterion in Intelligence Community Policy Guidance Number 704.2. (See Chapter 11)

To deny or revoke a clearance the Government must initially establish, by substantial evidence, conditions in the personal or professional history of the applicant that may disqualify the applicant from being eligible for access to classified information. The Government has the burden of establishing controverted facts alleged in the SOR. *"Substantial evidence" is "more than a scintilla but less than a preponderance. It is equivalent to prima-facie evidence,"* which is defined as evidence that is sufficient to raise a presumption of fact or to establish the fact in question unless rebutted. The *Adjudicative*

---

[27] United States Government Accountability Office (GAO), Report to the Ranking Member, Committee on Armed Services, House of Representatives, entitled: DOD Personnel: More Consistency Needed in Determining Eligibility for Top Secret Security Clearances, GAO-01-465, April 18, 2001.

Guidelines presumes a nexus or rational connection between proven conduct under any of the criteria listed therein and an applicant's security suitability. The burden of disproving a mitigating condition never shifts to the Government.

Security clearance eligibility is also affected by the Bond Amendment (50 USC 435b, Section 3002). This law prohibits all federal agencies from granting or renewing any security clearance to a person who is an unlawful user of a controlled substance or an addict. It also prohibits all federal agencies from granting or renewing access eligibility for Special Access Programs, Restricted Data, or Sensitive Compartmented Information for anyone who has been:

1. *Convicted of a crime, sentenced, and incarcerated for a term exceeding 1 year,*

2. *Discharged or dismissed from the Armed Forces under dishonorable conditions, or*

3. *Determined to be mentally incompetent by a government approved mental health professional.*

Waivers can be granted for these 3 listed conditions; however, a waiver cannot be granted to a person who **is** an unlawful user of a controlled substance or **is** an addict. Some adjudicative facilities may be unable to always predict future access to Restricted Data and certain other SAPs. So as a practical matter some have chosen to apply all the Bond Amendment requirements to the adjudication of all security clearances. Within DoD, adjudicators have been delegated the authority to grant waivers for the Bond Amendment restrictions (except drug use/addiction) and grant these clearances with a "waiver" annotated in the applicable field of the person's security clearance database record.

When adverse suitability information surfaces regarding an individual who currently holds a security clearance, the adjudicator must consider whether the person:

- *Voluntarily reported the information*
- *Was truthful and complete in responding to questions;*
- *Sought assistance and followed professional guidance, where appropriate;*
- *Resolved or appears likely to favorably resolve the security concern;*
- *Has demonstrated positive changes in behavior and employment;*
- *Should have his or her access temporarily suspended pending final adjudication of the information.*

If the adjudicator decides that the adverse suitability information is not serious enough to recommend denial or revocation of the clearance, the clearance may be granted or continued with a warning that future incidents of a similar nature may result in a revocation.

REBUTTING AND APPEALING
SECURITY CLEARANCE DENIALS

DISCO processes about 150,000 personnel security clearances each year for DoD contractors and contractors of 23 other federal agencies. These are referred to as industrial cases. DISCO favorably adjudicates about 90% to 95% of these cases after the investigations are conducted by OPM. If DISCO cannot affirmatively find that it is clearly consistent with the national interest to grant or continue a personnel security clearance, the case is referred to DOHA for further review. DOHA has the option to request further investigation, send out written interrogatories, interview the applicant, and/or require the applicant to undergo a psychological evaluation. Of the approximately 8,000 cases received from DISCO in 2009, DOHA favorably adjudicated about 72.5% (5,800 cases) and directed DISCO to grant or continue the clearances. DOHA made preliminary decisions to deny or revoke clearances on the remaining 27.5% (2,200 cases). When this occurs, DOHA sends the applicant a "Statement of Reasons" detailing the specific reasons why it intends to deny or revoke the clearance and advises the applicant of their right to submit a written rebuttal and their right to a hearing.

Statement of Reasons (SOR)—About 23% of applicants who receive an SOR from DOHA drop out of the process by not responding to the SOR; their clearances are denied or revoked without further action. For an applicant who chooses to rebut the SOR, the written rebuttal must be received at DOHA within 20 days from the date the applicant receives the SOR. This rebuttal can be made with or without a request for a hearing. Applicants may request an extension of time to file a rebuttal to the SOR, but they must have a good reason. The rebuttal must include a detailed written answer that admits or denies each allegation in the SOR. The applicant may include information that rebuts, explains, or mitigates each allegation. The SOR rebuttal may also include affidavits from friends and associates corroborating the applicant's claims or attesting to the applicant's character, reliability, and honesty. The applicant may also submit other documents with the SOR rebuttal that might influence a favorable determination under a "whole person" assessment, such as employment performance reviews and recognition for professional, academic and other achievements. If a review of the SOR rebuttal determines that the applicant has fully mitigated the potentially disqualifying conditions, DOHA directs DISCO to grant the clearance.

Judgment without a hearing—About 30% of applicants who respond to an SOR do not request hearings. If DOHA determines that the applicant's SOR response has not mitigated the potentially disqualifying conditions and the applicant has not requested a hearing, the case is assigned to a DOHA administrative judge within 20 days of receipt of the SOR rebuttal and the applicant is sent a File Of Relevant Materials (FORM). The FORM consists of all material that will be submitted by the DOHA Department Counsel to the DOHA Administrative Judge for a decision based solely on the written record. The applicant has 30 days from receipt of the FORM to submit a written response to the FORM, setting forth objections, rebuttal, extenuation, mitigation, or explanation, as appropriate. About 88% of case decisions based only on a review of the written record by a DOHA Administrative Judge result in clearance denial or revocation.

Judgment with a hearing—About 70% of applicants who respond to an SOR request hearings. Either the applicant or a DOHA Department Counsel can request a hearing. If a hearing is requested, the applicant will be notified at least 15 days in advance of the time and place of the hearing. The hearing will be held at a location within a major city near the applicant's place of employment or residence. The Administrative Judge may require a pre-hearing conference. The applicant must appear at the hearing in person with or without an attorney or a personal representative. Hearings are generally open, except when the applicant requests that it be closed, or when the Administrative Judge determines that there is good cause for keeping the proceedings closed.

As far in advance as practical, the DOHA Department Counsel and the applicant may request information from the opposing party regarding witnesses or other evidence to support or rebut, explain, extenuate or mitigate information contained in the SOR that may be presented at the hearing. This is essentially the same as the information presented in the FORM and the applicant's response to the FORM when no hearing is requested, plus a list of witnesses and the nature of the testimony they will provide. At the hearing witnesses and other evidence are subject to cross examination, and a verbatim transcript is made of the hearing.

After the hearing, the Administrative Judge makes a written decision that includes not only the clearance decision but also all findings of fact, policies, and conclusions regarding the allegations in the SOR. This written decision is sent to both the applicant and the DOHA Department Counsel. DOHA then directs DISCO to make appropriate notification to the applicant's employer. If the clearance is denied or revoked, the applicant is notified of appeal procedures. About 60% of case decisions based on a hearing result in clearance denial or revocation. A copy of the DOHA Prehearing Guidance is at Appendix L.

The Appeal—Either the applicant or the DOHA Department Counsel can appeal the DOHA Administrative Judge's decision. About 20% to 30% of these decisions are appealed. This must be done in writing within 15 days of the Administrative Judge's decision. Appeals go before a DOHA Appeal Board of three Administrative Judges. A written appeal brief must be received by the Appeal Board within 45 days from the date of the Administrative Judge's original decision. If the DOHA Department Counsel submits an appeal, a copy of the appeal brief is sent to the applicant and the applicant has 20 days to submit a written reply brief, if any. No new evidence is received or considered by the Appeal Board; therefore, most appeals claim that the judge's decision was arbitrary, capricious, or contrary to law because the evidence did not support the decision and/or insufficient weight was given to applicant's mitigating evidence. Except for rare circumstances where there were procedural errors, an Appeal Board's decision is final. The Appeal Board issues a written decision addressing the material issues raised on appeal, and a copy is sent to both parties. The Appeal Board can affirm, reverse, or remand a case to the original Administrative Judge with instructions for further review.

In the majority of appeals, the DOHA Appeal Board affirms clearance denials. Industrial and non-industrial applicants do not have a right to contest security clearance denials or revocations in the courts. A copy of the DOHA Appeal Instructions is at Appendix M.

Department of Energy (DOE)—DOE procedures are similar to DISCO/DOHA procedures. DOE has a number of security offices that grant security clearances and make preliminary decisions to deny or revoke clearances for both federal employees and contractors. When one of DOE's security offices is unable to grant a clearance and the applicant requests a hearing, the case is referred to DOE's Office of Hearing and Appeals for adjudication.

Other Adjudication Facilities—There are differences between the adjudication of most federal contractor (industrial) cases and the adjudication of cases involving military/federal civilian applicants and cases involving Special Access Programs.

In non-industrial cases, applicants who receive an SOR (also known as a Letter of Intent or LOI) do not have a right to a hearing. The applicant's written rebuttal to the SOR is reviewed by a supervisory adjudicator who makes the clearance decision.

DoD Regulation 5200.2-R, *Personnel Security Program*, states that an applicant has 10 days to notify the CAF of his/her intent to rebut the SOR and 30 days to submit the rebuttal. An extension of 30 days can be granted by the CAF. CAFs must provide applicants a written decision to their SOR rebuttal promptly, but not more than 60 days from the date of receipt of the SOR rebuttal, unless additional investigative action is necessary. If a decision cannot be issued with 60 days, the applicant must be notified and in no case will the decision take more than a total of 90 days.

If the applicant's clearance is denied or revoked based on a review of the SOR rebuttal, the applicant then has a right to appeal. In making the appeal, applicants have the choice of submitting a written appeal with supporting documents directly to their Personnel Security Appeal Board (PSAB) or requesting a personal appearance before a DOHA Administrative Judge. Procedures and timelines for SOR rebuttals and appeals differ slightly for each CAF/PSAB. DoD specifies 10 days to notify the PSAB of an intent to appeal with or without a personal appearance, and 40 days to submit an appeal brief when a personal appearance is not request. Applicants who choose to appear before a DOHA Administrative Judge to present their appeal are permitted to explain their case (with or without an attorney or personal representative), submit supporting documents, and present witnesses,[28] but it is not a hearing and there is usually no opposing counsel. The DOHA Administrative Judge evaluates all the information presented and makes a written clearance recommendation to the applicant's PSAB generally within 60 days of receiving the request for a personal ap-

---

[28] Prior to Under Secretary of Defense for Intelligence, Memorandum of 19 November 2007, "Amendment to DoD Regulation 5200.2-R to Delete Bar on Witnesses," applicants were not permitted to present witness at a personal appearance.

pearance. PSABs are composed of 3 members and decisions are made by a majority vote. PSABs notify applicants of their final decision and include reasons for their decision.

At first glance it may seem that applicants in industrial cases have greater procedural protections and administrative remedies than in non-industrial cases, because of their right to a hearing. But that hearing is an adversarial process in which the government is represented by an attorney experienced in security clearance matters, and the applicant may not be able to afford equal representation. When industrial applicants appeal their cases, they cannot introduce new evidence; whereas, applicants in non-industrial cases can submit new evidence, and the PSAB can take an entirely fresh look at the case and make what they believe to be the appropriate decision without regard for the lower-level decision. Lastly, in industrial cases, either party (the applicant or the DOHA Department Counsel) can appeal the decision of a DOHA Administrative Judge.

ADJUDICATION OF SCI ELIGIBILITY

SCI eligibility can only be granted or denied by an Intelligence Community (IC) agency. Most industrial applicants needing SCI, are initially processed through DISCO, and their investigations are conducted by OPM. OPM sends the completed investigations to DISCO, but DISCO does not adjudicate the investigations.[29] DISCO forwards the investigations to the sponsoring IC agency for adjudication. If SCI eligibility is granted, a collateral Top Secret clearance is also granted at the same time. If the SCI eligibility is denied for an industrial applicant, but the applicant needs a non-SCI clearance, the investigation is returned to DISCO for adjudication of the non-SCI clearance.

If a sponsoring IC agency makes a preliminary decision to deny SCI eligibility for an industrial or non-industrial applicant, the applicant is sent an SOR (or equivalent letter) and advised of the right to submit a rebuttal within 45 days. If a review of the response to the SOR results in an unfavorable determination, the applicant is notified of the decision (including reasons for the decision) and advised of the right to appeal the decision in writing to the head of the IC agency, who can make the final decision himself or refer it to a 3-member

---

[29] The Defense Security Service states on their website that if the request is for an initial clearance, DISCO may issue the collateral clearance eligibility prior to forwarding to the SCI CAF, but this rarely seems to occur.

PSAB. The applicant is also given the opportunity to appear personally before the PSAB or other adjudicative authority, such as a DOHA Administrative Judge.[30] The decision of a DOHA Administrative Judge is only a recommendation, which can be accepted or rejected by the PSAB and/or IC agency head.

FINAL DENIAL OR REVOCATION
OF A SECURITY CLEARANCE

An applicant whose security clearance has been finally denied or revoked is barred from reapplication for one year from the date of the unfavorable clearance decision. A reapplication for a security clearance must be sponsored by a federal agency or federal contractor and is subject to the same processing requirements as those required for a new security clearance application. After an industrial applicant reapplies for a clearance, he/she is notified of the requirement to provide the Director of DOHA a copy of the prior adverse clearance decision together with evidence that circumstances or conditions previously found against the applicant have been rectified or sufficiently mitigated to warrant reconsideration. If the Director of DOHA decides that reconsideration is warranted, DISCO will be directed to request a new investigation. Otherwise the applicant is barred from reapplying for another year. Other federal agencies have similar procedures.

EMPLOYMENT SUITABILITY/FITNESS
VERSUS SECURITY CLEARANCE

When you accept a federal job offer that requires a security clearance, you will be required to submit an SF86. For most positions you will have to wait until you are granted either an interim security clearance or a final security clearance before you are actually hired and report for duty. That can be a matter of a few days or several months depending on the type of security clearance required. The federal agency's security office will review your SF86 for completeness, check federal investigations/clearance databases, and provide a copy of the SF86 to their Human Resources (HR) office. The HR office will review your SF86 to insure that you meet the minimum employment suitabil-

---

[30] Intelligence Community Policy Guidance Number 704-3, October 2008, "Denial or Revocation of Access to Sensitive Compartmented Information, Other Controlled Access Program Information, and Appeals Processes.

ity or fitness criteria for the position. If the HR review is favorable, the security office will forward your SF86 to the organization that will conduct the rest of your background investigation. At this point if the federal agency considers an interim clearance is necessary, the agency's security office can grant or decline to grant an interim Secret clearance. A determination for an interim Top Secret clearance cannot be made until additional preliminary checks are completed. These checks usually take a few weeks. When the entire investigation is completed, it is usually forwarded to the agency's HR office for employment suitability adjudication. If the employment suitability adjudication by the HR office is favorable, the investigation is then adjudicated for a security clearance. These two adjudications are usually separate processes by separate offices using different criteria.

There arc 3 stages at which the offer of employment you accepted can be withdrawn by the agency—the initial HR review,[31] the HR adjudication, and the security clearance adjudication. If you are rejected because you failed to meet employment suitability criteria, your right to 1) be informed of the specific reasons, 2) rebut the reasons, and 3) appeal a final adverse decision to the Merit System Protection Board (MSPB) will depend on the type of the position you were offered. Federal agencies are required to use employment suitability standards and procedures for all appointments to "competitive service" positions. OPM recommends, but does not require, that these same standards and procedures be used for appointments to excepted service positions and temporary positions, as well as contractor positions.

Most IC agency jobs and some other federal jobs that require security clearances are "excepted service" positions. Consequently if an agency withdraws a job offer for an excepted service position due to employment fitness reasons, they generally only inform you that you were found to be unfit for the position without providing any specific reason. Applicants often confuse this with being denied a security clearance, because the job offer was withdrawn after they submitted a security clearance application.

Federal contractor positions that require both a Public Trust and a security clearance are subject to the same processing as federal excepted service positions that require a security clearance, except that contractor applicants submit their application forms to their companies'

---

[31] Polygraph screening exams, when required, can be done as part of the initial HR review or as part of the background investigation subsequent to the initial HR review.

security offices where they are reviewed for completeness, then forwarded to a federal agency for further processing.

Title 5 Code of Federal Regulations Part 731 (5 CFR 731) governs federal employment suitability standards and procedures. Section 731.202 of 5 CFR 731 covers specific suitability criteria. For excepted service positions some disqualifying factors are listed at 5 CFR 302.203. The *Adjudicative Guidelines* governs federal security clearance criteria. Employment suitability/fitness and security clearance criteria are very similar, but differences exist.

One major difference is that suitability and fitness criteria can be influenced by the nature of the position for which you are applying, whereas security clearance criteria is unaffected by the nature of the position (except that SAP eligibility can be affected by unique country-specific SAP Foreign Influence factors). As previously stated there must be a nexus between the additional criteria, the agency's mission, and the position duties. This difference can result in being rejected due to suitability or fitness criteria in situations where a security clearance would have been granted had the person not been eliminated from the hiring process before the case was adjudicated for a security clearance. When this happens, it is possible to be subsequently hired as federal contractor employee in a position that does not require an employment fitness determination (e.g. Public Trust position) and be granted a security clearance at the same level required for the federal job. For example, the Drug Enforcement Agency (DEA) considers applicants unsuitable for employment, if they have ever illegally used any drug. The only exception to this is for self-disclosed "limited youthful and experimental use of marijuana." The FBI has a similar policy that limits drug involvement to experimental marijuana use more than 3 years ago and experimental use of other drugs more than 10 years ago. Both the DEA's and the FBI's employment suitability criteria for drug involvement are significantly more restrictive than security clearance criteria currently being applied by federal agencies.

If a federal agency notifies you that you were found unsuitable or unfit for the position without providing any other explanation, the position was either an excepted service position, a temporary position, or a contractor position not covered under 5 CFR 731. It is possible that this adverse suitability/fitness determination may not have any effect on future security clearance eligibility or on future suitability or fitness determinations for employment with a different federal agency.

If a federal agency intends to withdraw an offer of employment for a competitive service position due to suitability criteria, they must notify you in writing (Notice of Proposed Action—NOPA) and state the reasons they believe you are unsuitable. The NOPA must explain your right to receive the information used to make this decision and your right to make a written rebuttal. If the agency makes a final adverse suitability decision, they must notify you of that decision in writing and inform you of your right to appeal the decision to the MSPB.

Being denied employment due to an unfavorable suitability or fitness determination is not considered a clearance denial or revocation and you are not required to list it on an SF86 or SF85P. If an unfavorable suitability determination also resulted in debarment from federal service, it must be listed on the SF86, SF85P, and Optional Form 306—OF306 (Declaration for Federal Employment). There is no question on the SF85 regarding prior federal background investigations, debarments or clearance denials/revocations. In any event, all prior federal background investigations must be listed on the SF86 and SF85P. When applying for a job that requires both suitability/fitness and security clearance determinations, it is difficult to know at what point an agency records the initiation of a background investigation. Since the review of a clearance application form is the first step of every background investigation, applicants must assume that when they submit a clearance application form to a federal agency, a background investigation has been initiated.

If your case receives a favorable suitability or fitness determination, your background investigation will be adjudicated for a security clearance. All security clearance adjudications are required to provide essentially the same "due process" rights, regardless of whether the job is for a competitive service position, excepted service position, or contractor position. If there is a preliminary decision to deny a clearance, you will be sent an SOR or an LOI detailing specific reasons why granting you a clearance may not be clearly consistent with the interests of national security. The SOR or LOI will include instructions for submitting a rebuttal and in some cases requesting a hearing. If there is a final decision to deny a clearance, you will be sent a "Letter of Denial" (LOD) that contains instructions for submitting an appeal. (Sample SORs and LOD are at Appendix J, K, and N.)

CHAPTER 6

REQUESTING CASE FILES

Anyone who has been investigated for a clearance can request a copy of their investigative and adjudicative case files under the provisions of the Federal Privacy Act. More than 90% of all background investigations have been conducted by DSS or OPM. DSS stopped conducting background investigations on 20 February 2005. Prior to that they conducted background investigations on all personnel affiliated with DoD, except for employment suitability investigations, which were conducted by OPM. On 20 February 2005 OPM assumed responsibility for conducting all background investigations formerly conducted by DSS. Between 2002 and 2005 OPM conducted some background investigations for DSS, but DSS retained control of the investigations. There are 21 other federal agencies that have delegated or statutory authority to conduct their own investigations, but in total they conduct less than 10% of all investigations.

There are limitations to the release of copies of investigative files to the Subject of the investigation. Because each investigation is unique, it is difficult to provide a comprehensive list of information that might be redacted from your investigative file before it is released to you. The most common redacted information falls into one of these three general areas:

- Information that pertains to another person and release of which would, constitute a violation of their privacy.

- Information that is currently and properly classified.

- Information that may tend to identify a source to whom a promise of confidentiality was granted.

Copies of open investigations are generally not released until the case is closed. In certain instances, medical information may be withheld. In those cases you can request that the medical information be sent to a physician of your choice, so the physician can explain the information to you.

REQUESTS FOR INVESTIGATIVE RECORDS

OPM Investigations—To obtain a copy of your background investigation conducted by OPM, mail your request to:

> FOI/P, OPM-FIPC
> P.O. Box 618
> 1137 Branchton Road
> Boyers, PA 16018-0618

Your request must include your hand written signature and all of the following information:

- Full name
- Social Security Number
- Date of birth
- Place of birth
- Current home address (a Post Office Box is not acceptable; the records are sent by certified mail and require your signature).

Alternatively, you may FAX your hand signed request to 724-794-4590. If you have any questions, you can call OPM at 724-794-5612.

DSS Investigations—Due to the transfer of the DSS personnel security investigations function to OPM on February 20, 2005, any requests for investigations completed after February 20, 2005 should be sent to OPM. DSS only maintains those personnel security investigations completed by the agency prior to the February 20, 2005 transfer.

If you wish to request a copy of your DSS investigation, you must send a written request containing the following:

- Full current name
- Any other names you may have used in the past

- Date of Birth
- Social Security Number
- An originally notarized signature
- A brief description of the records you are seeking
- Any other information that you believe may be useful in searching for records pertaining to you
- Whether you want someone else to receive the records on your behalf (include name and address of the other party)

Mail your request to:

> Defense Security Service
> Privacy Act Branch
> 938 Elkridge Landing Road
> Linthicum, MD 21090-2917

Please note, that due to privacy concerns, facsimile and electronic mail requests for investigative files are **not** accepted by DSS. Only originally signed and properly notarized requests will be accepted via postal mail.

Requests for Adjudicative Files—Although OPM currently conducts over 90% of all federal background investigation, they adjudicate only a fraction of 1% of all investigations. OPM adjudicates security clearance and suitability cases for OPM personnel and OPM contractor personnel, as well as limited number of suitability cases referred to OPM by other agencies.

Requests for copies of adjudication/clearance records must be submitted to the agency that adjudicated the investigation, not the agency that conducted the investigation, unless the same agency conducted the investigation and adjudicated it. Records of suitability, fitness and HSPD12 credentialing determinations are generally held by the federal agency's Human Resources office. Records of security clearance determinations are held by the agency's Central Adjudication Facility.

PART II

ISSUES
&
MITIGATION

CHAPTER 7

INTRODUCTION TO PART II

In the following chapters potentially disqualifying conditions for credentialing, employment suitability, fitness, and security clearances are listed along with mitigating factors. Because the list of potentially disqualifying conditions for security clearances is the most comprehensive, they are presented in the order listed in the "*Adjudicative Guidelines for Determining Eligibility for Access to Classified Information*," along with their applicability to each of the different types of clearances. With the exception of Chapter 13, none of the chapter titles requires explanation. Chapter 13, "Personal Conduct & Regulatory Bars," includes the issues of deliberate omission, concealment, and falsification of relevant facts; work-related misconduct; susceptibility to blackmail; association with criminals; some whole-person factors; and conditions that can result in a bar to federal employment. A list of bars to federal employment is included in Appendix D.

There are differences in the disqualifying conditions listed at 5 CFR 731.202 (suitability) and 5 CFR 302.203 (fitness). Neither list is comprehensive, and there are conditions that do not appear on either list that could result in disqualification. Although 5 CFR 731.202 states that only factors listed in 5 CFR 731.202 will be considered a "basis for finding a person unsuitable;" the "criminal or dishonest conduct" factor can be interpreted very broadly. For example 5 CFR 731.202 does not specifically list delinquent debt as a disqualifying factor; however, dishonest conduct encompasses intentional failure to pay one's debts, even if the failure was due to inability to pay the debt. Many applicants are found unsuitable for employment when they have significant delinquent debt that does not involve criminal or dishonest behavior per se. The factors listed in 5 CFR 302.203 are only examples of some disqualifying reasons that may be used to find an applicant unfit, and agencies are authorized to use any other regulations or practices that are necessary.

OPM's "Final Credentialing Standards for Issuing Personal Identity Verifications Cards under HSPD-12" purports to be a comprehensive list of disqualifying conditions that all federal agencies must follow. However, the standards do not address financial considerations or mental health.

Unlike the *Adjudicative Guidelines* for security clearances, there are no issue-specific mitigating conditions for federal employment suitability determinations under 5 CFR 731.202. Only the following general factors are listed at 5 CFR 731.202 as "Additional considerations":

(1) The nature of the position for which the person is applying or in which the person is employed;

(2) The nature and seriousness of the conduct;

(3) The circumstances surrounding the conduct;

(4) The recency of the conduct;

(5) The age of the person involved at the time of the conduct;

(6) Contributing societal conditions; and

(7) The absence or presence of rehabilitation or efforts toward rehabilitation.

Neither OPM's *Final Credentialing Standards* for PIV card issuance, nor 5 CFR 302.203 (federal employment fitness), contains any general or specific mitigating factors. However as previously stated, OPM recommends that all federal agencies apply the employment suitability criteria at 5 CFR 731.202 (including the 7 factors listed above) for making employment fitness determinations. Many federal agencies have incorporated these criteria into their internal policy documents for making fitness determinations for excepted service appointments and contractor personnel. Because of this, it is recommended that all mitigating conditions for security clearance issues be viewed as equally applicable to security clearance, suitability, fitness, and credentialing determinations.

Throughout Part II of this book applicability of potentially disqualifying conditions for each type of clearance is presented in accordance with government standards and guidelines. Explanations of potentially disqualifying conditions as they apply to each of the 3 federal personnel security programs appearing in italics at the beginning of Chapters 9 through 21 are taken from the OPM's January 14, 2008 *"Credentialing, Suitability, and Security Clearance Decision-Making Guide,"* which uses criteria established in the OPM's *Final Credentialing Standards*, 5 CFR 731.202, and the *Adjudicative Guidelines for Determining Eligibility for Access to Classified Information*.

Paragraphs 1, 2(b), 2(c), 2(d), 2(e), and 2(f) of December 2005 *Adjudicative Guidelines* are reprinted below, because they do not appear elsewhere in this book:

ADJUDICATIVE GUIDELINES FOR DETERMINING ELIGIBILITY FOR ACCESS TO CLASSIFIED INFORMATION

1. Introduction. The following adjudicative guidelines are established for all U.S. government civilian and military personnel, consultants, contractors, employees of contractors, licensees, certificate holders or grantees and their employees and other individuals who require access to classified information. They apply to persons being considered for initial or continued eligibility for access to classified information, to include sensitive compartmented information and special access programs, and are to be used by government departments and agencies in all final clearance determinations. Government departments and agencies may also choose to apply these guidelines to analogous situations regarding persons being considered for access to other types of protected information.

Decisions regarding eligibility for access to classified information take into account factors that could cause a conflict of interest and place a person in the position of having to choose between his or her commitment to the United States, including the commitment to protect classified information, and any other compelling loyalty. Access decisions also take into account a person's reliability, trustworthiness and ability to protect classified information. No coercive policing could replace the self-discipline and integrity of the person entrusted with the nation's secrets as the most effective means of protecting them. When a person's life history shows evidence of unreliability or untrustworthiness, questions arise whether the person can be relied on and trusted to exercise the responsibility necessary for working in a secure environment where protecting classified information is paramount.

2. The Adjudicative Process.
(a) (removed—see Chapter 8 of this book)
(b) Each case must be judged on its own merits, and final determination remains the responsibility of the specific department or agency. Any doubt concerning personnel being considered for access to classified information will be resolved in favor of the national security.

(c) The ability to develop specific thresholds for action under these guidelines is limited by the nature and complexity of human behavior. The ultimate determination of whether the granting or continuing of eligibility for a security clearance is clearly consistent with the interests of national security must be an overall common sense judgment based upon careful consideration of the following guidelines, each of which is to be evaluated in the context of the whole person.

(1) GUIDELINE A: Allegiance to the United States;

(2) GUIDELINE B: Foreign Influence;

(3) GUIDELINE C: Foreign Preference;

(4) GUIDELINE D: Sexual Behavior;

(5) GUIDELINE E: Personal Conduct;

(6) GUIDELINE F: Financial Considerations;

(7) GUIDELINE G: Alcohol Consumption;

(8) GUIDELINE H: Drug Involvement;

(9) GUIDELINE I: Psychological Conditions;

(10) GUIDELINE J: Criminal Conduct;

(11) GUIDELINE K: Handling Protected Information;

(12) GUIDELINE L: Outside Activities;

(13) GUIDELINE M: Use of Information Technology Systems

(d) Although adverse information concerning a single criterion may not be sufficient for an unfavorable determination, the individual may be disqualified if available information reflects a recent or recurring pattern of questionable judgment, irresponsibility, or emotionally unstable behavior. Notwithstanding the whole-person concept, pursuit of further investigation may be terminated by an appropriate adjudicative agency in the face of reliable, significant, disqualifying, adverse information.

(e) When information of security concern becomes known about an individual who is currently eligible for access to classified information, the adjudicator should consider whether the person:

(1) voluntarily reported the information;

(2) was truthful and complete in responding to questions;

(3) sought assistance and followed professional guidance, where appropriate;

(4) resolved or appears likely to favorably resolve the security concern;

(5) has demonstrated positive changes in behavior and employment;

(6) should have his or her access temporarily suspended pending final adjudication of the information.

(f) If after evaluating information of security concern, the adjudicator decides that the information is not serious enough to warrant a recommendation of disapproval or revocation of the security clearance, it may be appropriate to recommend approval with a warning that future incidents of a similar nature may result in revocation of access.

Adjudicative Desk Reference (ADR)

In applying the standards listed in the *Adjudicative Guidelines*, adjudicators may also use the ADR, developed by the Defense Personnel Security Research Center (PERSEREC) for additional guidance. The ADR contains the Adjudication Guidelines and extensive background information on the relevance and applicability of security issue information. PERSEREC updated the ADR in June 2010, and it is available to the public on the internet. The following disclaimer is included in the ADR: "The background information about the adjudicative issue areas [in the ADR] is not U.S. Government policy and may not be cited as authority for denial or suspension of access. The Security Executive Agent Advisory Committee approved this program and encouraged its use as a job aid to assist security personnel in making informed judgments to implement policy." [The Security Executive Agent is the Director of National Intelligence.]

ELECTRONIC QUESTIONNAIRE FOR INVESTIGATIONS PROCESSING (E-QIP)

Since more than 90% of all SF86s (and equally high percentages of the SF85 and SF85P) are submitted using e-QIP, no reference is made elsewhere in Section II of this book regarding the use of the paper version of the forms. The primary difference between the paper version and the e-QIP version is the branching questions on the e-QIP version. An applicant who answers "no" to a threshold question in the e-QIP will not see the additional follow-on questions that ask for details regarding a "yes" response. Each section and sub-section of the e-QIP version has an "Optional Comment" field that allows the applicant to add a narrative explanation and more details regarding a potential issue. On the paper version there are only a few questions that have space next to them to enter information other than the details specifically requested by the question. On the SF85 and SF86 the "Continuation Space" on the last page of the paper version (and additional sheets of blank paper) is used for entering additional information. The paper version of the SF85P has no "Continuation Space," so it is necessary to provide mitigating information on a separate sheet of paper and attach it to the SF85P as an addendum. Throughout this book applicants are advised to provide as much mitigating information as possible using the "Optional Comment" fields. For applicants using the paper version of the forms, this same information will have to be entered into the

"Continuation Space" and/or on separate attached sheets of paper with the applicant's name and SSN at the top of each sheet.

OPM is currently revising the SF85P and anticipates a new version of the form will be implemented in late 2011. This new version of the SF85P will include questions that are currently on the SF85P-S, thus eliminating the need for the SF85P-S for selected positions, but increasing the scope of the questions on the SF85P. A revision to the SF85 is also planned, but not until a revised SF85P has been approved.

USE OF SPECIFIC TERMINOLOGY FOR MITIGATION

Mitigating information can be provided by the applicant during the following stages of the security clearance process:

1. When completing the clearance application form.

2. During a face-to-face interview with an investigator.

3. In response to a "Written Interrogatory" from an adjudicator.

4. In response to an SOR.

5. In response to a "File of Relevant Material"[32] or at a hearing.

For suitability, fitness, and credentialing determinations only some of these stages for submitting information are available.

When providing mitigation for security/suitability issues it is advisable to couch the wording in a way that it directly relates to the wording of the disqualifying or mitigating conditions as they are stated in the adjudicative criteria. The following are samples of simple statements that can be made on an SF86 or during an interview with an investigator, when providing mitigation for the "Foreign Preference" issue:

- My foreign citizenship is based solely on my parents' citizenship at the time of my birth.

- My foreign citizenship is based solely on birth aboard to U.S. citizen parents.

---

[32] The File of Relevant Materials (FORM) contains all the information that will be presented to a DOHA Administrative Judge by the DOHA Department Counsel (attorney) when a hearing has not been requested. It is equivalent to the information that must be disclosed by the Department Counsel prior to a hearing.

- I am ready and willing to renounce my foreign citizenship.

- I no longer possess a foreign passport. I surrendered it to (<u>name & position title</u>) on (<u>date</u>).

- My foreign passport was obtained for me by my parents when I was a minor. I have never used my foreign passport to enter or exit any country.

- I have not used my foreign passport since I became a naturalized U.S. citizen on (<u>date</u>).

- I have never exercised any rights, privileges, or obligations of foreign citizenship, and I have no intention of doing so in the future.

- I have not exercised any rights, privileges, or obligations of foreign citizenship, since I became a naturalized U.S. citizen.

- I have never performed or attempted to perform duties or otherwise acted so as to serve the interest of a foreign person, group, organization, or government in conflict with the national security interest of the United States, and I have no intention of doing so in the future.

- I have never been in the military service of a foreign country, and I have no intention of doing so in the future. I am unwilling to bear arms for any foreign country.

For a reply to a Written Interrogatory, SOR, or FORM, a more detailed response that includes all information that rebuts, explains, extenuates, and/or mitigates the potentially disqualifying conditions should be provide in narrative form.

It is not the purpose of suitability and security vetting processes to penalize applicants for existing conditions or mistakes they may have made in the past; the purpose is to attempt to predict future conduct based on past and present conduct and conditions. With regard to conduct-related issues, acknowledging the suitability/security significance of the behavior, accepting responsibility for it, obtaining professional counseling, and following the advice of the counselor to change the behavior always increases the possibility of fully mitigating the issue, as does other positive steps to alleviate the stressors, circumstances, or factors that caused the behavior.

CHAPTER 8

WHOLE-PERSON CONCEPT

The "Whole-Person" concept has become widely known among those who have been involved with national security clearances and is often misunderstood.[33] Applicants for security clearance are evaluated on potentially disqualifying and mitigating conditions listed under 13 separate guidelines in the *"Adjudicative Guidelines for Determining Eligibility for Access to Classified Information."* At paragraph 2(a), "The Adjudicative Process," the *Adjudicative Guidelines* additionally admonished adjudicators that:

(a) The adjudicative process is an examination of a sufficient period of a person's life to make an affirmative determination that the person is an acceptable security risk. Eligibility for access to classified information is predicated upon the individual meeting these personnel security guidelines. **The adjudication process is the careful weighing of a number of variables known as the whole-person concept. Available, reliable information about the person, past and present, favorable and unfavorable, should be considered in reaching a determination.** In evaluating the relevance of an individual's conduct, the adjudicator should consider the following factors: (emphasis added)

(1) The nature, extent, and seriousness of the conduct;

(2) the circumstances surrounding the conduct, to include knowledgeable participation;

(3) the frequency and recency of the conduct;

(4) the individual's age and maturity at the time of the conduct;

---

[33] Although the use of "whole-person" concept is clearly a requirement for security clearance adjudications; its use is not addressed in the standards for federal employment suitability/fitness or HSPD-12 credentialing determinations.

(5) the extent to which participation is voluntary;

(6) the presence or absence of rehabilitation and other permanent behavioral changes;

(7) the motivation for the conduct;

(8) the potential for pressure, coercion, exploitation, or duress; and

(9) the likelihood of continuation or recurrence.

These 9 factors, often referred to as the "General Criteria," must be considered together with applicable disqualifying and mitigating conditions listed under each of the 13 guidelines. But these are not the only factors and conditions that may be considered. A clearance decision should not be based on a finding that one or more disqualifying or mitigating conditions apply to the particular facts of a case. The adjudicator should consider all aspects of the case that are relevant and material to the applicant's trustworthiness and reliability. Unlike all the other mitigating factors that might apply to a security/suitability issue, only the last general criterion—*(9) the likelihood of continuation or recurrence*—suggests consideration of a person's general behavior before and after the conduct that resulted in the potentially disqualifying condition.

The problem of applying the whole-person concept is **availability** of information not directly related to the disqualifying condition(s) and **availability** of information regarding some issue-specific mitigating conditions unique to each of the 13 adjudicative criteria.

Adjudication that results in a preliminary decision to deny or revoke a clearance is based on a review of the applicant's SF86 and the results of the investigation—the NAC results, credit report, and Reports of Investigation (ROI). NAC results and credit reports never contain information regarding whole-person factors. ROIs rarely include information regarding whole-person factors, other than those listed under the General Criteria, and the General Criteria primarily list factors directly related to disqualifying conduct. ROIs sometime record personal references as stating that an applicant is "reliable, trustworthy, and honest," but ROIs almost never include specific examples reliable, trustworthy, or honest conduct. This is because most investigative agencies use an abbreviated report writing style that focuses almost entirely on security/suitability issues.

Investigators are trained to report potentially disqualifying conditions, as well as information related to the General Criteria, but they receive little or no training on issue-specific mitigating conditions listed in the 13 guidelines. Consequently issue-specific mitigating conditions, such as remorse/restitution or constructive community involvement for the issue of criminal conduct and total financial net worth as an indicator the relative value of foreign financial interests, are seldom recorded in ROIs.

Such things as recognition for professional accomplishments, consistent exemplary work performance, and academic achievements are usually not recorded in ROIs, unless there is an allegation of work- or school-related misconduct, and even then there is a possibility that they might not be recorded. Participation in civic, social, professional, educational, religious, and charitable organizations, as well as other forms of constructive community involvement usually does not appear in ROIs, unless an interviewee's knowledge of the applicant was based on contact related to one of these activities.

Without corroboration by an investigator or supporting documents, information on positive whole-person factors added to the comment sections of an SF86 has little adjudicative value. In some cases it is possible to submit supporting documents as an addendum to the SF86 for consideration during an interim clearance decision. It is also possible to provide supporting documents to an investigator during an ESI or SPIN, but it is difficult for an investigator to submit attachments with an ROI. Documents given to an investigator can be transcribed by the investigator into the narrative text of the ROI. Unfortunately in most cases the submission of documents that support positive whole-person factors usually does not occur until an applicant responds to a written notification (i.e. Letter of Intent or Letter of Instruction—LOI) that a government agency intends to deny or revoke his/her clearance. The LOI includes a "Statement of Reasons—SOR" detailing the applicable disqualifying conditions and conduct.

Most applicants are unaware that evidence of positive whole-person factors unrelated to disqualifying condition(s) is rarely considered by adjudicators unless applicants provide it themselves. This type of information is not elicited by the questions on an SF86, nor is it requested by an investigator during an ESI or SPIN. LOIs generally include instructions advising that the applicant must submit a detailed written answer to the SOR under oath or affirmation that admit or deny each listed allegation and that a general denial or other similar answer is insufficient.[34] *DoD Instructions for Responding to State-*

---

[34] An answer to a DOHA SOR can be a simple "I admit" or "I deny" response to each allegation, if the applicant requests a hearing. However this will preclude the possibil-

ment of Reasons (SOR),"[35] contains one sentence concerning the submission of documents related to whole-person factors:

> *"You may provide statements from co-workers, supervisors, your commander, friends, neighbors and others concerning your judgment, reliability and trustworthiness, and any other information that you think ought to be considered before a final decision is made."*

This sentence can easily be overlooked, because the instructions repeatedly emphasize submitting information that refutes, mitigates, extenuates, or explains the specific disqualifying information listed in the SOR.

DoD Instructions for Appealing a Letter of Denial/Revocation (LOD)[36] does not address whole-person factors at all and provides little guidance on the substance of appeals, but it makes reference to the information contained in the instructions for responding to an SOR.

Information that directly mitigates the potentially disqualifying condition(s) listed in the SOR is more important than positive whole-person factors. But positive whole-person factors can be used as the basis for supporting a favorable determination when information that directly mitigates a specific disqualifying condition does not exist or is insufficient.

Many applicants do not consider submitting evidence of positive whole-person factors until they have to respond to an SOR or appeal an LOD. SOR responses by federal contractors can include a request for a hearing before an administrative judge. Others only have the option for a "personal appearance" before an administrative judge or Personnel Security Appeal Board (PSAB), if they choose to appeal an LOD. Consequently this evidence is not available to adjudicators who can make a favorable determination at earlier stages of the adjudicative process. In cases involving major derogatory information, submitting this evidence at the earliest possible stage of the clearance process can reduce the time and increase the chance of a favorable determination.

---

ity of a favorable determination based on a review of the answer to the SOR and necessitate a hearing.

[35] See Appendix J.

[36] See Appendix N. In November 2007 DoD 5200.2-R was changed to allow witnesses to testify at "Personal Appearances."

As stated in the *DoD Instructions for Responding to an SOR*, "You may provide statements from co-workers, supervisors, your commander, friends, neighbors and others concerning your judgment, reliability and trustworthiness, and any other information that you think ought to be considered before a final decision is made." These statements can be in the form of a signed and dated letter, but sworn affidavits have greater probative value. It's probably wise to ask your friends and associates for a statement in the form of a letter. If needed, you can later transcribe the content of the letters into affidavit format on your own, and have your associates meet you at the office of a notary public where they can sign the affidavits under oath. Ideally you should submit one statement to cover each major aspect of your life—work, home, school, and other activities (e.g. civic, social, charitable, religious, etc.). These statements should be from people who know you well and, if possible, who know about the potentially disqualifying condition(s). It does not matter if they were previously interviewed as part of your background investigation. The statements should cover as much of your adult life as possible, but usually not more than 10 years. If you have live, worked, and attended school in more than one location during the period you need to cover, you will need to obtain additional statements. When submitting other documents, such as letters of commendation/appreciation, awards, certificates, diplomas, educational transcripts, etc., it is preferable to submit certified copies of originals. A notary public can certify copies of most original documents.

Appendix H is a sample Reference Affidavit and Appendix I is a sample Subject Affidavit. It may be appropriate to submit copies of affidavits as separate attachments to an SF86, when possible, to increase the chance of receiving an interim clearance. Alternatively, copies of affidavits can be given to an investigator during an ESI or SPIN. When answering an SOR from any federal agency it is better to use the DOHA SOR response format at Appendix K and submit Reference Affidavits (and other documents) as supporting documents to the SOR response.

CHAPTER 9

ALLEGIANCE TO THE UNITED STATES

ADJUDICATIVE CRITERIA

HSPD-12 Credentialing:
Individuals entrusted with access to Federal property and information systems must not put the government at risk or provide an avenue for terrorism. A PIV card will not be issued to a person if:

The individual is known to be or reasonably suspected of being a terrorist.

The following consideration may apply:

The individual has knowingly and willfully engaged in acts or activities designed to overthrow the U.S. Government by force.

Employment Suitability/Fitness:
All Federal employees must be loyal to the United States. The following suitability factor may apply:

Knowing and willful engagement in acts or activities designed to overthrow the U.S. Government by force. Information to consider when using this factor:

  (a) *Disqualifying acts must be overt, defined illegal acts.*

  (b) *Disqualifying advocacy must be the incitement or indoctrination to commit defined illegal acts.*

(c) *Disqualifying associations require the individual to know of the organization's unlawful goals, and for the individual to be an active member of the organization or to have the specific intent to further its unlawful goals.*

Security Clearance (Guideline A):

3.   *The Concern.* An individual must be of unquestioned allegiance to the United States. The willingness to safeguard classified information is in doubt if there is any reason to suspect an individual's allegiance to the United States.

4. *Conditions that could raise a security concern and may be disqualifying include:*

(a) *involvement in, support of, training to commit, or advocacy of any act of sabotage, espionage, treason, terrorism, or sedition against the United States of America;*

(b) *association or sympathy with persons who are attempting to commit, or who are committing, any of the above acts;*

(c) *association or sympathy with persons or organizations that advocate, threaten, or use force or violence, or use any other illegal or unconstitutional means, in an effort to:*

(1) *overthrow or influence the government of the United States or any state or local government;*

(2) *prevent Federal, state, or local government personnel from performing their official duties;*

(3) *gain retribution for perceived wrongs caused by the Federal, state, or local government;*

(4) *prevent others from exercising their rights under the Constitution or laws of the United States or of any state.*

5. *Conditions that could mitigate security concerns include:*

(a) *the individual was unaware of the unlawful aims of the individual or organization and severed ties upon learning of these;*

(b) *the individual's involvement was only with the lawful or humanitarian aspects of such an organization;*

(c) involvement in the above activities occurred for only a short period of time and was attributable to curiosity or academic interest;

(d) the involvement or association with such activities occurred under such unusual circumstances, or so much times has elapsed, that it is unlikely to recur and does not cast doubt on the individual's current reliability, trustworthiness, or loyalty.

DISCUSSION

For federal security clearance, Guideline A covers "Allegiance to the United States;" however, most issues perceived as involving "Allegiance to the United States" are actually covered under "Foreign Influence" (Guideline B) and "Foreign Preference" (Guideline C). Guideline A primarily concerns unlawful speech or action to influence, harm, or overthrow local, state or federal government or to prevent others from exercising their Constitutional rights.

Criticism of government policy or government agencies is protected by the First Amendment to the U.S. Constitution. Even abstract or purely hypothetical advocacy of violent overthrow of the government is Constitutionally protected speech, provided it does not seek to incite imminent unlawful action (sedition). Merely voicing opposition to the government or existing laws is not unlawful and not a security concern. However, when military personnel or public employees voice opposition to the government or existing laws, it could be potentially disqualifying conduct for a security clearance under Guideline E (Personal Conduct) or for a suitability determination under the "misconduct or negligence in employment" factor (see Chapter 13). Court cases and DoD regulations support disciplinary action against government employees and military personnel when their speech harms their organizations' efficiency or effectiveness. 37

Everyone understands that involvement in unlawful activities to support foreign interests to the detriment of U.S. national security could result in the denial of a clearance. Almost everyone understands

---

37 Recognizing the state's need to maintain order and efficiency, the U.S. Supreme Court stated in *Pickering v. Board of Education*, 391 U.S. 563 (1968) that a public employee's "interest as a citizen in making public comment must be balanced against the State's interest in promoting the efficiency of its employees' public services." This concept was later applied in *Connick v.Myers*, 461 U.S. 138, 146 (1983). DoD Instruction 1325.06, Dated: November 27, 2009, Subject: *Handling Dissident and Protest Activities Among Members of the Armed Forces*, describes impermissible conduct that would otherwise be Constitutionally protected.

that sympathetic association with people involved in these types of activities could also result in clearance denial. However, sympathetic association with groups that use or advocate violence to achieve domestic political or social objectives may be less clearly understood as a potentially disqualifying condition for a clearance. Involvement in extremist organizations, such as hate groups, antigovernment patriot groups, and single-issue groups (e.g. Animal Liberation Front and Earth Liberation Front) fall into this category.

The tactics used by these groups vary greatly. Some operate completely within the law, using non-violent demonstrations to further their cause. Others organize lawful demonstrations with the intent of causing violence through vociferous, confrontational speech to gain greater media attention. A few advocate and use unlawful "direct action." Membership in an organization that seemingly advocates only lawful, non-violent means to attain its objectives can be complicated by the existence of an underground faction of the organization that engages in unlawful direct action, and some members can be unaware that their contributions are funneled to the underground faction.

Even if a person does not participate in illegal activities, membership in an organization that advocates or supports illegal activities can create an allegiance issue. In this type of situation clearance investigators and adjudicators must attempt to determine whether the person knew of and adhered to the group's support of illegal activities.

Cases involving potentially disqualifying activities related to allegiance (where clear and persuasive mitigation is not present) are rarely adjudicated for credentialing, suitability, fitness, or security clearance determinations. In the past 15 years there has not been one case involving the issue of "allegiance" decided by a DOHA Administrative Judge. In most cases if a federal background investigation surfaces credible information of conduct specified under Guideline A, the background investigation would be promptly closed and the case would be referred to a federal criminal/counterintelligence agency for further investigation.

CHAPTER 10

FOREIGN INFLUENCE

ADJUDICATIVE CRITERIA

HSPD-12 Credentialing: No applicable criteria.

Employment Suitability/Fitness: No applicable criteria.

Security Clearance (Guideline B):
6. *The Concern.* Foreign contacts and interests may be a security concern if the individual has divided loyalties or foreign financial interests, may be manipulated or induced to help a foreign person, group, organization, or government in a way that is not in U.S. interests, or is vulnerable to pressure or coercion by any foreign interest. Adjudication under this Guideline can and should consider the identity of the foreign country in which the foreign contact or financial interest is located, including, but not limited to, such considerations as whether the foreign country is known to target United States citizens to obtain protected information and/or is associated with a risk of terrorism.

7. *Conditions that could raise a security concern and may be disqualifying include:*

(a) contact with a foreign family member, business or professional associate, friend, or other person who is a citizen of or resident in a foreign country if that contact creates a heightened risk of foreign exploitation, inducement, manipulation, pressure, or coercion;

(b) connections to a foreign person, group, government, or country that create a potential conflict of interest between the individual's

obligation to protect sensitive information or technology and the individual's desire to help a foreign person, group, or country by providing that information;

(c) counterintelligence information, that may be classified, indicates that the individual's access to protected information may involve unacceptable risk to national security;

(d) sharing living quarters with a person or persons, regardless of citizenship status, if that relationship creates a heightened risk of foreign inducement, manipulation, pressure, or coercion;

(e) a substantial business, financial, or property interest in a foreign country, or in any foreign-owned or foreign-operated business, which could subject the individual to heightened risk of foreign influence or exploitation;

(f) failure to report, when required, association with a foreign national;

(g) unauthorized association with a suspected or known agent, associate, or employee of a foreign intelligence service;

(h) indications that representatives or nationals from a foreign country are acting to increase the vulnerability of the individual to possible future exploitation, inducement, manipulation, pressure, or coercion;

(i) conduct, especially while traveling outside the U.S., which may make the individual vulnerable to exploitation, pressure, or coercion by a foreign person, group, government, or country.

8. Conditions that could mitigate security concerns include:

(a) the nature of the relationships with foreign persons, the country in which these persons are located, or the positions or activities of those persons in that country are such that it is unlikely the individual will be placed in a position of having to choose between the interests of a foreign individual, group, organization, or government and the interests of the U.S.;

(b) there is no conflict of interest, either because the individual's sense of loyalty or obligation to the foreign person, group, government, or country is so minimal, or the individual has such deep and longstanding relationships and loyalties in the U.S., that the individual can be

expected to resolve any conflict of interest in favor of the U.S. interest;

(c) contact or communication with foreign citizens is so casual and infrequent that there is little likelihood that it could create a risk for foreign influence or exploitation;

(d) the foreign contacts and activities are on U.S. Government business or are approved by the cognizant security authority;

(e) the individual has promptly complied with existing agency requirements regarding the reporting of contacts, requests, or threats from persons, groups, or organizations from a foreign country;

(f) the value or routine nature of the foreign business, financial, or property interests is such that they are unlikely to result in a conflict and could not be used effectively to influence, manipulate, or pressure the individual.

DISCUSSION

The "Foreign Influence" criterion, Guideline B, of the "Adjudicative Guidelines," affects many security clearance applicants, particularly those who are naturalized U.S. citizens or whose parents immigrated to the U.S. Others who marry (or reside with) a foreign national, who have foreign financial/business interests, or who maintain close and continuing contact with foreigners are also affected. There are two other related criteria—Foreign Preference and Outside Activities—that sometimes affect these same applicants.[38]

SECURITY CONCERN

Foreign Influence has been an increasingly significant concern when considering people for security clearances. This has been due in part to changes in motivation of those who have chosen to spy against the U.S. A March 2008 government study, "Changes in Espionage by Americans: 1947 – 2007"[39] reported that since 1990 offenders who are naturalized citizens rose to 35%, those with relatives or close friends

---

[38] See Chapters 9 and 20 for information on the "Foreign Preference" and "Outside Activities" criteria.

[39] Technical Report 08-05, Defense Personnel Security Research Center, March 2008 at http://www.dhra.mil/perserec/reports/tr08-05.pdf.

overseas increased to 58%, and those with foreign business or professional connections increased to 50%. The increased concern with Foreign Influence is reflected in the greatly increased level of detail in the information required in the newest version (March 2010) of the SF86 for questions regarding foreign relatives and contacts.

The *Adjudicative Guidelines* specifies that "foreign contacts and interests may be a security concern if the individual has divided loyalties or foreign financial interests; may be manipulated or induced to help a foreign person, group, organization, or government in a way that is not in U.S. interests; or is vulnerable to pressure or coercion by any foreign interest." The *Adjudicative Guidelines* further specifies that "Adjudication . . . should consider the identity of the foreign country in which the foreign contact or financial interest is located, including but not limited to, such considerations as whether the foreign country is known to target United States citizens to obtain protected information and/or is associated with a risk of terrorism." However the location of a person's contacts or interest is not by itself a disqualifying condition.

MITIGATING SECURITY CONCERNS

Section 19 of the March 2010 version of the SF86 asks, *"Do you have, or have you had, close and/or continuing contact with a foreign national within the **last seven (7) years** with whom you, or your spouse, or cohabitant are bound by affection, influence, common interests, and/or obligation? Include associates as well as relatives, not previously listed in Section 18."* This question has 2 conditions.

One condition is that a bond of affection, influence, common interest, and/or obligation exists. If such a bond does not exist, you are not required to list the foreign national under Section 19, regardless of whether there has been close and/or continuing contact. Whether or not such a bond exists depends entirely on how an applicant or applicant's spouse/cohabitant feels about the relationship with the foreign national. When answering the question on the SF86, the applicant is not required to guess how the relationship will be perceived by an adjudicator.

If an applicant feels such a bond exists, then the question's other condition, *"close and/or continuing contact,"* must be met before the foreign national needs to be listed at Section 19. *Continuing contact* is relatively easy to interpret. If you or your spouse/cohabitant had contact with the person in the past few years and anticipate future contact, then it probably meets the definition of continuing contact. There is no definition for *close contact*. In a close relationship there is usually mutual knowledge of personal information, often including personal and family history. It is up to the applicant to decide whether to interpret "close" as having the additional meaning of physical or emotional closeness (or a combination of both). If a bond exists, you will have to list any foreign national with whom there has been close contact anytime in the past 7 years, even if you do not anticipate future contact.

The March 2010 version of the SF86 added the term "common interest" to the question at Section 19. Previously it was possible to exclude foreign nationals with whom an applicant only had casual contact through social media websites, because there was rarely a bond of affection, influence, and/or obligation. The addition of the term "common interest" could significantly increase the number of foreign national contacts that have to be listed at Section 19.

Honest, forthright responses are required on the SF86, but common sense should be applied to Section 19. If you do not know personal information about the foreign national with whom you have or have had contact, and you are uncertain whether a bond exists, think twice before you list them at Section 19. Merely listing or not listing foreign national contacts might affect the granting of an interim security clearance.

Do not contact foreign nationals to obtain information about them so you can answer questions at Section 19. This also applies to foreign national relatives at Section 18. Most of the questions regarding foreign national relatives and contacts have a check box for "I don't know." If your contact with a foreign national becomes an issue, the more you know about a foreign national, the more difficult it will be to claim that your relationship to them is not close and that you cannot be influenced by them to do anything detrimental to the security interests of the United States. Similarly, if you list a foreign national at Section 19, it will be difficult to later disavow that a "bond" exists. If your investigation includes an ESI or a SPIN for foreign contact, you will be asked about all foreign contacts, not just those with whom a "bond" exists. Be prepared to provide information about foreign national contacts that you did not list on your SF86 and your reasons for not listing them.

The location, relationship, occupation, activities, and interests of the foreign person, as well as the recency, frequency and nature of the contact are all relevant. Anticipated future contact is also relevant. The security significance of these foreign contacts is measured by the **extent** to which an applicant or the applicant's spouse/cohabitant:[40]

- Maintains contact with foreign friends, family members, or professional associates.

- Provides or receives material support to/from contacts outside the U.S.

- Travels to the foreign country.

- Maintains property or financial interests (including inheritance rights) outside the U.S.

- Fails to report association with foreigners when required.

Foreign connections that "create a potential conflict of interest between the individual's obligation to protect sensitive information and the individual's desire to help a foreign person, group, government, or country by providing that information" are security concerns. Absent a potential for a conflict of interest, foreign connections must present a "heightened" risk of foreign influence to be a security concern. A heightened risk can be created either by the nature of the foreign contact and/or by the perception that the applicant lacks substantial ability to resist foreign influence. The closer a relationship is with the foreign national, the greater the potential for foreign influence. In assessing an applicant's ability to resist foreign influence adjudicators may consider the degree to which an applicant (and spouse/cohabitant) has assimilated American culture and displayed undivided loyalty to the United States by:

- Applying for U.S. citizenship as soon as they are eligible.

- Expressing their intention to live permanently in the U.S. even after retirement.

- Observing American holidays.

- Participating in local non-ethnic social, community, political, or charitable groups.

---

[40] A "cohabitant" is anyone residing with the applicant in a spouse-like relationship. The SF86 defines cohabitant as "a person with whom you share bonds of affection, obligation, or other commitment, as opposed to a person with whom you live for reasons of convenience (a roommate)."

- Socializing with people outside their ethnic group.

Additionally, circumstances or behavior that could attract the attention of foreign intelligence are also potentially disqualifying factors. Foreign travel for the purpose of tourism or education is generally not a security concern, but can be a concern when the foreign travel involves contact with foreign friends or relatives or managing foreign financial interest.

The "whole-person" concept is usually at the heart of the analysis of whether an applicant should be eligible for a clearance under Guideline B. In such cases the whole-person analysis may address "evidence of an applicant's personal loyalties; the nature and extent of an applicant's family's ties to the U.S. relative to his ties to a foreign country; his or her social ties within the U.S.; and many others raised by the facts of a given case."[41]

Being married to or cohabiting with an undocumented alien may or may not be a "Foreign Influence" issue; however, it is a serious "Personal Conduct" and possibly a "Criminal Conduct" issue. (See Chapter 13 for further information.)

INTERIM CLEARANCES

The existence of certain types of current foreign connections can create a presumption of foreign influence. Frequent contact with a Canadian cousin who works on a farm will probably not create such a presumption and would not require any specific mitigation; whereas, minimal contact with Chinese father who is a colonel in the People's Liberation Army would. Absent any potential for "conflict of interest," foreign financial interests that represent a very small percentage of an applicant's net worth are generally not considered a significant concern. Often foreign influence concerns can be mitigated by the information collected during a security clearance investigation. But interim clearances require issue mitigation before the investigation is completed. The SF86 asks about foreign activities, associates, financial interests, and travel. But the SF86 asks for only minimal information that might mitigate indicators of potential foreign influence. To improve the chance of getting an interim clearance it is necessary provide additional comments describing a foreign financial interest as a percentage of an applicant's total net worth. The new (March 2010) version of the

---

[41] DOHA ISCR Case No. 04-11414.1a (App. Bd., March 5, 2007)

SF86 now asks if a foreign relative or foreign contact is "affiliated with a foreign government, military, security, defense industry, or intelligence service" and if so, the nature of the affiliation. It also asks for the name of a foreign relative's employer. It's advisable to use the "optional comment" field on e-QIP to provide the occupation (if known) of all foreign relatives and contacts. Also use the optional comment field to provide a narrative description of the exact nature and extent of your relationship to them, as well as your anticipated future contact.

SENSITIVE COMPARTMENT INFORMATION (SCI)

For first- and second-generation immigrants and for other applicants who are married to or cohabit with foreign nationals, employment with the U.S. Intelligence Community (IC) has often been out of reach. This is because the disqualifying condition created by the existence of non-U.S. citizen immediate family members[42] cannot be mitigated for SCI eligibility as it can for collateral clearances. And SCI eligibility is almost always a requirement for IC employment. This obstacle can only be overcome with a "waiver" from a Senior Official of the IC. This risk avoidance policy within the IC changed somewhat in October 2008 with the issuance of Director of National Intelligence (DNI), Intelligence Community Directive (ICD) Number 704. ICD 704 has made it a little easier for those with a non-U.S. citizen immediate family member to receive SCI eligibility. Previously under Director of Central Intelligence Directive 6/14, a waiver required both a "certification of compelling need" and a favorable counterintelligence "risk assessment." ICD 704 eliminated the requirement for a "certification of compelling need."

On the other hand, dual citizenship and foreign passports (both Foreign Preference issues) are treated more leniently under DNI regulations for SCI. (See Chapter 11, Foreign Preference.)

---

[42] Immediate family members are defined as the spouse, parents, siblings, children, and cohabitant of the individual requiring SCI access.

CHAPTER 11

FOREIGN PREFERENCE

ADJUDICATIVE CRITERIA

HSPD-12 Credentialing: No applicable criteria.

Employment Suitability/Fitness: No applicable criteria.

Security Clearance (Guideline C):
9. *The Concern*. When an individual acts in such a way as to indicate a preference for a foreign country over the United States, then he or she may be prone to provide information or make decisions that are harmful to the interests of the United States.

10. *Conditions that could raise a security concern and may be disqualifying include:*

(a) exercise of any right, privilege or obligation of foreign citizenship after becoming a U.S. citizen or through the foreign citizenship of a family member. This includes but is not limited to:

(1) possession of a current foreign passport;

(2) military service or a willingness to bear arms for a foreign country;

(3) accepting educational, medical, retirement, social welfare, or other such benefits from a foreign country;

(4) residence in a foreign country to meet citizenship requirements;

(5) *using foreign citizenship to protect financial or business interests in another country;*

(6) *seeking or holding political office in a foreign country;*

(7) *voting in a foreign election;*

(b) *action to acquire or obtain recognition of a foreign citizenship by an American citizen;*

(c) *performing or attempting to perform duties, or otherwise acting, so as to serve the interests of a foreign person, group, organization, or government in conflict with the national security interest;*

(d) *any statement or action that shows allegiance to a country other than the United States: for example, declaration of intent to renounce United States citizenship; renunciation of United States citizenship*

11. *Conditions that could mitigate security concerns include:*

(a) *dual citizenship is based solely on parents' citizenship or birth in a foreign country;*

(b) *the individual has expressed a willingness to renounce dual citizenship;*

(c) *exercise of the rights, privileges, or obligations of foreign citizenship occurred before the individual became a U.S. citizen or when the individual was a minor;*

(d) *use of a foreign passport is approved by the cognizant security authority;*

(e) *the passport has been destroyed, surrendered to the cognizant security authority, or otherwise invalidated;*

(f) *the vote in a foreign election was encouraged by the United States Government.*

Sensitive Compartmented Information (SCI):
The follow is extracted from paragraph III.C of Annex A to Director of National Intelligence (DNI), Intelligence Community Policy Guidance (ICPG) Number 704.2, *"Personnel Security Adjudication Guidelines for Determining Eligibility for Access to Sensitive Compartmented Information and Other Controlled Access Program Information,"* 2 October 2008. This version of Guideline C of the *Adjudicative Guidelines* is significantly different than Guideline C of the *Adjudicative*

Guidelines approved by the President of the United States in December 2005 (shown above).

1. The Concern. When an individual acts in such a way as to establish a preference for a foreign country over the United States, he or she may provide information or make decisions that are harmful to the interests of the United States. The principal goal of the Foreign Preference assessment is to determine the risk based on foreign associations that information may be compromised if access is approved; it is not a measurement of how loyal a subject is to the United States. Therefore, a finding that there is a preference must be established by adequate evidence of heightened risks related to national security.

Furthermore, the fact that a U .S. citizen is or has become a citizen of another country does not establish a preference for a foreign country. Being a U.S. citizen and a citizen of another country is not prohibited or disqualifying absent a showing of heightened risks related to national security. The same is true for the exercise of any right, privilege or obligation of foreign citizenship or action to acquire or obtain recognition of a foreign citizenship by a U.S. citizen.

2. Conditions that could raise a security concern and may be disqualifying include:

a. Failure to disclose to an appropriate security official the known possession of citizenship in any other country;

b. Failure to disclose to an appropriate security official the acquisition of citizenship in any other country;

c. Failure to report to an appropriate security official the possession of a passport issued by any other country;

d. Failure to use a U.S. passport while entering or exiting the United States;

e. Performing or attempting to perform duties, or otherwise acting, so as to serve the interests of a foreign person, group, organization, or government in conflict with U.S. national security interests;

f. Intentional act of expatriation from the United States such as declaration of intent to renounce United States citizenship or renunciation of U.S. citizenship, with the exception of routine oaths associated with citizenship in another country;

g. Seeking or holding political office in a foreign country; or,

h. Military service or a willingness to bear arms for a foreign country.

3. Conditions that could mitigate security concerns include:

a. Any of the potentially disqualifying activities noted in paragraph two above occurred before the initial request for a security clearance granting access to SCI;

b. Any of the potentially disqualifying activities noted in paragraph two above that occurred after the initial request for a security clearance granting access to SCI were sanctioned by a cognizant security authority;

c. The perceived foreign preference involves a foreign country, entity, or association that poses a low security risk.

DISCUSSION

The Foreign Preference issue basically concerns foreign citizenship and the exercise of foreign citizenship. Some people who are U.S. citizens at birth believe they are dual citizens simply because they were born in a foreign country. Some naturalized U.S. citizens believe that when they took the oath of allegiance to the U.S., it effectively renounced their former citizenship. Either situation may or may not be true, depending on the foreign country involved. Foreign citizenship laws are varied and complicated. Security clearance applicants who are uncertain about dual citizenship should research the matter before answering the citizenship question on the SF86. A good place to start is OPM's March 2001 "Citizenship Laws of the World" posted at their website.

RELEVANCE TO SECURITY

The "Foreign Preference" criterion, Guideline C of the "Adjudicative Guidelines," makes the "exercise of any right, privilege or obligation of foreign citizenship after becoming a U.S. citizen" a potentially disqualifying condition for a security clearance. Guideline C also states:

When an individual acts in such a way as to indicate a preference for a foreign country over the United States, then he or she may be prone to provide information or make decisions that are harmful to the interests of the United States.

In 1998 only 11 DOHA cases involved Foreign Preference. In 2008 it increased to 272 cases. This change occurred primarily because of the issuance of the "Money Memorandum"[43] in August 2000 that stated:

The security concerns underlying this guideline are that the possession and use of a foreign passport in preference to a U.S. passport raises doubt as to whether the person's allegiance to the United States is paramount and it could also facilitate foreign travel unverifiable by the United States. Therefore consistent application of the guideline requires that any [DoD] clearance be denied or revoked unless the applicant surrenders the foreign passport or obtains official approval for its use from the appropriate agency of the United States Government.

Guideline C does not specifically indicate that the mere existence of dual citizenship is a potentially disqualifying condition. It uses the words "exercise" and "acts," indicating there must be conduct that demonstrates a preference for a foreign country. However, Guideline C lists mitigating conditions for dual citizenship unrelated to conduct, thereby implying that dual citizenship by itself is a potential security concern. Merely having dual citizenship will not automatically result in a security clearance denial, nor will simply renouncing foreign citizenship necessarily result in a security clearance approval. Generally people who acquired dual citizenship at birth and have done nothing to obtain recognition of the foreign citizenship will encounter little or no problem in obtaining a clearance, unless there are other security issues in their case.

EVALUATING DUAL CITIZENSHIP

The foreign country where citizenship is held is not relevant. DOHA decisions regarding applicants who were unwilling to renounce Iranian or Chinese citizenship were the same as for those who were unwilling to renounce Canadian or British citizenship. When an immi-

[43] Memorandum from Arthur L. Money, Assistant Secretary of Defense for Command, Control, Communications, and Intelligence; dated August 16, 2000; Subject: Guidance to DoD Central Adjudication Facilities (CAF) Clarifying the Application of the Foreign Preference Adjudicative Guideline. This policy was later incorporated into the Adjudicative Guidelines.

grant becomes a naturalized U.S. citizen and takes the oath of allegiance in which they "absolutely and entirely renounce and abjure all allegiance and fidelity to any foreign prince, potentate, state, or sovereignty of whom or which I have heretofore been a subject or citizen," they rarely take the additional step of insuring that their former citizenship has been effectively renounced. Some even apply to have their foreign passport renewed and use it to travel to their native country. This creates serious problems when applying for a security clearance.

MITIGATING SECURITY CONCERNS

Guideline C does not contain any specific mitigating conditions similar to those in other Guidelines where potentially disqualifying conduct can be mitigated based on voluntariness, motivation, frequency, recency, and unusual circumstances. However, the "General Criteria" (see page 76) described in "The Adjudicative Process" paragraph of the Adjudicative Guidelines applies to the adjudication of all cases and requires that these factors be considered.

Expressing a willingness to renounce foreign citizenship and surrendering a foreign passport, is often sufficient to mitigate the potentially disqualifying condition of "possession of a current foreign passport," when no other aggravating or complicating factors are involved. But it is necessary to express willingness to renounce foreign citizenship on the SF86 and surrender the foreign passport before the clearance application is submitted, if an applicant wants to avoid delays in obtaining a clearance. DSS recommends surrendering the foreign passport to the security officer who initially processes the clearance application form. The applicant should indicate on the application form when and to whom the passport was surrendered.

Some countries prohibit their citizens from entering or leaving their country using a foreign passport. Some make it practically impossible to renounce citizenship. Personal safety concerns while traveling in certain areas of the world sometimes makes it unwise to use a U.S. passport. These reasons can further mitigate the dual citizenship and possession of a foreign passport after becoming a U.S. citizen.

It is possible to mitigate some of the other potentially disqualifying conditions using the General Criteria. For instance, if a college student obtains recognition of foreign citizenship to receive foreign educational or medical benefits to facilitate a year of attendance at a foreign university, this can be mitigated by the circumstances and age at the time of the conduct.

Security clearance decisions posted at the DOHA website are replete with cases where security clearance decisions hinged on an applicant's willingness to renounce foreign citizenship and surrender their foreign passport. However, because of potential counterintelligence implications, it is not advisable to contact a foreign embassy or consulate for this purpose without first obtaining guidance from the U.S. Government. On the SF86 and during a security interview, it is only necessary to express a willingness to renounce foreign citizenship.

The following was taken from the U.S. Department of State document entitled: "Dual Citizenship – Security Clearance Implications," posted at their website. In the document "DS" refers to the State Department's Bureau of Diplomatic Security:

To illustrate the DS evaluation process regarding dual citizenship, some past examples that have arisen recently are provided below. DS' goal is to maintain consistency in its determinations. There may appear to be many similarities between cases; however individual circumstances vary greatly and may not be known to the hiring entity. While not all inclusive, the following examples give an indication of how such factors are evaluated and determinations made:

1. Example A. A subject derived foreign citizenship from his or her parents. In this case, DS would examine whether or not the subject has exercised the foreign citizenship: by accepting educational, medical or social welfare benefits for himself/herself or family; possessing and using the foreign passport; serving in the foreign military; working for the foreign government; etc. In the absence of the subject's exercising foreign citizenship, and if subject's current and past actions consistently demonstrated preference for and allegiance to the United States, then dual citizenship would not preclude a security clearance.

2. Example B. A subject only recently became a naturalized U.S. citizen through marriage and has no previous ties to the United States. In this case, DS could not likely grant an immediate security clearance, since the demonstrated loyalty requirement could not be satisfied immediately. Eligibility for access could be reconsidered after a passage of time during which the subject would have the opportunity to clearly demonstrate preference for and unquestioned allegiance to the United States, and the absence of any undue conflicting influence, as required by the referenced guidelines.

3. Example C. A subject was born in the U.S. as the child of foreign visitors. The subject left the U.S. in infancy, never returned and has no ties or history which indicate a preference for and allegiance to the United States. DS would not have the background information required to grant a security clearance.

4. Example D. A subject is a naturalized U.S. citizen and dual national who is willing to relinquish his foreign passport but is not/not willing to renounce for-

*eign citizenship of birth. The subject explains that the reason for this position
Is: (1) so that children can continue to enjoy free foreign education benefits;
(2) for possible future employment opportunities; and (3) for foreign inheritance purposes. DS would not be able to clearly determine the individual's
preference for the United States, sufficient to grant a security clearance.*

INTERIM CLEARANCES

Without proper mitigation, dual citizenship, like other security issues, can create a presumption that a disqualifying condition exists and result in having an interim clearance declined. Stating in the SF86 a willingness to renounce foreign citizenship and that the foreign passport has been surrender to the appropriate security officer can significantly mitigate security concerns. Explaining in the SF86 the reasons dual citizenship and/or other potentially disqualifying conditions exist will also improve the chance of obtaining an interim clearance. See page 74 for examples of other statements that can be included in the SF86.

SENSITIVE COMPARTMENT INFORMATION (SCI)

Annex A to ICPG 704.2 is identified as the *Adjudicative Guidelines* as approved by the President and issued by the Assistant for National Security Affairs on 29 December 2005. However, this version of Guideline C is significantly different than Guideline C in the *Adjudicative Guidelines* that was actually issued on 29 December 2005.

All but one of the potentially disqualifying conditions related to dual citizenship in the ICPG 704.2 version of Guideline C are totally different than those listed in the original December 2005 version of the *Adjudicative Guidelines*. There has been no indication of which version of Guideline C Intelligence Community agencies are actually using. If the Adjudicative Guidelines in ICPG 704.2 are being used to adjudicate SCI eligibility, it can cause a great deal of uncertainty regarding reciprocity of clearances until these two versions of the "Foreign Preference" guideline are reconciled.

As previously stated the *Adjudicative Guidelines* are currently being revised, but it unknown when the revisions will be completed, approved, and implemented. It is anticipated that the number of criteria will be reduced through consolidation, other redundancies will be removed, and the differences that exists with the "Foreign Preference" criterion in ICPG 704.2 will be reconciled.

CHAPTER 12

SEXUAL BEHAVIOR

ADJUDICATIVE CRITERIA

HSPD-12 Credentialing:
Sexual behavior of a criminal nature that poses an unacceptable risk if access is granted to federally-controlled facilities and information systems. The following consideration may apply:

<u>*There is a reasonable basis to believe, based on the individual's criminal or dishonest conduct, that issuance of a PIV card poses an unacceptable risk.*</u>
[F]or example, convictions for sexual assault may indicate that granting a PIV poses an unacceptable risk to the life and safety of persons on Government facilities, while a documented history of misusing workplace information systems to distribute pornography may indicate that granting a PIV poses an unacceptable risk to the Government's information systems.

Employment Suitability/Fitness:
Persons who engage in sexual behavior of a criminal nature may not demonstrate the character and conduct required to promote the efficiency or protect the integrity of the service. The following suitability factor may apply:

<u>*Criminal or dishonest conduct.*</u>
The following are examples of conduct that may be disqualifying (Note: This list is not meant to be all inclusive):

   (a) a recent, serious criminal offense

(b) a pattern of sexual behavior of a criminal nature

Security Clearance (Guideline D):

12. *The Concern.* Sexual behavior that involves a criminal offense, indicates a personality or emotional disorder, reflects lack of judgment or discretion, or which may subject the individual to undue influence or coercion, exploitation, or duress can raise questions about an individual's reliability, trustworthiness and ability to protect classified information. No adverse inference concerning the standards in the Guideline may be raised solely on the basis of the sexual orientation of the individual.

13. *Conditions that could raise a security concern and may be disqualifying include:*

(a) sexual behavior of a criminal nature, whether or not the individual has been prosecuted;

(b) a pattern of compulsive, self-destructive, or high-risk sexual behavior that the person is unable to stop or that may be symptomatic of a personality disorder;

(c) sexual behavior that causes an individual to be vulnerable to coercion, exploitation, or duress;

(d) sexual behavior of a public nature and/or that which reflects lack of discretion or judgment.

14. *Conditions that could mitigate security concerns include:*

(a) the behavior occurred prior to or during adolescence and there is no evidence of subsequent conduct of a similar nature;

(b) the sexual behavior happened so long ago, so infrequently, or under such unusual circumstances, that it is unlikely to recur and does not cast doubt on the individual's current reliability, trustworthiness, or good judgment;

(c) the behavior no longer serves as a basis for coercion, exploitation, or duress;

(d) the sexual behavior is strictly private, consensual, and discreet.

DISCUSSION

Many people have concerns about how their past sexual indiscretions may negatively affect their clearance eligibility. Most sexual misconduct is either not a potentially disqualifying condition for a clearance or can be fully mitigated by "passage of time without recurrence" and the absence of any susceptibility to blackmail or coercion.

Of the approximately 1160 cases decided by Administrative Judges at DOHA in 2009 only 36 cited "Sexual Behavior" as a security/suitability issue. Almost all of these 36 cases involved criminal conduct, and about half involved criminal convictions for sexual offenses. Only 2 cases cited extramarital affairs, and both of the applicants in these cases were involved in current sexual relationships about which their spouses were unaware. Involvement with prostitutes was cited in 4 cases, 5 cases cited possession of child pornography, and 15 cases cited sexual acts with children. The remaining cases involved voyeurism, exhibitionism, and compulsive, self-destructive viewing of pornography. Eight-nine percent of the cases citing sexual behavior resulted in clearance denials. Many of these issues did not surface during standard investigations for security clearances, but surfaced during polygraph examinations required as part of the processing for Sensitive Compartment Information (SCI) eligibility.

Prior to 1992 the Adjudicative Guidelines made "*acts of sexual misconduct or perversion indicative of moral turpitude, poor judgment, or lack of regard for the laws of society*" disqualifying. This included sodomy, heterosexual promiscuity, wife-swapping, transvestism, transsexualism, and aberrant, deviant, or bizarre sexual conduct.

Much has changed since 1992. When assessing sexual behavior, adjudicators must first consider whether the behavior is relevant to a security clearance determination before they consider whether it is true. Today sexual behavior is relevant when it is compulsive, self-destructive, high-risk, or criminal; creates susceptibility to coercion; occurs in public; or shows poor judgment. If at least one of these factors is not present, sodomy, promiscuity, adultery, group sex, cybersex, swinging, pornography, sadism, masochism, fetishism, bondage and degradation, Dominance and submission, homosexuality, bisexuality, transsexualism, and transvestism are not disqualifying conditions for a security clearance. Potentially disqualifying sexual behavior is usually a complex issue and often involves other adjudicative criteria, such as Criminal Conduct, Personal Conduct, Use of Information Technology Systems and sometimes Foreign Influence.

Mitigating Security Concerns

Absent the potential for coercion, adultery or an isolated incident involving use of a prostitute usually does not result in the denial of a security clearance under Guideline D. However, when two or more criminal convictions exist, a conviction for soliciting prostitution can be a Guideline J (Criminal Conduct) issue. Under certain circumstances adultery in the military can also be a criminal offense. Eliminating the potential for coercion usually requires disclosing the conduct to a spouse and possibly to others, such as an employer if a work associate is involved or the spouse of the other person.

Allegations of sexual harassment are usually considered under Guideline E (Personal Conduct) rather than Guideline D, because they occur in the workplace, involve rule violation, and may be indicative of questionable judgment. Compulsive, self-destructive involvement with pornography outside the workplace seldom becomes a Guideline D issue, because it is rarely discovered during a standard background investigation. Viewing or downloading pornography on an employer's computer is a Guideline M (Use of Information Technology Systems) issue, because it is almost always an unauthorized use of an employer's computer. It can also be a Guideline E issue, because it is a misuse of an employer's time and usually a violation of work rules. Sexual misconduct occurring in foreign countries or involving foreigners can increase susceptibility to foreign exploitation and therefore create additional security concerns under Guideline B (Foreign Influence).

When sexual behavior is a potential disqualifying condition, adjudicators must consider the 9 General Criteria (see page 76) in addition to the specific disqualifying and mitigating conditions listed paragraph 14 at Guideline D.

As mentioned earlier, the *Adjudicative Guidelines* are currently being revised. It is anticipated that the revised *Adjudicative Guidelines* will probably not have a separate criterion specifically for Sexual Behavior. Conduct described under the Sexual Behavior criterion can be adequately addressed by the disqualifying and mitigating conditions listed under the Personal Conduct, Psychological Conditions, and Criminal Conduct criteria. (See Chapters 13, 17, and 18)

Do all adjudicators consistently apply the *Adjudicative Guidelines* when making security clearance determinations, particularly when sexual behavior is an issue? Do some adjudicators sometimes measure an applicant's conduct against their own personal moral standards?

Occasionally an adjudicator's decision can be arbitrary or capricious. Fortunately every security clearance applicant has a right to appeal an adverse decision to a Personnel Security Appeal Board (PSAB). If the evidence did not support the decision and/or sufficient weight was not given to the applicant's mitigating evidence, the applicant may be successful in having the decision reversed by a PSAB.

CHAPTER 13

PERSONAL CONDUCT & REGULATORY BARS

ADJUDICATIVE CRITERIA

HSPD-12 Credentialing:
An individual's employment misconduct or negligence may put people, property, or information systems at risk. The following consideration may apply:

There is a reasonable basis to believe, based on the individual's misconduct or negligence in employment, that issuance of a PIV card poses an unacceptable risk.
[F]or example, documented misconduct in prior employment related to unauthorized access to customer medical or financial records may indicate that granting a PIV poses an unacceptable risk to the Government's records.

Federal statutes and/or regulations may prevent lawful employment. The following consideration may apply:

A statutory or regulatory bar prevents the individual's contract employment; or would prevent Federal employment under circumstances that furnish a reasonable basis to believe that issuance of a PIV card poses an unacceptable risk.
[F]or example, a person's 5-year bar on Federal employment based on a felony conviction related to inciting a riot or civil disorder, as specified under 5 U.S.C. 7313, may indicate that granting a PIV poses an unacceptable risk to persons, property, and assets in Government facilities.

To be considered eligible for an Identity Credential, the individual's claimed identity must be clearly authenticated. If the individual refuses to cooperate with the documentation and investigative requirements to validate his or her identity, or if the investigation fails to confirm the individual's claimed identity or there is evidence the information provided by the individual to authenticate his or her identity is fraudulent, an identity credential must not be issued. A PIV card will not be issued to a person if:

The employer is unable to verify the individual's claimed identity, or

There is reasonable basis to believe the individual has submitted fraudulent information concerning his or her identity

Conduct involving questionable judgment, lack of candor, dishonesty, or unwillingness to comply with rules and regulations can raise questions about an individual's reliability, trustworthiness, and put people, property or information systems at risk. The following consideration may apply:

There is a reasonable basis to believe, based on the individual's material, intentional false statement, deception, or fraud in connection with Federal or contract employment, that issuance of a PIV card poses an unacceptable risk.
[F]or example, a person's documented history of forging academic transcripts or military service records to obtain employment may indicate that granting a PIV poses an unacceptable risk to the integrity of Government records to which the employee or contractor employee will have access.

Employment Suitability/Fitness:
The appointment of an individual to a competitive service position when his/her employment record shows he/she has engaged in misconduct or negligence may not promote the efficiency or protect the integrity of the service. The following suitability factor may apply:

Misconduct or negligence in employment
The following are examples of conduct that may be disqualifying (Note: This list is not meant to be all inclusive):

  (a) poor attendance without cause

(b) *insubordination*

(c) *other suitability issues that occur in employment (such as theft, etc.)*

(d) *a pattern of misconduct or negligence in employment as reflected in employment history*

Note: Misconduct involves doing something wrong in the employer's estimation, while negligence is the failure to do something expected by the employer. Performance (i.e. an inability to perform) or other qualification issues are not included.

Competitive service applicants or employees are required to give OPM, MSPB, or the Special Counsel all information, testimony, documents, and materials requested in matters inquired of under the civil service laws, rules and regulations, the disclosure of which is not otherwise prohibited by law. Therefore, failure to provide testimony when requested may be disqualifying. The following suitability factor may apply:

<u>*Refusal to furnish testimony as required by sec. 5.4 of 5 CFR*</u> *(OPM Use Only)*

Federal statutes and/or regulations may prevent lawful employment. The following suitability factor may apply:

<u>*Any statutory or regulatory bar which prevents the lawful employment of the person involved in the position in question*</u>
The following are examples of conduct that may result in a statutory debarment (Note: This list is not meant to be all inclusive):

(a) *participation in a strike against the government*

(b) *conviction of misdemeanor crime (under Federal or State law) of domestic violence (use or attempted use of physical force, or the threatened use of a deadly weapon, committed by current or former spouse, parent, or guardian of the victim, by a person with whom the victim shares a child in common, by a person who is cohabiting or who has cohabited with the victim as a spouse, parent, or guardian, or by a person similarly situated to a spouse, parent, or guardian of the victim)*

(c) *employment is determined to be in violation of the anti-nepotism statute*

Providing intentional false statements or engaging in deception or fraud in the competitive hiring process circumvents the Federal hiring procedures created to ensure fair and open competition. The following suitability factor may apply:

Material, intentional false statement or deception or fraud in examination or appointment (OPM Use Only)
The following are examples of conduct that may be disqualifying (this list is not meant to be all inclusive):

(a) *intentional attempt to withhold information, or furnish false information that is capable of influencing decisions about the individual's suitability, qualifications, or other matters related to the appointment process*

(b) *material, intentional false answers to questions on application or appointment documents*

(c) *materially, intentionally falsifying experience, education, etc. that could influence an official decision*

(d) *impeding or interfering with fair and open competition in the competitive examining system*

(e) *impeding or interfering with conditions or qualifications for appointment or restrictions on appointment in the competitive service*

Note: A "material" statement (as used in the phrase "material, intentional false statement") is one that is capable of influencing, or has a natural tendency to affect, an official decision. The test of materiality does not rest on whether the agency actually relied on the statement.

Dishonesty not covered by the above factor raises questions about an individual's character that may indicate his or her employment would not promote the efficiency of the service or protect its integrity. The following suitability factor may apply:

Criminal or dishonest conduct
The following are examples of conduct that may be disqualifying (this list is not meant to be all inclusive):

(a) *intentional lies, fraud, or deceit other than in connection with examination or appointment*

(b) *illegal activities resulting from dishonest acts*

(c) *intentional falsification of non-federal documents*

Note:
(1) Criminal Conduct. The primary emphasis is on the nature of the criminal conduct, which may or may not have resulted in conviction. The details and/or reasons for dismissal of the offense must be considered. The expungement of, and/or pardons for offense would not nullify the conduct, unless granted on the basis of the person's innocence. Pending charges (of a nature that would potentially be disqualifying) cannot be adjudicated until the case is disposed.
(2) Dishonest Conduct. Dishonest conduct includes, but is not limited to deliberate lies, fraud, or deceit for personal benefit. Examples may include acceptance of a bribe, falsification of records, falsification of employment documents, deliberate financial irresponsibility with continuing, valid debts of a significant nature, etc.

Security Clearance (Guideline E):

<u>15. The Concern</u>. *Conduct involving questionable judgment, lack of candor, dishonesty, or unwillingness to comply with rules and regulations can raise questions about an individual's reliability, trustworthiness and ability to protect classified information. Of special interest is any failure to provide truthful and candid answers during the security clearance process or any other failure to cooperate with the security clearance process.*

The following will normally result in an unfavorable clearance action or administrative termination of further processing for clearance eligibility:

(a) refusal, or failure without reasonable cause, to undergo or cooperate with security processing, including but not limited to meeting with a security investigator for subject interview, completing security forms or releases, and cooperation with medical or psychological evaluation;

(b) refusal to provide full, frank and truthful answers to lawful questions of investigators, security officials, or other official representa-

tives in connection with a personnel security or trustworthiness determination.

<u>**16.**   *Conditions that could raise a security concern and may be disqualifying also include:*</u>

(a) deliberate omission, concealment, or falsification of relevant facts from any personnel security questionnaire, personal history statement, or similar form used to conduct investigations, determine employment qualifications, award benefits or status, determine security clearance eligibility or trustworthiness, or award fiduciary responsibilities;

(b) deliberately providing false or misleading information concerning relevant facts to an employer, investigator, security official, competent medical authority, or other official government representative;

(c) credible adverse information in several adjudicative issue areas that is not sufficient for an adverse determination under any other single guideline, but which, when considered as a whole, supports a whole-person assessment of questionable judgment, untrustworthiness, unreliability, lack of candor, unwillingness to comply with rules and regulations, or other characteristics indicating that the person may not properly safeguard protected information;

(d) credible adverse information that is not explicitly covered under any other guideline and may not be sufficient by itself for an adverse determination, but which, when combined with all available information supports a whole-person assessment of questionable judgment, untrustworthiness, unreliability, lack of candor, unwillingness to comply with rules and regulations, or other characteristics indicating that the person may not properly safeguard protected information. This includes but is not limited to consideration of:

(1) untrustworthy or unreliable behavior to include breach of client confidentiality, release of proprietary information, unauthorized release of sensitive corporate or other government protected information;

(2) disruptive, violent, or other inappropriate behavior in the workplace;

(3) a pattern of dishonesty or rule violations;

(4) evidence of significant misuse of Government or other employer's time or resources;

(e) personal conduct or concealment of information about one's conduct, that creates a vulnerability to exploitation, manipulation, or duress, such as (1) engaging in activities which, if known, may affect the person's personal, professional, or community standing, or (2) while in another country, engaging in any activity that is illegal in that country or that is legal in that country but illegal in the United States and may serve as a basis for exploitation or pressure by the foreign security or intelligence service or other group;

(f) violation of a written or recorded commitment made by the individual to the employer as a condition of employment;

(g) association with persons involved in criminal activity.

17. Conditions that could mitigate security concerns include:

(a) the individual made prompt, good-faith efforts to correct the omission, concealment, or falsification before being confronted with the facts;

(b) the refusal or failure to cooperate, omission, or concealment was caused or significantly contributed to by improper or inadequate advice of authorized personnel or legal counsel advising or instructing the individual specifically concerning the security clearance process. Upon being made aware of the requirement to cooperate or provide the information, the individual cooperated fully and truthfully;

(c) the offense is so minor, or so much time has passed, or the behavior is so infrequent, or it happened under such unique circumstances that it is unlikely to recur and does not cast doubt on the individual's reliability, trustworthiness, or good judgment;

(d) the individual has acknowledged the behavior and obtained counseling to change the behavior or taken other positive steps to alleviate the stressors, circumstances, or factors that caused untrustworthy, unreliable, or other inappropriate behavior, and such behavior is unlikely to recur;

(e) the individual has taken positive steps to reduce or eliminate vulnerability to exploitation, manipulation, or duress;

(f) association with persons involved in criminal activities has ceased or occurs under circumstances that do not cast doubt upon the individual's reliability, trustworthiness, judgment, or willingness to comply with rules and regulations.

DISCUSSION

FALSIFICATION/CONCEALMENT

"Failure to provide truthful and candid answers during the security clearance process" is one of the most common reasons for the denial or revocation of security clearances. Of the approximately 1,300 security clearance cases decided by DOHA Administrative Judges during FY2008, Guideline E (Personal Conduct) was the second most frequently cited issue and appeared in 497 (38%) of the cases. It was frequently cited due to applicants concealing information related to one of the other issues, such as criminal conduct, drug involvement, and alcohol consumption.

Unfortunately in many falsification cases, the information the applicants tried to conceal would not have resulted in clearance denials. But the act of providing false information on clearance application forms was often fatal to the cases.

If an applicant does not provide full and truthful answers to questions on a clearance application or to government security officials, it is extremely difficult to trust the applicant with classified national security information or in other positions of trust. Most conduct-related security issues can be mitigated by rehabilitation as evidenced by passage of time without recurrence of the conduct. However, concealing relevant unfavorable information or claiming unearned qualifications or achievements on a clearance application indicates a current unwillingness to comply with security requirements and casts serious doubts on an applicant's honesty, trustworthiness, and judgment.

For security clearance the potentially disqualifying conditions related to falsification are listed at paragraphs 16a and 16b of the Adjudicative Guidelines, above. In the current version of the Adjudicative Guidelines the word, "material" was removed from the phrase, "falsification of relevant and material facts." Since all questions on clearance forms are considered relevant, any deliberate omission, concealment, or falsification, including information that would not have made any difference in the adjudication, may be cause for clearance denial.

For employment suitability the adjudicative criteria for falsification requires that the falsification be "material;" however falsification can also be considered under the "dishonest conduct" criterion, which does not require that falsification be "material" to be disqualifying.

In recent years the misrepresentation of educational qualifications on government forms has gained increased importance in clearance investigations and adjudication. Previously educational degrees were merely verified. Today the bona fides of questionable post-secondary schools are being scrutinized.

Submitting false information to private, state and local entities is also a potentially disqualifying condition for all three federal personnel security programs. This includes falsification of employment, school, financial, legal, and other documents, as well as making false oral statements. The relative weight attached to these types of untruthful utterances depends on the recency and frequency, as well as any professional or legal proscriptions and personal gain.

OTHER ASPECTS OF PERSONAL CONDUCT

Other aspects of the "Personal Conduct" criterion encompass a wide variety of dishonest or unreliable behavior not specifically covered under other adjudicative criteria. It also addresses multiple instances of minor misconduct covered under other criteria where the misconduct fails to reach the threshold of being considered a potentially disqualifying condition under any one criterion. Other "Personal Conduct" issues are:

- Failure to cooperate with investigation

- Pattern of dishonest, unreliable, or rule-breaking behavior

- Vulnerability to coercion

- Association with persons involved in criminal activity

- Violation of a written commitment made as a condition of clearance or employment

Failure to cooperate with investigation—A clearance is a privilege, not a right. Applicants cannot be compelled to provide information or submit to other examinations, but refusal to fully cooperate in the security clearance process usually results in a clearance denial, because it creates the presumption that the applicant is hiding relevant information. Asserting the Fifth Amendment right against self-incrimination will not mitigate a refusal to cooperate or provide information. The SF86 provides some protection against criminal prosecution. Question #23 (Illegal Use of Drugs or Drug Activity) and question #27 (Use of Information Technology Systems) both included the caveat, "Neither your truthful responses nor information derived from your responses will be used as evidence against you in any subsequent criminal proceeding."

Pattern of dishonest, unreliable, or rule-breaking behavior—
When an applicant has been involved in multiple incidents of conduct that individually fall below the threshold for denying a clearance, the conduct can be evaluated in its totality to determine the applicant's clearance eligibility. When reviewed separately, such things as traffic infractions, a single misdemeanor arrest for shoplifting, issuing bad checks, and minimal participation in copyrighted file sharing on a peer-to-peer network usually would not result in a clearance denial. But when reviewed under the Personal Conduct criterion, the sum of the conduct can become a potentially disqualifying condition.

Misconduct not specifically addressed under other adjudicative criteria can also be evaluated under Personal Conduct. This includes such things as work- or school-related misconduct, rule violations, and dishonesty. It can also include failure to act in a responsible manner in one's relationship to family, friends, neighbors and associates. As with conduct that falls below the threshold for clearance denial under a specific adjudicative criterion, this type of conduct is evaluated in its totality. Specifically addressed under Personal Conduct are:

- Misuse of employer's time and resources

- Disruptive, violent, or other inappropriate behavior in the workplace

- Untrustworthy or unreliable behavior

- Pattern of dishonesty or rule violation

Vulnerability to coercion—Whenever a person attempts to conceal conduct that could cause serious embarrassment or problems with a spouse, family member, employer, or law enforcement/security agency, the potential for vulnerability to coercion exists. Examples include:

- Misrepresentation of professional or educational qualifications
- Concealment of potentially disqualifying conditions on any employment or security form
- Concealment of business or financial problems from family members
- Involvement in undetected criminal activity

When a person engages in seriously embarrassing or prohibited conduct in a foreign country or such conduct becomes known to foreign nationals, it significantly increases the possibility of exploitation by a foreign intelligence or security service and creates heightened security risk.

Association with persons involved in criminal activity—Close and continuing contact with anyone involved in criminal activity is a potentially disqualifying condition. Contact or communication with a person who is no long involved in criminal conduct, including people in prison, is not a disqualifying condition. Association with an immediate family member involved in criminal activity is evaluated based on the nature of the association, the nature of the criminal activity, and the potential for undesirable influence.

Violation of a written commitment made as a condition of clearance or employment—Occasionally security clearances are granted with conditions. Such conditions can include the requirement to sever a relationship with a foreign business or organization, pay off delinquent debts by a certain date, or abstain from illegal drug involvement. A violation of a written condition for a clearance can be the basis for immediate clearance revocation. Violations of written commitments made by individuals to employers as a condition of employment can also be a potentially disqualifying condition.

Often "Personal Conduct" is cited in addition to or instead of other potentially disqualifying conditions, such as criminal conduct, financial considerations, alcohol consumption, etc., because of the broad wording of this adjudicative criterion. For example paragraph 15 of the *Adjudicative Guidelines* states:

Conduct involving questionable judgment, lack of candor, dishonesty, or unwillingness to comply with rules and regulations can raise questions about an individual's reliability, trustworthiness and ability to protect classified information.

Criminal activity almost always indicates questionable judgment and/or an unwillingness to comply with rules and regulations. But some criminal activity does not always meet the statutory definition of a crime. In these situations the "Personal Conduct" criterion allows the adjudicator to apply common sense to situations that might fall outside the "Criminal Conduct" criterion. In a recent DOHA case (No. 10-00503) the Administrative Judge denied a clearance to a woman who had been married to and living with an undocumented alien.

Applicant is a native-born citizen of the United States. She and her husband, who is unemployed, have been married for nine years. Applicant's husband was born in Mexico, and he is a citizen of Mexico. Applicant's husband is neither a U.S. registered alien nor a naturalized United States citizen. He resides with Applicant in the home they share in the United States. Applicant's husband has no legal documents that verify or permit his residency in the United States.

[S]ection 1324 of Title 8 of the United States Code, a federal statute that makes it a felony crime to harbor an illegal alien. The statute reads, in pertinent part:

Sec. 1324. Bringing in and harboring certain aliens

(1) (A) Any person who –

> *(iii) knowing or in reckless disregard of the fact that an alien has come to, entered, or remains in the United States in violation of law, conceals, harbors, or shields from detection, or attempts to conceal, harbor, or shield from detection, such alien in any place, including any building or any means of transportation;*

shall be punished as provided in subparagraph (B).

(B) A person who violates subparagraph (A) shall, for each alien in respect to whom such a violation occurs –

> *(ii) in the case of a violation of subparagraph (A)(ii), (iii), (iv), or (v)(II), be fined under title 18, imprisoned not more than 5 years, or both.*

The word "harbor" as used in this section is intended to encompass conduct tending to substantially facilitate the alien's remaining in the U.S. illegally, provided the person charged has knowledge of the alien's unlawful status. . . . The term "harbor" also means to afford shelter to and is not limited to clandestine sheltering.

The Administrative Judge cited disqualifying conditions 16(d), 16(c), and 16(d) of the *Adjudicative Guidelines* as reasons for denying the applicant a clearance, which essentially cover a pattern of rule violations, vulnerability to exploitation, and association with persons involved in criminal activity. Although applicant's spouse was described as unemployed, DOHA Department apparently chose not to allege "Criminal Conduct," probably because there was nothing in the record to show that the applicant's spouse (through some unknown independent financial means) did not pay for the house in which he and the applicant lived. Unless it could be shown that the applicant provided the house in which her spouse lived and/or other substantial financial support, it would be difficult to prove that the applicant harbored or substantially facilitated his remaining in the U.S. illegally. Applicant's spouse could have been well established in the U.S. at the time of their marriage, and applicant could have moved into the house that he rented or otherwise controlled.

For individuals who already possess a security clearance, failure to self-report potentially disqualifying information and other required information to their Facility Security Officer, Security Manager, and/or Special Security Officer is also covered under "Personal Conduct," as well as Guideline K (Handling Protected Information). (See Chapter 19)

MITIGATING SECURITY CONCERNS

Many applicants treat a clearance application form as just another bureaucratic form and fill it out quickly without attention to accuracy or detail. Others view it as being comparable to a resume where a certain amount of "huffing and puffing," as well as selective presenting and withholding of information are normal. Some honestly misunderstand the wording and the intent of the questions. Lawyers, work and school associates, and military recruiters occasionally give applicants bad advice about what must be disclose and what may be withheld on a clearance application form.

Mitigating alleged falsification is possible, if the applicant did not deliberately provide false information on a clearance form. Mistake of fact, faulty memory, and misunderstanding can be plausible reasons for unintentionally providing false information. When applicants are given an opportunity to correct false information but repeat their false assertions, mitigation becomes impossible even if they later tell the truth. "Prompt, good-faith efforts to correct the omission, concealment, or falsification before being confronted with the facts" are critical to successfully mitigating this issue.

For security clearances, adjudicators are admonished to consider "available, reliable information about the person, past and present, favorable and unfavorable" in reaching a clearance determination. This "whole-person" concept is often applied when assessing applicants' intent to falsify and their subsequent actions to correct false information.

Mature, highly educated individuals are less likely than young military recruits to convince an adjudicator that they misunderstood questions, inadvertently made mistakes, or incorrectly relied on the advice of other people.

When falsification is admittedly deliberate but the applicant promptly attempts to correct it before being confronted, adjudicators can sometimes make a favorable decision if the falsification was an isolated, uncharacteristic lapse in judgment by an otherwise responsible, honest individual.

Under Guideline E the only mitigation for "failure to cooperate with investigation" is to cooperate fully when advised of the requirement to do so. Mitigation for "vulnerability to coercion" is generally limited to elimination of the vulnerability by disclosing the previously concealed information to family, close friends, employers, and/or others, as appropriate.

A "pattern of dishonest, unreliable, or rule-breaking behavior" can usually only be mitigated by acknowledging the misbehavior and showing rehabilitation through passage of time without recurrence or successful professional counseling.

A *"violation of a written commitment made as a condition of clearance or employment"* can be mitigated by acknowledging the violation and showing rehabilitation through passage of time without recurrence or successful counseling/training. It can be mitigated by showing that the violation was an isolated incident or that it occurred under such unusual circumstances that it is unlikely to recur.

"Association with persons involved in criminal activity" can only be mitigated by showing that the potential for adverse influence does not exist. Close and continuing contact with such persons probably cannot be mitigated, except by discontinuing all contact and making a statement of intent to this effect or by limiting the nature and frequency of future contact to a few brief impersonal encounters a year at family or social gatherings the applicant has an obligation to attend but has no control over who the other attendees are.

APPLICANT HONESTY AND CREDIBILITY

Often the truth can be somewhat nebulous. The best a background investigator can hope for is to nail down a person's honest perception of reality. The various sources of information relied upon to produce a Report of Investigation may provide differing perceptions of an event or condition. It's the job of the adjudicator to decide which versions most accurately resemble the truth. Applicants have a legal duty to be honest in the information they provide on clearance application forms and to the questions of federal security officials. Unlike most employers and educators who often have to accept an employee's or student's explanation of events at face value, the Government has the resources and capability to gather information that verifies or refutes information provided by an applicant.

At times the decision to grant or deny a clearance hinges on an applicant's credibility—not just the plausibility of the information provided regarding a specific issue, but the applicant's overall credibility based on all the information and specific details provided, as well as his/her sincerity, demeanor, and attitude. One of the reasons applicants are more successful in obtaining a favorable clearance determination if they appear in person before an Administrative Judge, is because it gives the judge an opportunity to make a better assessment of their overall credibility.

Applicants can destroy their own credibility by embellishing the facts or minimizing their culpability. Investigators and adjudicators are adept at gauging the plausibility of an applicant's explanation of events and can quickly pick out any flaws or inconsistencies. It's their job. They're trained and experienced at it. There's a good example of a case (ISCR Case No. 06-26489) in Chapter 19 where an applicant was denied a clearance, because he continued to assert that his failure to comply with a security reporting requirement was unintentional. The Administrative Judge made it fairly clear that the security violation by itself would not have resulted in a clearance denial, if the applicant had acknowledged that he knowingly committed the violation.

CHAPTER 14

FINANCIAL CONSIDERATIONS

ADJUDICATIVE CRITERIA

HSPD-12 Credentialing:
Failure to live within one's means, satisfy debts, and meet financial obligations may raise questions about the individual's honesty and put people, property or information systems at risk. The following consideration may apply:

<u>*There is a reasonable basis to believe, based on the individual's criminal or dishonest conduct, that issuance of a PIV card poses an unacceptable risk*</u>
[F]or example, a person's consistent failure to satisfy significant debts may indicate that granting a PIV poses an unacceptable risk to Government financial assets and information systems to which the individual will have access.

Employment Suitability/Fitness:
Failure to live within one's means, satisfy debts, and meet financial obligations may raise questions about the individual's honesty. The following suitability factor may apply:

<u>*Criminal or dishonest conduct*</u>
The following are examples of conduct that may be disqualifying (Note: This list is not meant to be all inclusive):

  (a) *unwillingness to satisfy debts*

(b) indebtedness caused by frivolous or irresponsible spending and
the absence of any evidence of willingness or intent to pay the
debt or establish a realistic plan to pay the debt

(c) a history of not meeting financial obligations

(d) deceptive or illegal financial practices such as embezzlement,
employee theft, check fraud, income tax evasion, expense account fraud, filing deceptive loan statements, other intentional
financial breaches of trust

Security clearance (Guideline F):

18. *The Concern*. Failure or inability to live within one's means,
satisfy debts, and meet financial obligations may indicate poor self-
control, lack of judgment, or unwillingness to abide by rules and
regulations, all of which can raise questions about an individual's
reliability, trustworthiness and ability to protect classified information. An individual who is financially overextended is at risk of
having to engage in illegal acts to generate funds. Compulsive gambling is a concern as it may lead to financial crimes including espionage. Affluence that cannot be explained by known sources of income
is also a security concern. It may indicate proceeds from financially
profitable criminal acts.

19. *Conditions that could raise a security concern and may be dis-*
qualifying include:

(a) inability or unwillingness to satisfy debts;

(b) indebtedness caused by frivolous or irresponsible spending and
the absence of any evidence of willingness or intent to pay the debt or
establish a realistic plan to pay the debt.

(c) a history of not meeting financial obligations;

(d) deceptive or illegal financial practices such as embezzlement,
employee theft, check fraud, income tax evasion, expense account
fraud, filing deceptive loan statements, and other intentional financial breaches of trust;

(e) consistent spending beyond one's means, which may be indicated
by excessive indebtedness, significant negative cash flow, high debt-
to-income ratio, and/or other financial analysis;

(f) financial problems that are linked to drug abuse, alcoholism,
gambling problems, or other issues of security concern.

(g) failure to file annual Federal, state, or local income tax returns as required or the fraudulent filing of the same;

(h) unexplained affluence, as shown by a lifestyle or standard of living, increase in net worth, or money transfers that cannot be explained by subject's known legal sources of income;

(i) compulsive or addictive gambling as indicated by an unsuccessful attempt to stop gambling, "chasing losses" (i.e. increasing the bets or returning another day in an effort to get even), concealment of gambling losses, borrowing money to fund gambling or pay gambling debts, family conflict or other problems caused by gambling.

20. Conditions that could mitigate security concerns include:

(a) the behavior happened so long ago, was so infrequent, or occurred under such circumstances that it is unlikely to recur and does not cast doubt on the individual's current reliability, trustworthiness, or good judgment;

(b) the conditions that resulted in the financial problem were largely beyond the person's control (e.g. loss of employment, a business downturn, unexpected medical emergency, or a death, divorce or separation), and the individual acted responsibly under the circumstances;

(c) the person has received or is receiving counseling for the problem and/or there are clear indications that the problem is being resolved or is under control;

(d) the individual initiated a good-faith effort to repay overdue creditors or otherwise resolve debts;

(e) the individual has a reasonable basis to dispute the legitimacy of the past-due debt which is the cause of the problem and provides documented proof to substantiate the basis of the dispute or provides evidence of actions to resolve the issue;

(f) the affluence resulted from a legal source of income.

DISCUSSION

A sampling of recent DOHA security clearance cases showed that about 50 percent involved "Financial Considerations." This was two times greater than the next most frequently listed security/suitability issue.[44] The Department of Navy CAF reported that 81% of their security clearance denials and revocations in FY2008 were due to *Financial Considerations*.

Excessive indebtedness increases the temptation to commit unethical or illegal acts in order to obtain funds to pay off the debts. Concealment of debt from family members is particularly significant because it is related to stress or desperation regarding debt and increases the possibility of illegal or unethical acts. It is noteworthy that most Americans who betrayed their country did it for financial gain— about half were motivated by a real or perceived urgent need for money and about half by personal greed.

For some people financial problems result from situations that are largely beyond their control. For others financial problems are often symptoms of irresponsibility, poor judgment, or reckless behavior. Reckless behavior includes such things as excessive use of alcohol, drug abuse, and compulsive gambling. In these cases "Personal Conduct" and other criteria may also apply.

The Financial Considerations criterion for security clearances lists 9 examples of potentially disqualifying conditions. Aside from compulsive gambling, deceptive or illegal financial practices, and unexplained affluence, the 9 conditions can generally be boiled down to 1 security concern—significant delinquent debt. Although a high debt to income ratio is listed as a potentially disqualifying condition; it rarely comes into play absent any past or present delinquent debt or signs of unexplained income. Low credit scores are not listed as a potentially disqualifying condition, because factors other than delinquent debt affect credit scores. In fact a FICO credit score does not appear on the credit report used for security clearance purposes.

DELINQUENT DEBT

Delinquent debt is by far the most common financial concern. It is often complicated by other adjudicative concerns, such as carelessness, irresponsibility, and substance abuse. Unlike most other adjudicative criteria, financial indebtedness issues tend to be current problems, and therefore the most common mitigating factor, passage

---

[44] *Guideline E: Personal Conduct* was cited in about 45 percent of the cases, but was frequently an issue involving falsification or irresponsibility directly related to other adjudicative criteria. *Personal Conduct* as an issue appeared most frequently in conjunction with *Financial Considerations*.

of time, does not apply. Additionally, the fact that a debt is no longer legally collectable, due to a state's statute of limitations, will not be considered a mitigating condition. In adjudicating such cases the following factors are taken into consideration:

- Cause of debt

- Response to debt

- Amount of debt

Cause of debt is generally more important than the amount of debt, because it reveals more about a person's reliability, trustworthiness, and judgment. Of people who seek credit counseling, roughly 50 percent are due to irresponsibility, about 25 percent due to loss of income, about 10 percent due to divorce/separation; and about 10 percent due to unexpected medical expenses.

If the debt was caused by irresponsibility (including compulsive or addictive behavior) that is likely to continue, the problem is magnified. If the debt occurred due to situations beyond the applicant's control, and the applicant is handling it in a responsible manner (including bankruptcy or debt consolidation, if appropriate), the significance of the problem is substantially reduced.

Response to debt is evaluated by the things people do (or don't do) about delinquent debt. How people deal with debt is often a decisive consideration. Those who ignore their financial responsibilities may also ignore their responsibility to safeguard classified information. Classic indicators of irresponsibility and unethical behavior are:

- Changing addresses without notifying creditors

- Failure to take reasonable measures to pay or reduce debts

- Knowingly issuing bad checks

- Increased credit card use immediately before filing for bankruptcy

Surprisingly the word, "bankruptcy" does not appear anywhere in the *Adjudicative Guidelines*. This is because bankruptcy can be considered a positive effort to get one's finances under control. What is important is the underlying reason for the bankruptcy. Credit counseling is also considered a positive effort.

Amount of debt focuses primarily on the delinquent amount, but total debt can also be taken into consideration. Most delinquent debt is a security concern. For total debt there is a rule of thumb used by credit counselors—if an individual's minimum monthly payments for consumer credit (excluding credit cards that are paid in full at the end of each billing cycle and mortgages on primary homes) total more than 20 percent of monthly take-home pay, there is a financial problem. This does not apply to unmarried military personnel who live in barracks and eat in mess halls and others who are similarly situated. As mentioned before, debt-to-income ratio is seldom considered unless there are significant past or present delinquent debts or obvious signs of unexplained income.

OPM, which conducts 90 percent of all security clearance investigations, uses the following criteria for expansion of investigations for financial issues:[45]

- Credit report reflects current delinquencies (120 days or more) on combined delinquent debt totaling $3,500 and any single account is $1,000 or more delinquent (including judgments and liens) or

- Bankruptcy within the past 2 years or

- Bankruptcy within the past 3 to 5 years with evidence of current credit problems.

This does not mean that delinquent debt totaling less than $3,500 is not adjudicatively significant, but it does suggest that, absent any aggravating circumstances or other security issues, the government is not overly concerned about small amounts of delinquent debt. OPM considers bankruptcy for case expansion purposes; it is only a trigger for further inquiry. Bankruptcy is a legal means of liquidating debts, except for taxes and student loans. The amount absolved through bankruptcy should not be counted under amount of debt.

MITIGATING DELINQUENT DEBT

The following conditions generally mitigate the delinquent debt and related Personal Conduct concerns:

---

[45] OPM Federal Investigations Notice No. 06-07, August 29, 2006.

Not Likely to Recur: Likelihood of recurrence is greatly reduced if the conduct occurred long ago, occurred under unusual circumstances, or was an isolated incident. Examples of these type of situations include, writing one or two clusters of unintentional insufficient fund checks, loosing track of a couple of bills as a result of relocating, or having "paid collection" accounts from a few years ago. Favorable changes in financial habits and lifestyle over a period of time can mitigate more serious past financial irresponsibility. Formerly delinquent debts (delinquent debts that were eventually fully satisfied) are given more or less weight depending on the applicant's more recent credit dealings. The existence of current debt problems increases the significance of past debt problems.

Beyond Applicant's Control: Financial problems often arise due to situations beyond a person's control, such as medical debts, divorce, loss of income, victim of crime, bad investments, business downturn, and natural disasters. In these situations if a person acts reasonably and responsibly (including bankruptcy or debt consolidation, when necessary) to resolve their debts, the financial issue can be mitigated. The debts do not have to be fully resolved at the time of adjudication, but there should be verifiable uninterrupted efforts toward this goal. Being a victim of predatory lending practices, particularly involving subprime mortgages, may fall into the category of situations beyond an applicant's control. Applicants who are lawyers, accountants, and people with experience in the financial services industry will have difficulty convincing anyone that they were victims.

Foreclosures and Short Sales: A study was published by Sheldon I. Cohen, a prominent Washington D.C. area attorney specializing in national security clearances, entitled *"Debt and Home Foreclosures: Their Effect on National Security Clearances."* Cohen reviewed 62 case decisions by DOHA between 2006 and 2010 involving foreclosures and short sales. He also reviewed 71 DOHA Appeal Board cases involving Financial Considerations. Regarding 22 case decisions that resulted in the granting of security clearances, Cohen stated, "The common thread in all of these cases is that:

(1) applicants were victims of circumstances not of their own doing;

(2) they had not been speculators in the housing market who were caught when the bubble burst;

(3) they had not succumbed to fraudulent schemes "too good to be true" as a result of their own greed; and

(4) they had made good faith efforts to meet their other debts after the loss of their homes by foreclosure or short sale."

Counseling/Good Faith Effort to Repay: Conscientious participation in credit counseling or a debt consolidation program can significantly mitigate financial concerns. Without formal counseling consistent, systematic, good faith efforts to repay or otherwise resolve debts will have the same effect. The debts do not have to be fully resolved at the time of adjudication, but there should be verifiable uninterrupted efforts toward this goal. Occasionally clearances are granted with a "condition." In cases involving delinquent debts, the condition can be that the applicant must continue paying off the debts in a prescribed manner until the debts are paid in full by a certain date without incurring new debts.

Disputed Debts: When business records, including credit reports, indicate that an applicant owes money, the burden of proof shifts to the applicant to disprove the claim. If an applicant has several sizable credit accounts listed as "paid as agreed" and only one delinquent account, adjudicators are much more inclined to accept even minimal evidence from the applicant that the account information is erroneous. Conversely, if an applicant disputes half of the accounts listed on their credit report, adjudicator will want to see convincing evidence to support the applicant's claim. Efforts to dispute erroneous credit report entries immediately after learning of them will also help to substantiate the applicant's position.

Personal Conduct: When delinquent debt is caused by irresponsible or careless conduct, the potentially disqualifying factors under the "Personal Conduct" criterion will usually also be considered by adjudicators. These factors focus on trustworthiness, reliability, and judgment as they relate to the handling of financial matters. To mitigate these concerns it is necessary to show a positive change in attitude regarding debt. Such change needs to be shown through documented, consistent efforts to meet one's financial obligations. If it appears that an applicant is only taking action because they know that it is required to obtain a security clearance, it will not convince an adjudicator that the problem is unlikely to recur after the clearance is granted. Therefore, efforts to resolve financial problems should begin a reasonable amount of time prior to applying for a clearance. What is reasonable varies greatly depending on individual circumstances. Obviously the earlier corrective action is taken, the more likely the problem can be fully mitigated. In some instances credit counseling, initiated only a few months prior to applying for a clearance can substantially mitigate security concerns.

DELINQUENT DEBT & INTERIM CLEARANCE

Mitigating financial issues is significantly more difficult for interim clearances than for final clearances. For final clearances adjudicators consider all case information, including comprehensive investigative reports. If a Subject Interview was conducted as part of the investigation, the report will contain explanation, documentation, and mitigation offered by an applicant. People do a better job of providing mitigating information when allowed to tell their story face to face to an investigator, particularly if the investigator is skillful in eliciting the pertinent facts. The investigator should be familiar with general mitigating conditions and know how to get the applicant to address these without asking leading questions.

For interim security clearances, government officials must rely primarily on the clearance application form and sometimes on a credit report. If an applicant completes an SF86 or SF85P (the SF85 does not have any financial questions) and provides only the information requested on the form, the form will contain little or no mitigating information. To have mitigating information considered for an interim clearance determination, the information must be entered into the "Optional Comment" field following the appropriate financial questions on the e-QIP version of the forms. And, the information must directly address one or more of the mitigating conditions listed under Guideline F (Financial Considerations) and, if appropriate, Guideline E (Personal Conduct) of the *Adjudicative Guidelines*. Sometimes it is possible to submit documents as attachments to an SF86 or SF85P. This is particular true for non-industrial cases. If you have had a bankruptcy in the past 2 years and your credit report shows: 1) accounts included in the bankruptcy correctly, 2) that you have not incurred substantial new debt, and 3) that you have been paying all debts as agreed since the bankruptcy, then submitting a copy of the bankruptcy and a copy of your credit report with your SF86 or SF85P will increase your chance of receiving an interim clearance.

WHAT TO DO IF YOU HAVE DELINQUENT DEBT

1. Get credit reports from all three national credit reporting companies and use the reports to make a list of all your creditors, but understand its limits:

    Unpaid alimony, tax delinquencies, automobile leases, gambling debts, personal loans, bad checks, and debts to medical practitioners, utility companies, and local stores don't always appear on credit reports. Occasionally account information on the wrong person appears on a report and frequently duplicate entries of the same account appear on a report. Although the SF86 only asks for 7 year's worth of financial data (except for financial problems due to gambling); adjudicators may consider all financial information available to them. Some financial data that may not appear on your credit report can be obtained by field investigators from court records, rental/utility records, real estate records, employment records, etc.

2. Immediately take action to dispute any erroneous information on your credit report.

3. Consistently make at least minimum monthly payments to all creditors.

4. Contact those creditors that have unpaid claims against you, insure that the claims are legitimate, and set up a repayment schedule as soon as possible. Try to communicate in writing and keep copies of all correspondence. If you communicate by telephone, make a written record of the telephone call and include the date, name of the person you spoke to, and a gist of the conversation.

5. Get credit counseling if necessary, preferably with an agency that is a member of the National Foundation for Credit Counseling. They may be able to negotiate better repayment terms and lower interest rates than you can obtain by yourself.

6. Don't be afraid of bankruptcy, if your situation warrants it. If you seek the services of a reputable credit counseling service first, they will advise you whether your situation can be resolved better through bankruptcy or debt consolidation.

CHAPTER 15

ALCOHOL CONSUMPTION

ADJUDICATIVE CRITERIA

HSPD-12 Credentialing:
An individual's abuse of alcohol may put people, property, or information systems at risk. The following consideration may apply:

There is a reasonable basis to believe, based on the nature or duration of the individual's alcohol abuse without evidence of substantial rehabilitation, that issuance of a PIV card poses an unacceptable risk. [F]or example, a person's long-term alcohol abuse without evidence of substantial rehabilitation may indicate that granting a PIV poses an unacceptable safety risk in a Government facility.

Employment Suitability/Fitness:
An individual's abuse of alcohol may impact on his or her ability to complete the duties of the job and/or raise questions about his or her reliability and trustworthiness, thus indicating that his or her employment would not promote the efficiency of the service or protect its integrity. The following suitability factor may apply:

Alcohol abuse of a nature and duration which suggests that the applicant or appointee would be prevented from performing the duties of the position in question, or would constitute a direct threat to property or safety of others.
The following are examples of conduct that may be disqualifying (Note: This list is not meant to be all inclusive):

  (a) current continuing use of alcohol [sic][to excess]

(b) a pattern of alcohol-related arrests and/or problems in employment

(Note: Less serious alcohol-related conduct may still be a concern under the criminal conduct or misconduct or negligence in employment
factors, and should first be considered in concert with any other suitability issues to determine if a suitability disqualification is warranted
before being evaluated under the security criteria.)

Security Clearance (Guideline G):
21. *The Concern*. Excessive alcohol consumption often leads to the
exercise of questionable judgment or the failure to control impulses,
and can raise questions about an individual's reliability and trustworthiness.

22. *Conditions that could raise a security concern and may be disqualifying include:*

(a) alcohol-related incidents away from work, such as driving while
under the influence, fighting, child or spouse abuse, disturbing the
peace, or other incidents of concern, regardless of whether the individual is diagnosed as an alcohol abuser or alcohol dependent;

(b) alcohol-related incidents at work, such as reporting for work or
duty in an intoxicated or impaired condition, or drinking on the job,
regardless of whether the individual is diagnosed as an alcohol abuser or alcohol dependent;

(c) habitual or binge consumption of alcohol to the point of impaired
judgment, regardless of whether the individual is diagnosed as an
alcohol abuser or alcohol dependent;

(d) diagnosis by a duly qualified medical professional (e.g., physician, clinical psychologist, or psychiatrist) of alcohol abuse or alcohol
dependence;

(e) evaluation of alcohol abuse or alcohol dependence by a licensed
clinical social worker who is a staff member of a recognized alcohol
treatment program;

(f) relapse after diagnosis of alcohol abuse or dependence and completion of an alcohol rehabilitation program;

(g) failure to follow any court order regarding alcohol education,
evaluation, treatment, or abstinence.

23. Conditions that could mitigate security concerns include:

(a) so much time has passed, or the behavior was so infrequent, or it happened under such unusual circumstances that it is unlikely to recur or does not cast doubt on the individual's current reliability, trustworthiness, or good judgment;

(b) the individual acknowledges his or her alcoholism or issues of alcohol abuse, provides evidence of actions taken to overcome this problem, and has established a pattern of abstinence (if alcohol dependent) or responsible use (if an alcohol abuser);

(c) the individual is a current employee who is participating in a counseling or treatment program, has no history of previous treatment and relapse, and is making satisfactory progress;

(d) the individual has successfully completed inpatient or outpatient counseling or rehabilitation along with any required aftercare, has demonstrated a clear and established pattern of modified consumption or abstinence in accordance with treatment recommendations, such as participation in meetings of Alcoholics Anonymous or a similar organization and has received a favorable prognosis by a duly qualified medical professional or a licensed clinical social worker who is a staff member of a recognized alcohol treatment program.

DISCUSSION

The "Alcohol Consumption" criterion affects many clearance applicants, particularly those who have received alcohol counseling and those who have been involved in alcohol-related incidents, such as drunk driving, disorderly conduct, and public intoxication. Others who have been cautioned by a superior about alcohol use or experienced work, social, legal, financial, or health problems as a result of drinking can also be affected.

The *Adjudicative Guidelines* states that "Excessive alcohol consumption often leads to the exercise of questionable judgment or the failure to control impulses, and can raise questions about an individual's reliability and trustworthiness." Simply stated, alcohol abusers are more likely than others to engage in careless or impulsive behavior that can create an increased risk of unauthorized disclosure of classified information.

EVALUATING ALCOHOL CONSUMPTION

When does drinking become a security concern? Alcohol is legal and its consumption, regardless of quantity, does not by itself trigger a security concern. Alcohol becomes a concern when there has been:

- Alcohol-related incident or other evidence of impaired judgment or misconduct while under the influence of alcohol.

- Negative impact on work/school performance, finances, personal or professional relationships.

- Failure to comply with court-ordered alcohol education, evaluation, treatment, or abstinence.

- Diagnosis of alcohol abuse or alcohol dependence by a qualified medical professional.

- Relapse after completion of an alcohol treatment program.

Absent a diagnosis of alcohol abuse or alcohol dependence, investigators and adjudicators look for indicators of current abuse or dependence. These indicators include:

- Attempts or perceived need to cut down on drinking.

- Annoyance or anger when criticized about drinking.

- Feelings of guilty about drinking and how it affects other aspects of life.

- Drinking first thing in the morning to steady nerves or get rid of a hangover.

- Claims of high tolerance for alcohol.

- Drinking prior to social events.

- Drinking extensively alone.

- Drinking that causes or increases social, work, school, financial, legal or heath problem.

MITIGATING SECURITY CONCERNS

The following conditions may mitigate Alcohol Consumption concerns:

Problem is not serious—A single recent alcohol-related incident (or even two incidents spaced a few years apart) may not suggest a serious alcohol problem, provided there has not been a diagnosis of alcohol abuse or dependence and there are no other indicators of current abuse or dependence.

Problem is not recent—Absent any recent indications of abuse, serious problems that occurred more than 2 years ago (depending on seriousness/number and change in drinking habits/lifestyle) may no longer be an issue.

Positive changes in behavior—The applicant acknowledges their alcohol dependence or abuse and has demonstrated consistent abstinence (if alcohol dependent) or responsible use (if alcohol abuser). There have been positive lifestyle changes and other actions to overcome the problem. These could involve alcohol education, avoiding people, places, and activities associated with drinking, changing residences, leaving school and entering the workforce, changing jobs, getting married, having children, as well as involvement with healthy recreational activities or volunteer/social organizations. At least 6 months of positive changes in drinking habits and lifestyle may mitigate 1 or 2 recent alcohol-related incidents.

Rehabilitation—Successful completion of a treatment program (including any required aftercare program), consistent pattern of reduced consumption or abstinence in accordance with treatment recommendations for at least 12 months after treatment, and a favorable prognosis by a qualified medical professional may mitigate security concerns. When there has been no formal treatment, persuasive evidence of abstinence or consistent responsible alcohol use for at least 12 months may also mitigate security concerns.

Alcohol problems involving people who already have a security clearance may be sufficiently mitigated, if they participate in a treatment program with satisfactory progress and have no previous history of treatment and relapse.

INTERIM CLEARANCES

Disclosure of alcohol-related counseling or any alcohol-related incident on an SF86 (the SF85P only has questions about criminal conduct and the SF85 has no criminal or alcohol questions) can create a presumption of an alcohol consumption issue. Often this issue can be mitigated by the information collected during a security clearance investigation. But as previously stated, interim clearances require issue mitigation before the investigation is completed. The SF86 asks about alcohol-related counseling, incidents, and "negative impact," but it does not ask for information that might mitigate alcohol concerns. Applicants are allowed to include mitigating information in the e-QIP version of the SF86 by using the "Optional Comment" field following each section and sub-section. Including mitigating information in this manner is often a determining factor in the granting of an interim clearance.

CHAPTER 16

DRUG INVOLVEMENT

ADJUDICATIVE CRITERIA

HSPD-12 Credentialing:
An individual's abuse of drugs[46] may put people, property, or information systems at risk. The following consideration may apply:

<u>There is a reasonable basis to believe, based on the nature or duration of the individual's illegal use of narcotics, drugs, or other controlled substances without evidence of substantial rehabilitation, that issuance of a PIV card poses an unacceptable risk.</u>
[F]or example, a person's long-term illegal use of narcotics without evidence of substantial rehabilitation may indicate that granting a PIV poses an unacceptable safety risk in a Government facility.

Employment Suitability/Fitness:
Drug involvement can raise questions about an individual's reliability and trustworthiness and ability or willingness to comply with laws, rules, and regulations, thus indicating that his or her employment would not promote the efficiency of the service or protect its integrity. The following suitability factor may apply:

<u>Illegal use of narcotics, drugs or other controlled substances, without evidence of substantial rehabilitation.</u>

---

[46] Drugs are defined as mood and behavior altering substances, and include: (1) Drugs, materials, and other chemical compounds identified and listed in the Controlled Substances Act of 1970, as amended (e.g. marijuana or cannabis, depressants, narcotics, stimulants, and hallucinogens) and (2) inhalants and other similar substances.

The following are examples of conduct that may be disqualifying (Note: This list is not meant to be all inclusive):

  (a) *a recent, serious offense*

  (b) *a pattern of drug-related arrests and/or problems in employment*

  (Note: Less serious drug-related conduct may still be a concern under the criminal conduct or misconduct or negligence in employment suitability factors, and should first be considered in concert with any other suitability issues to determine if a suitability disqualification is warranted before being evaluated under the security criteria.)

Security Clearance (Guideline H):

<u>24. The Concern</u>. *Use of an illegal drug or misuse of a prescription drug can raise questions about an individual's reliability and trustworthiness, both because it may impair judgment and because it raises questions about a person's ability or willingness to comply with laws, rules, and regulations.*

(a) Drugs are defined as mood and behavior altering substances, and include:

  (1) Drugs, materials, and other chemical compounds identified and listed in the Controlled Substances Act of 1970, as amended (e.g., marijuana or cannabis, depressants, narcotics, stimulants, and hallucinogens), and (2) inhalants and other similar substances;

(b) drug abuse is the illegal use of a drug or use of a legal drug in a manner that deviates from approved medical direction.

<u>25. Conditions that could raise a security concern and may be disqualifying include:</u>

(a) Any drug abuse (see above definition);[47]

---

[47] The provisions of 50 U.S.C. 435b, section 3002 (Bond Amendment, see page 54 of this book) prohibit all federal agencies from granting or renewing any security clearance to a person who <u>is</u> an unlawful user of a controlled substance or <u>is</u> an addict. Waivers cannot be granted for this prohibition.

(b) testing positive for illegal drug use;

(c) illegal drug possession, including cultivation, processing, manufacture, purchase, sale, or distribution; or possession of drug paraphernalia;

(d) diagnosis by a duly qualified medical professional (e.g., physician, clinical psychologist, or psychiatrist) of drug abuse or drug dependence;

(e) evaluation of drug abuse or drug dependence by a licensed clinical social worker who is a staff member of a recognized drug treatment program;

(f) failure to successfully complete a drug treatment program prescribed by a duly qualified medical professional;

(g) any illegal drug use after being granted a security clearance;

(h) expressed intent to continue illegal drug use, or failure to clearly and convincingly commit to discontinue drug use.

26. *Conditions that could mitigate security concerns include:*

(a) the behavior happened so long ago, was so infrequent, or happened under such circumstances that it is unlikely to recur or does not cast doubt on the individual's current reliability, trustworthiness, or good judgment;

(b) a demonstrated intent not to abuse any drugs in the future, such as:

> *(1) dissociation from drug-using associates and contacts;*
>
> *(2) changing or avoiding the environment where drugs were used;*
>
> *(3) an appropriate period of abstinence;*
>
> *(4) a signed statement of intent with automatic revocation of clearance for any violation;*

(c) abuse of prescription drugs was after a severe or prolonged illness during which these drugs were prescribed, and abuse has since ended;

(d) satisfactory completion of a prescribed drug treatment program, including but not limited to rehabilitation and aftercare requirements, without recurrence of abuse, and a favorable prognosis by a duly qualified medical professional.

DISCUSSION

A 2003 national survey[48] of drug use showed that about 60% of Americans between 19 and 30 years of age had used an illegal drug and about 20% had used a prescription drug for nonmedical reasons some time in their lives. The "Drug Involvement" criterion affects the clearance eligibility of many applicants by making any illegal use of drugs a potentially disqualifying condition. It also makes cultivation, manufacture, purchase, sale, distribution; and simple possession of illegal drugs or drug paraphernalia potentially disqualifying conditions.

The *Adjudicative Guidelines* states that drug abuse ". . . can raise questions about an individual's reliability and trustworthiness, both because it may impair judgment and because it raises questions about a person's ability or willingness to comply with laws, rules, and regulations." Drug abuse also raises concerns about an individual's susceptibility to blackmail and the possible presence of mental health issues. Drug use can cause financial problems, sometimes leading to other criminal activity to support a drug habit.

Like many other issues, the security concern related to past drug abuse focuses more on applicants' demonstrated willingness and ability to abstain from future drug involvement than on their past conduct. Experimentation with drugs, particularly marijuana, is fairly common behavior during a person's formative years. Such experimentation is usually benign and does not result in chronic or long-term use for most people.

EVALUATING DRUG INVOLVEMENT

When does drug abuse become a security concern? Under federal law (Section 3002 of 50 U.S.C. 435b) a current user of illegal drugs cannot be granted a security clearance. Using illegal drugs a few months prior to submitting a clearance application form can be considered current use. Evaluation of past drug abuse is based on:

- Which drugs were used.
- Frequency of drug use.
- Recency of drug use.

---

[48] Department of Health and Human Services, Substance Abuse and Mental Health Services Administration, "2003 National Survey on Drug Use & Health: Results."

- Circumstances of drug use.

- Effects of drug use (e.g. mental health, employment, finances, and arrests).

MITIGATING SECURITY CONCERNS

Illegal drug involvement can be mitigated if it is shown that the applicant is no longer has any illegal drug involvement and it is highly probable that the applicant will not become illegally involved with drugs in the future. Determining whether an applicant is likely to have future drug involvement is primarily based on the type, frequency, and recency of past drug involvement. The following is extracted from the Defense Personnel Security Research Center's 2010 *Adjudicative Desk Reference* used by many government adjudicators:

> *The following examples of time periods [of abstinence] that might mitigate various types and frequencies of past drug use . . . are provided for consideration in the context of all the other information available about the person. They are not a formula to be applied mechanically in all cases.*
>
> ***At Least Six Months:*** *The only drug use was experimental or occasional use of marijuana, and there are no aggravating circumstances.*
>
> ***At Least One Year:*** *Marijuana was used frequently, or any other drug was used experimentally, and there are no aggravating circumstances.*
>
> ***At Least Two Years:*** *Marijuana was used regularly, or any other drug was used occasionally, and there are no aggravating circumstances. There was no evidence of psychological or physical dependence at the time subject was using drugs, and subject has demonstrated a stable lifestyle with satisfactory employment record since then.*
>
> ***At Least Three Years:*** *Any drug other than marijuana was used frequently or regularly, or marijuana was used regularly with signs of psychological dependence. There are no other aggravating circumstances. Subject has maintained a stable lifestyle, satisfactory employment record, and a completely clean record in all other issue areas during the past three years.*
>
> ***At Least Five Years:*** *A minor involvement in drug trafficking for profit or failure to complete a drug treatment program. Subject has maintained a stable lifestyle, satisfactory employment record, and a completely clean record in all other issue areas during the past five years.*
>
> *Every case has unique factors that must be considered in addition to these time guidelines. Adjudicators should adjust the time periods in order to take into account circumstances of past drug use and whether the individual is a current clearance holder or an applicant. When in doubt, ask the following question: Has subject demonstrated "strength of character, trustworthiness,*

honesty, reliability, discretion, and sound judgment" as required by Executive Order 12968? If so, access may be approved. If not, it may be denied.

The *Adjudicative Desk Reference* uses the following definitions for levels of drug use:

Experimental Use: *Initial use for a maximum of six times, or more intensive use for a maximum of one month.*

Occasional Use: *Once a month or less.*

Frequent Use: *Once a week or less, but more than once a month.*

Regular or Habitual Use: *More than once a week.*

Aggravating factors that could require longer periods of abstinence to mitigate drug abuse include: drug use while holding a security clearance, solitary drug use, growing or making one's own drugs, relapse after completion of a drug treatment program, and other misconduct related to illegal drugs.

Factors that support the minimum period of abstinence include: disassociation from drug-using associates, drug use occurred between late teens and late twenties, avoiding the environment where drugs were used, successful completion of a drug treatment program with a favorable prognosis, and a signed "statement of intent" not to illegally use drugs in the future and agreeing to an automatic revocation of clearance for any violation.

For frequent or regular use of drugs, purchase and/or possession of drugs incidental to personal use will not require separate or additional mitigation, nor will occasionally purchasing marijuana and sharing it with others. Other situations, where money or bartered items are exchanged for drugs, will be evaluated based on any actual or intended profit. Situations involving more than simple use and possession may require mitigation similar to that used for Criminal Conduct (Guideline J).

Even though an applicant can show an appropriate period of abstinence from illegal drug use and other mitigating conditions, it doesn't guarantee a successful outcome. Sometimes the attitude of the adjudicator and intangible case factors are a greater determinate of case outcome than the facts. There are two cases that exemplify this problem, and both were at DOHA. Even greater differences in applying the Adjudicative Guidelines are possible when similar cases are decided at different adjudicative facilities. The first is ISCR Case No. 04-10404 and the second is ISCR Case No. 09-00521. The drug use in both cases is similar. In the first case the applicant used marijuana about 70 times over a 5 year period, and in the second case the applicant used marijuana about 120 times over a 3 year period—both represent "frequent use." Both also used psilocybin mushrooms a few times. In the first case the applicant had abstained from drug use for less than 5 months (last use to date of hearing) and was granted a clearance. In the second case the applicant had abstained from drug use for 15 months (last use to date of hearing) and was denied a clearance. The only difference in the 2 cases was that the applicant in the first case had successfully completed substance abuse counseling and had more positive factors under the "whole-person" concept.

INTERIM CLEARANCES

For interim clearances some drug-related disqualifying conditions can sometimes be mitigated by merely listing the type, frequency, circumstances, and dates of drug use as required by the clearance application form. It is recommended that applicants include additional mitigating information in the "Optional Comment" field following each drug-related question on the e-QIP versions of the clearance application forms. The new March 2010 version of the SF86 now includes a question regarding an applicant's intent to illegally use drugs in the future; however, it is still advisable to include a statement in the "Optional Comment" field indicating an intent not to illegally use drugs in the future and agreeing to the automatic revocation of clearance for any violation.

CHAPTER 17

PSYCHOLOGICAL CONDITIONS

ADJUDICATIVE CRITERIA

HSPD-12 Credentialing:
While there is no specific HSPD-12 consideration related to psychological conditions, actions involving violence should be evaluated under the criminal or dishonest conduct consideration. Incidents on the job should be evaluated under the misconduct or negligence in employment consideration.

Employment Suitability/Fitness:
While there is no specific suitability factor related to psychological conditions, actions involving violence should be evaluated under the criminal or dishonest conduct factor. Incidents on the job should be evaluated under the misconduct or negligence in employment factor. Any other concerns about psychological conditions should be evaluated, as appropriate, to determine if the person is medically qualified and fit to hold the position in question.

Security Clearance (Guideline I):
<u>27. The Concern</u>. *Certain emotional, mental, and personality conditions can impair judgment, reliability, or trustworthiness. A formal diagnosis of a disorder is not required for there to be a concern under this guideline. A duly qualified mental health professional (e.g., clinical psychologist or psychiatrist) employed by, or acceptable to and approved by the U.S. Government, should be consulted when evaluat-*

ing potentially disqualifying and mitigating information under this guideline. No negative inference concerning the standards in this Guideline may be raised solely on the basis of seeking mental health counseling.

28. Conditions that could raise a security concern and may be disqualifying include:

(a) behavior that casts doubt on an individual's judgment, reliability, or trustworthiness that is not covered under any other guideline, including but not limited to emotionally unstable, irresponsible, dysfunctional, violent, paranoid, or bizarre behavior;

(b) an opinion by a duly qualified mental health professional that the individual has a condition not covered under any other guideline that may impair judgment, reliability, or trustworthiness;
(c) the individual has failed to follow treatment advice related to a diagnosed emotional, mental, or personality condition, e.g. failure to take prescribed medication.

29. Conditions that could mitigate security concerns include:

(a) the identified condition is readily controllable with treatment, and the individual has demonstrated ongoing and consistent compliance with the treatment plan;

(b) the individual has voluntarily entered a counseling or treatment program for a condition that is amenable to treatment, and the individual is currently receiving counseling or treatment with a favorable prognosis by a duly qualified mental health professional;

(c) recent opinion by a duly qualified mental health professional employed by, or acceptable to and approved by the U.S. Government that an individual's previous condition is under control or in remission, and has a low probability of recurrence or exacerbation;

(d) the past emotional instability was a temporary condition (e.g., one caused by a death, illness, or marital breakup), the situation has been resolved, and the individual no longer shows indications of emotional instability;

(e) there is no indication of a current problem.

DISCUSSION

"An estimated 26.2 percent of Americans . . . suffer from a diagnosable mental disorder in a given year."[49] Nearly two-thirds of these people do not seek treatment, some because of the stigma that is associated with mental health treatment.[50] Mental health issues can adversely affect an individual's eligibility for a federal security clearance, but many clearance applicants worry unnecessarily and sometimes choose not to seek treatment due to fears that it could result in the denial or revocation of a clearance.

The "Psychological Conditions" criterion of the *Adjudicative Guidelines* is one of the least understood criteria for being granted a security clearance. Regarding the standards for eligibility for access to classified information, Executive Order 12968 states:

> "No negative inference concerning the standards in this section may be raised solely on the basis of mental health counseling. . . . However, mental health counseling, where relevant to the adjudication of access to classified information, may justify further inquiry to determine whether the standards of subsection (b) of this section are satisfied, and mental health may be considered where it directly relates to those standards."

This policy is restated in slightly different words in Guideline I and on the SF86.

Of the 150,000 security clearance applications processed each year by DISCO only 5 applicants were denied clearances in 2009 by DOHA Administrative Judges because of *Psychological Conditions*. A July 2009 article at www.Army.mil reported that the US Army Central Clearance Facility's "*adjudicative history indicates that 99.98 percent of cases with psychological concerns obtained/retained their security clearance eligibility.*"

A past or present mental, emotional, or personality disorder is not by itself a disqualifying condition for a final security clearance. A psychological condition does not have to be formally diagnosed as a disorder to be a security concern. The security concern arises when the possibility of future unreliable or dysfunctional behavior is indicated by either abnormal behavior or the opinion of a qualified mental

---

[49] The National Institute of Mental Health, "The Numbers Count: Mental Health Disorders in America," undated publication posted at: http://www.nimh.nih.gov/health/publications/the-numbers-count-mental-disorders-in-america/index.shtml.
[50] "Mental Health: A Report of the Surgeon General," undated, posted at: http://www.surgeongeneral.gov/library/mentalhealth/chapter1/sec1.html.

health practitioner. When a psychological condition (or the side effects of medication) adversely affects a person's judgment and behavior, such things as disappointment, failure, or perceive injustice or betrayal may cause reactions that are irresponsible, self-destructive, retaliatory, and/or unlawful. This can result in willful or negligent compromise of classified information, violence, sabotage, or espionage.

INVESTIGATION OF PSYCHOLOGICAL CONDITIONS

A "yes" response to the "Mental and Emotional Health" question on the SF86 usually results in the need for additional information beyond the dates of treatment and identification of the health care provider in order to make a final security clearance determination. The question at section 21 of the March 2010 version of SF86 can be somewhat confusing. It reads:

> Mental health counseling in and of itself **is not a reason** to revoke or deny eligibility for access to classified information or for a sensitive position, suitability or fitness to obtain or retain Federal employment, fitness to obtain or retain contract employment, or eligibility for physical or logical access to federally controlled facilities or information systems.

> **In the last seven (7) years**, have you consulted with a health care professional regarding an emotional or mental health condition or were you hospitalized for such a condition? Answer 'No' if the counseling was for any of the following reasons and was not court ordered:

> – strictly marital, family, grief not related to violence by you; or

> – strictly related to adjustments from service in a military combat environment.

There is no exception for relationship counseling that does not involve a spouse or other family member. In the question the word "strictly" is used to rule out situations where the applicant seeks mental health counseling for one of the exceptions and is diagnosed as having a different or separate problem. For example an applicant initially seeks marital counseling and is diagnosed as having bipolar disorder. If there is any doubt about whether counseling or hospitalization should be disclosed, it is always preferable to answer "yes" to the question and provide both the required information and a detailed explanation in the "Optional Comment" field.

When applicants answer "yes" to this question they are directed to complete an "Authorization for the Release of Medical Information."

This form is on the last page of the SF86 and authorizes a health care practitioner to answer 3 questions:[51]

> *Does the person under investigation have a condition that could impair his or her judgment, reliability or ability to properly safeguard classified national security information?*
>
> *If so, describe the nature of the condition and the extent and duration of the impairment or treatment.*
>
> *What is the prognosis?*

When the health care practitioner(s) answer(s) "no" to the first question, there is no further investigation of this issue, unless the investigation surfaces contradictory information from some other record or personal source. When there is a "yes" to the first question, the applicant is usually required to complete an OFI 16-A, *Specific Release*, which is used to obtain more detailed information regarding medication, other treatment, test results, and medical opinions regarding health, recovery and/or rehabilitation. If necessary a security adjudicator will consult with a qualified government mental health practitioner, and if any doubt remains about an applicant's reliability, the applicant can be required to undergo a medical evaluation by a psychiatric consultant.

There is a presumption that mental health treatment that occurred more than 7 years ago or any treatment related to one of the exceptions to the "Mental and Emotional Health" question on the SF86 is not relevant or material to a security clearance determination. However if information is developed during an investigation that unlisted mental health treatment is relevant, information about the treatment can be pursued.

ADJUDICATION OF PSYCHOLOGICAL CONDITIONS

The Psychological Conditions criterion lists 3 specific examples of potentially disqualifying conditions and 5 specific examples of mitigating conditions. Ultimately almost all cases where a final clearance is denied due to psychological conditions involve 1 of the 4 following situations:

---

[51] At the last page of the SF85P is a similarly worded "Authorization for the Release of Medical Information."

(1) The applicant has displayed dysfunctional or abnormal behavior, and the applicant refuses to seek treatment or refuses to undergo medical evaluation.

(2) A qualified medical practitioner has determined that the applicant's condition could impair his or her judgment or reliability, and the applicant has failed to take medication or participate in other treatment as prescribed.

(3) A qualified medical practitioner has determined that the applicant's condition could impair his or her judgment or reliability and the condition cannot be adequately treated.

(4) A qualified medical practitioner has determined that the applicant's condition could impair his or her judgment or reliability and there is a lack of persuasive evidence that the condition is under control and will remain so for the foreseeable future.

INTERIM CLEARANCES

The federal policy against drawing negative inferences solely on the basis of mental health treatment for final clearances does not apply to interim security clearances. Unless properly documented mitigating information is submitted with clearance applications, interim clearances are frequently declined when applicants list mental health treatment on their SF86. Denial or revocation of a final security clearance due to a mental health issue is very rare; however interim security clearances can be and often are "declined" solely on the basis of mental health treatment listed on an SF86. This potentially affects tens of thousands of clearance applicants each year.

All information required on an SF86 is considered relevant. The only types of mental health treatment presumed not to be relevant are those that fall into one of the two specific exceptions to Section #21, "Psychological and Emotional Health." The section starts with the sentence: "*Mental health counseling in and of itself **is not a reason** to revoke or deny eligibility. . . .*" However, the "declination" of an interim clearance is not considered denial of eligibility, so the sentence does not apply to interim clearance decisions.

Guideline I states, "*No negative inference concerning the standards in this Guideline may be raised solely on the basis of seeking mental health counseling.*" It is the policy of DSS to use the standards in the *Adjudicative Guidelines* for the granting both interim clearances and final clearances. In theory if the SF86 contains no information indicative of a current or past condition that could impair judgment, reliability or trustworthiness, there should be no basis for declining an interim clearance under this guideline. However, contrary to this policy, DISCO, which is a part of DSS, regularly declines interim clearances when mental health counseling is listed on the SF86.

The information provided at the DSS webpage on interim clearances, as it pertains to mental health, was obviously written for an older, obsolete version of the SF86. It identifies emotional, mental, and personality disorders as an example of one of the most common reasons for an interim clearance declination. It goes on to state:

> *Not all of the above examples will result in the decline of an interim eligibility. There can be mitigating factors such as a particular behavior was not recent, or it was an isolated incident. Or, in the case of emotional, mental and personality disorders, mental health treatment [was] for a temporary condition such as that caused by a death, illness or marital breakup. In this regard, it is important that an applicant for a personnel security clearance answer all questions fully as requested on the security application form. A remarks section exists on the form where information may be added if there is not room in the applicable section of the form to provide additional details. For example, an applicant may want to provide reasons for mental health treatment.*

This passage clearly indicates that mental health treatment by itself can result in the declination of an interim clearance. It also suggests mitigation is possible, if the treatment was only for a temporary condition caused by death, illness or marital breakup. It is uncertain what is meant by "illness," but bereavement/grief counseling and marital counseling no longer have to be listed on the SF86 and therefore would not enter into an interim clearance determination. The important point is that mitigation of this issue for an interim clearance is possible.

MITIGATING MENTAL HEALTH TREATMENT
FOR INTERIM CLEARANCES

Since interim clearance determinations are made very early in the security clearance process, to be successful it is necessary to provide information with the SF86 indicating that no potentially disqualifying condition exists or that such condition is fully mitigated. There are things that you should do before you actually fill out the SF86.

Discuss this matter with your doctor (psychiatrist or psychologist) before you apply for job that requires a security clearance. If your doctor feels that your past or present condition does not adversely affect your eligibility for a clearance, obtain a letter from your doctor on letterhead stationary stating either that:

- You do not have a condition or treatment that could impair your judgment, reliability or ability to properly safeguard classified national security information, or

- You have a condition that could impair your judgment, reliability or ability to properly safeguard classified national security information, but the condition is under control and will remain so for the foreseeable future.

The letter should include your doctor's address, telephone and fax numbers, and a statement indicating that he/she is willing to answer questions about your condition, treatment, and prognosis from any government security official by telephone, fax, mail, or in person. The letter should also describe your condition, treatment, and prognosis. The letter or an attached resume should provide the doctor's qualifications and/or experience in treating your type of condition. You should complete a medical information release form (one that is acceptable to your doctor) authorizing your doctor to discuss your case with government security officials and leave a copy of the release on file at your doctor's office. Also give your doctor a completed copy of the SF86 Authorization for the Release of Medical Information.

When filling out the SF86, indicate in the "Optional Comments" field of Section #21 that you are submitting a letter from your doctor regarding your mental health treatment. Give a copy of both releases and the original letter from your doctor to the person who processes your clearance application, so that these documents can be forwarded to the government official who makes your interim clearance determination. You can place the releases and the letter from your doctor in a properly marked, sealed envelope to prevent people, other than the appropriate government security official, from reading it.

CHAPTER 18

CRIMINAL CONDUCT

ADJUDICATIVE CRITERIA

HSPD-12 Credentialing:
A PIV card will not be issued to a person if:
<u>*There is a reasonable basis to believe the individual will use an identi-ty credential outside the workplace unlawfully or inappropriately.*</u>

An individual's criminal or dishonest conduct may put people, prop-erty, or information systems at risk. The following consideration may apply:

<u>*There is a reasonable basis to believe, based on the individual's crim-inal or dishonest conduct, that issuance of a PIV card poses an unac-ceptable risk.*</u>
[F]or example, a person's convictions for burglary may indicate that granting a PIV poses an unacceptable risk to the Government's phys-ical assets and to employees' personal property on a Government facility.

Employment Suitability/Fitness:
Criminal activity creates doubt about an individual's judgment, reliability, and trustworthiness and calls into question an individual's ability or willingness to comply with laws, rules, and regulations. This type of conduct may not promote the efficiency of the service or protect its integrity. The following factor may apply:

<u>*Criminal or dishonest conduct*</u>

The following are examples of conduct that may be disqualifying (Note: This list is not meant to be all inclusive):

   (a) a recent, serious offense

   (b) a pattern of criminal conduct that may or may not have resulted in arrests/charges/convictions

Security Clearance (Guideline J):

30. The Concern. Criminal activity creates doubt about a person's judgment, reliability and trustworthiness. By its very nature, it calls into question a person's ability or willingness to comply with laws, rules and regulations.

31. Conditions that could raise a security concern and may be disqualifying include:

(a) a single serious crime or multiple lesser offenses;

(b) discharge or dismissal from the Armed Forces under dishonorable conditions;[52]

(c) allegation or admission of criminal conduct, regardless of whether the person was formally charged, formally prosecuted or convicted;

(d) individual is currently on parole or probation;

(e) violation of parole or probation, or failure to complete a court-mandated rehabilitation program.

(f) conviction in a Federal or State court, including a court-martial of a crime, sentenced to imprisonment for a term exceeding one year and incarcerated as a result of that sentence for not less than a year.[53]

32 Conditions that could mitigate security concerns include:

---

[52] Under the provisions of 50 U.S.C. 435b, section 3002 (Bond Amendment, see page 54 of this book and later in this Chapter), eligibility for Special Access Programs, Sensitive Compartmented Information, and Restricted Data cannot be granted or renewed when this disqualifying condition exists. In meritorious cases waivers to this prohibition can be granted.

[53] Ibid.

(a) so much time has elapsed since the criminal behavior happened, or it happened under such unusual circumstances that it is unlikely to recur or does not cast doubt on the individual's reliability, trustworthiness, or good judgment;

(b) the person was pressured or coerced into committing the act and those pressures are no longer present in the person's life;

(c) evidence that the person did not commit the offense;

(d) there is evidence of successful rehabilitation; including but not limited to the passage of time without recurrence of criminal activity, remorse or restitution, job training or higher education, good employment record, or constructive community involvement.

DISCUSSION

The "Criminal Conduct" criterion affects clearance applicants who have been suspected, arrested, charged or convicted of a single serious crime or multiple lesser offenses. Others who have intentionally provided false information on their clearance application forms, who have had illegal drug involvement, or who have been involved in previously unreported crime can also be affected. Over the years Criminal Conduct has consistently been among the 4 most common reasons for security clearance denial.

The *Adjudicative Guidelines* states that *"Criminal activity creates doubt about a person's judgment, reliability and trustworthiness. By its very nature, it calls into question a person's ability or willingness to comply with laws, rules and regulations."* Because of the high rate of adult criminal recidivism, this issue is perhaps one of the best predictors of future compliance with rules for handling classified information.

CRIMINAL OFFENSES

Criminal offenses are divided into three categories—infractions, misdemeanors, and felonies. For security clearance purposes, an infraction is a crime for which the maximum possible penalty is a fine; a misdemeanor is a crime for which the maximum possible penalty is incarceration for up to 1 year; and a felony is a crime for which the maximum possible penalty is incarceration for more than 1 year.

The March 2010 version of the SF86 asks the following threshold questions regarding criminal conduct:

1 yr + 1 day = Felon

- *In the past seven (7) years have you been issued a summons, citation, or ticket to appear in court in a criminal proceeding against you? (Do not check if all the citations involved traffic infractions where the fine was less than $300 and did not include alcohol or drugs.)*

- *In the past seven (7) years have you been arrested by any police officer, sheriff, marshal or any other type of law enforcement official?*

- *In the past seven (7) years have you been charged, convicted, or sentenced of a crime in any court? (Include all qualifying charges, convictions or sentences in any Federal, state, local, military, or non-U.S. court, even if previously listed on this form).*

- *In the past seven (7) years have you been or are you currently on probation or parole?*

- *Are you currently on trial or awaiting a trial on criminal charges?*

- *Have you EVER been convicted in any court of the United States of a crime, sentenced to imprisonment for a term exceeding 1 year for that crime, and incarcerated as a result of that sentence for not less than 1 year? (Include all qualifying convictions in Federal, state, local, or military court, even if previously listed on this form.)*

- *Have you EVER been charged with any felony offense? (Include those under the Uniform Code of Military Justice and non-military/civilian felony offenses.)*

- *Have you EVER been convicted of an offense involving domestic violence or a crime of violence (such as battery or assault) against your child, dependent, cohabitant, spouse, former spouse, or someone with whom you share a child in common?*

- *Have you EVER been charged with an offense involving firearms or explosives?*

- *Have you EVER been charged with an offense involving alcohol or drugs?*

The distinction between "arrested" and "charged" can be important for anyone arrested more than 7 years ago for a felony or any offense involving alcohol, drugs, firearms or explosives, but not formally charged with one of these offenses. Applicants often mistake the charge or offense listed on the police report as a charge that must be listed on the SF86. Since a charge can be changed or dropped between the time of an arrest and the defendant's initial court appearance, the best definition of a "charge" for SF86 purposes is any accusation of criminal conduct as it is initially presented at court.

For SF86 purposes an arrest is any situation in which a law enforcement officer restricts a person's freedom, then either takes them into custody or releases them on their promise to appear in court (i.e.

issues a citation). Under this definition a traffic offense resulting in a citation is technically an arrest; however, minor traffic citations resulting in a fine of $300 or less can be omitted from the SF86, unless they involved drugs or alcohol.

There are certain circumstances where a person can be taken into custody, but not technically arrested. This typically occurs when a person is initially arrested for being drunk in public, placed in a jail cell until sober, then released without any conditions or further action. In their report police record this as a detention not amounting to an arrest (or some similar wording). This type of incident must be listed in the "Use of Alcohol" section of the SF86, and it is recommended that such incidents also be disclosed in the "Police Record" section of the SF86.

In the SF86 there is an exception that permits withholding information about certain expunged drug convictions. This exception only applies to drug convictions and expungement orders in a federal court. Consequently, clearance applicants must list all applicable dismissed charges and convictions even if the record was sealed, expunged, or otherwise stricken from a state or local court record.

COMPLIANCE WITH BOND AMENDMENT

The Bond Amendment (50 U.S.C. 435b, Section 3002), which became law in January 2008, prohibits all federal agencies from granting or renewing eligibility for access to Sensitive Compartmented Information, Special Access Programs, and Restricted Data for anyone who has been: 1) convicted, sentenced, and incarcerated for a term exceeding 1 year for any crime or 2) discharged/dismissed from the Armed Forces under dishonorable conditions. As a practical matter, due to the inability to always predict future access to Restricted Data, these Bond Amendment restrictions may be applied to the adjudication of all levels of security clearances. In many agencies senior adjudicators have the authority to waive these Bond Amendment restrictions. When an adjudicator would have arrived at a favorable decision but for a Bond Amendment disqualification, the adjudicator may grant a meritorious waiver if deemed appropriate.

CRIMINAL ASPECTS OF OTHER ADJUDICATIVE CRITERIA

A knowing and willful false statement made in connection with a clearance application is a felony. Normally this offense is considered under the "Personal Conduct" criterion, which specifically addresses this issue. However adjudicators can cite both Personal Conduct and Criminal Conduct for this single criminal act. Likewise, an adjudicator may cite Criminal Conduct in addition to Alcohol Consumption, Drug Involvement, or Sexual Behavior when there has been a single felony or multiple misdemeanor offenses at least one of which involved alcohol, drugs, or sexual conduct.

MITIGATING SECURITY CONCERNS

The following conditions may mitigate Criminal Conduct concerns:

Multiple Lesser Offenses Not Serious—Multiple minor traffic infractions without allegations of other criminal conduct would not be an issue under the Criminal Conduct criterion. However, they can be considered under the Personal Conduct criterion along with any other dishonest, unreliable, or rule-breaking behavior.

Alleged Crime Not Committed—Security clearance adjudications do not use the same standard of evidence used in criminal proceedings. Once the government has substantial evidence that the applicant committed a crime, the burden of proof shifts to the applicant to present evidence to refute the allegation. To propound this mitigating condition there must be proof that the applicant did not commit the alleged offense. Being accused but not arrest, arrested but not prosecuted, or prosecuted but found not guilty, many not be sufficient to counter an allegation of criminal conduct. Law enforcement agencies often choose not to pursue action against a suspect, if there is insufficient evidence to meet the criminal standard to prove guilt or if a technical/procedural error was made that would prevent a successful criminal prosecution.

Successful Rehabilitation—Evidence of rehabilitation can simply be "passage of time" without recurrence of criminal activity or any other indicators of continued antisocial, irresponsible or violent behavior. There is no general rule for how much time must elapse since the last criminal offense for full mitigation solely through "passage of time." The amount of time depends on age when the crime occurred, how long criminal activity continued, the number and seriousness of the crimes, and the circumstances surrounding the crimes. Positive evidence of rehabilitation can significantly reduce the amount of time necessary to fully mitigate criminal conduct. Such evidence includes, "remorse or restitution, job training or higher education, good employment record, or constructive community involvement." Also taken into consideration are other positive changes in lifestyle, associates, and social responsibility. These factors can positively influence an adjudicator's determination that an applicant's past conduct is not likely to recur or no longer cast any doubt on the applicant's judgment, reliability or trustworthiness. Knowingly and willfully providing false information for a security clearance investigation and "currently being on parole or probation" are very difficult to mitigated, because there has been too little time to show rehabilitation. However, current unsupervised (or informal) probation by itself usually does not result in clearance denial, if the underlying criminal conduct has been fully mitigated.

Isolated Incident or Unique Circumstance—Many people commit a single non-violent criminal act due to an impulsive decision or an uncharacteristic lapse of judgment. Such crimes are sometimes prompted by a transitory situation. The presence of extenuating circumstances and/or a record of otherwise consistent reliability, trustworthiness, and good judgment over a significant period of time before or after the offense can mitigate suitability and security concerns by showing criminal conduct is not likely to recur, even though the crime may have occurred recently.

Pressured or Coerced—A single serious crime can be fully mitigated, if an applicant committed the crime due to threat of harm to himself or his family or other similar forms of duress. It is unlikely that this mitigating condition would be applicable to multiple criminal acts over a period of time, such as during a period of gang membership, unless it is propounded in combination with "successful rehabilitation." It would also not be applicable when the threat of harm or duress occurred as reprisal for some breech of promise or misconduct by the applicant.

STANDARDS OF EVIDENCE

Some people incorrectly believe that if they are found not guilty of a criminal offense or if the charge against them was dismissed or not prosecuted that it will not be a security or suitability issue. Being found not guilty or having a charge dismissed in a criminal proceeding does not mean that the person was determined to be innocent of the offense. It just means that there wasn't enough evidence to determine guilt. In order to be charged or convicted of a crime, the evidence must meet a criminal standard. The standard of evidence to support an unfavorable determination for a security clearance, suitability, fitness, or credentialing is less than the criminal standards for charging or convicting, but equal to or greater than the criminal standards for detaining and arresting.

Reasonable Suspicion—Suspicion of criminal activity that is based on specific and articulable facts. This is the standard required to justify a police officer's detention and questioning of a suspect.

Probable Cause—A reasonable belief that a person has committed a crime. This is the standard required to justify the arrest of a suspect.

Substantial Evidence—As used in security clearance adjudications this is evidence sufficient to establish that a disqualifying condition for a security clearance exists. Substantial evidence is defined as "more than a scintilla but less than preponderance," and consists of "such relevant evidence as a reasonable person would accept as adequate to support a conclusion." Substantial evidence is generally equivalent to "probable cause."

Preponderance of Evidence—The greater weight of the evidence required in a civil (non-criminal) lawsuit to decide in favor of one side or the other. Preponderance is based on the more convincing evidence and its probable truth or accuracy, and not on the amount of evidence. This is the standard used for employment suitability, fitness, and credentialing determinations.

Prima Facie—Proof that appears to be self-evident from the facts that the suspect committed a crime. Evidence which, unless credibly rebutted, would be sufficient to prove a crime. This is the standard required to justify charging a suspect with a criminal offense in court.

Beyond a Reasonable Doubt—No other logical explanation can be derived from the facts except that the defendant committed the crime. This is the standard required to prove guilt in a criminal proceeding.

Sometimes prosecutors decline to charge a suspect with a criminal offense even when there is *prima facie* evidence that the accused committed the offense. This occurs when the prosecutor knows he/she will be unable to satisfy the higher of standard of "Beyond a Reasonable

Doubt" to obtain a conviction, because there is credible contradictory evidence. Occasionally criminal charges are dismissed or not prosecuted because of a technicality such as a defective search warrant, improper arrest, faulty rights advisement, uncalibrated breathalyzer. Using the same set of facts an adjudicator might reach an unfavorable security or suitability determination. This is because security and suitability adjudicators are usually concerned about conduct more than criminal verdicts and other legal outcomes. They will accept a guilty verdict at face value, because guilt in a criminal case is based on a higher standard of evidence than required for a security clearance determination.

Although "Substantial Evidence" is required to establish a disqualifying condition for a security clearance; once credible rebuttal or mitigating evidence is available, an adjudicator bases his/her decision on a standard of evidence similar to a "Preponderance of Evidence."

CHAPTER 19

HANDLING PROTECTED INFORMATION

ADJUDICATIVE CRITERIA

HSPD-12 Credentialing:

Unauthorized access to government information or improper use of government information once access is granted may pose a significant risk to national security, may compromise the privacy of individuals, and may make public, information that is proprietary in nature, thus compromising the operations and missions of Federal entities. A PIV card will not be issued to a person if:

There is a reasonable basis to believe the individual will attempt to gain unauthorized access to classified documents, information protected by the Privacy Act, information that is proprietary in nature, or other sensitive or protected information

Employment Suitability/Fitness:

While there is no specific suitability factor, issues involving criminal acts should be evaluated under the Criminal Conduct criterion. Incidents on the job should be evaluated under the Personal Conduct criterion.

Security Clearance (Guideline K):

33. The Concern. Deliberate or negligent failure to comply with rules and regulations for protecting classified or other sensitive information raises doubt about an individual's trustworthiness, judgment, reliability, or willingness and ability to safeguard such information, and is a serious security concern.

<u>34. Conditions that could raise a security concern and may be disqualifying include:</u>

(a) deliberate or negligent disclosure of classified or other protected information to unauthorized persons, including but not limited to personal or business contacts, to the media, or to persons present at seminars, meetings, or conferences;

(b) collecting or storing classified or other protected information in any unauthorized location;

(c) loading, drafting, editing, modifying, storing, transmitting, or otherwise handling classified reports, data, or other information on any unapproved equipment including but not limited to any typewriter, word processor, or computer hardware, software, drive, system, gameboard, handheld, "palm" or pocket device or other adjunct equipment;

(d) inappropriate efforts to obtain or view classified or other protected information outside one's need to know;

(e) copying classified or other protected information in a manner designed to conceal or remove classification or other document control markings;

(f) viewing or downloading information from a secure system when the information is beyond the individual's need to know;

(g) any failure to comply with rules for the protection of classified or other sensitive information;

(h) negligence or lax security habits that persist despite counseling by management;

(i) failure to comply with rules or regulations that results in damage to the National Security, regardless of whether it was deliberate or negligent.

<u>35. Conditions that could mitigate security concerns include:</u>

(a) so much time has elapsed since the behavior, or it happened so infrequently or under such unusual circumstances that it is unlikely to recur or does not cast doubt on the individual's current reliability, trustworthiness, or good judgment;

(b) the individual responded favorably to counseling or remedial security training and now demonstrates a positive attitude toward the discharge of security responsibilities;

(c) the security violations were due to improper or inadequate training.

DISCUSSION

The security concerns listed under this criterion repeat some of the potentially disqualifying conditions for "Criminal Conduct" and for the work-related aspects of "Personal Conduct." The only difference is that criminal conduct and workplace rule violation involving "protected information" are more relevant to government clearances than other types of misconduct. Consequently, for security clearances this criterion provides many more examples of specific potentially disqualifying and mitigating conditions regarding security violations than listed for Criminal Conduct and workplace rule violations.

The *Handling Protected Information* criterion encompasses classified national security information, as well as sensitive but unclassified, embargoed technology, company proprietary, and Privacy Act information. Of the approximately 1300 initial case decisions posted at the DOHA website for January to December 2010, 15 cases involved Guideline K issues. Nine initial case decisions resulted in security clearance denials or revocations. One case that initially resulted in the granting of a clearance was later reversed on appeal. All of these cases also cited Guideline E (*Personal Conduct)* and/or Guideline M (*Use of Information Technology Systems)* as potentially disqualifying issues. These addition issues were usually directly related to the Guideline K conduct, because the conduct displayed questionable judgment and unreliable behavior and/or because the conduct involved computers.

The *Adjudicative Guidelines* states, *"Deliberate or negligent failure to comply with rules and regulations for protecting classified or other sensitive information raises doubt about an individual's trustworthiness, judgment, reliability, or willingness and ability to safeguard such information, and is a serious security concern."* Guideline K lists 9 specific examples of potentially disqualifying conduct. These 9 examples can be reduced to 2 general types of behaviors:

1. Intentional violation of security rules.

2. Repeated negligence, carelessness, or inattention in following security rules.

Cases involving either of these 2 types of behaviors often result in a clearance denial or revocation. Clearances are usually granted or continued in cases involving a single recent unintentional violation or where only a few unintentional violations occurred more than 2 years earlier and the applicant responded favorably to remedial training. DOHA Administrative Judges appear to impose a stricter standard when applying the most common mitigating condition of "passage of time without recurrence" to Guideline K cases.

Applying a stricter standard for mitigating security violations is justified. With most security clearance issues (e.g. alcohol, drugs, finances, criminal conduct, etc.) adjudicators try to evaluate the possibility of future recurrence of the problem, because the problem might in turn lead to deliberate or negligent compromise of classified information. Whereas, any recurrence of a security violation could by itself result in the unauthorized disclosure of classified information. In a somewhat extreme application of this stricter standard an applicant's clearance was revoked by DOHA in 2010 because of numerous unintentional security violations spanning several years, where the last violation occurred 12 years earlier.[54]

Another consideration for applying a stricter standard to these cases is that certain types of security violations are potential counterintelligence indicators that an individual might be disclosing protected information to unauthorized personnel. These behaviors include:

- Unauthorized removal of protected information from the office.

- Unauthorized introduction of cameras, recording devices, and wireless communication devices into areas storing protected material.

- Retention of protected information obtained at a previous employment without the authorization or the knowledge of that employer.

---

[54] This DOHA case (No. 04-12742) appears ripe for appeal. The Administrative Judge held that although the applicant had passive access to classified information at briefings and meetings during the past 12 years (without any security violations), she did not actively handle classified information, and therefore has not had an opportunity to demonstrate that the lax or sloppy security habits of the past will not recur. Using this logic, anyone whose clearance is revoked due to a security violation will never receive a clearance in the future, because they will not have an opportunity to demonstrate responsible handling of classified information without a clearance.

- Unauthorized copying of protected information.

- Concealing or removing protective markings when copying protected information.

- Efforts to view or obtain protected information clearly beyond one's need-to-know.

In early December 2010 numerous news sources reported that OMB sent a memo on December 3, 2010 to federal agencies forbidding unauthorized federal government employees and contractors from accessing classified documents publicly available on WikiLeaks and other websites. On December 13, 2010 DSS issued a notice to cleared federal contractors apparently in compliance with the OMB memo. The wording of the DSS notice did not specifically prohibit cleared contractors from viewing classified documents posted in the public domain, but stated that rules regarding the handling of classified information apply equally to such documents (i.e. cleared personnel are only authorized access to classified information for which they possess the proper clearance and need-to-know). Other news stories reported that university students were advised not to viewed classified information at WikiLeaks, because it could result in the denial of a security clearance in the future.

There has been some indignation regarding these warnings, but "The fact that classified information has been made public does not mean that it is automatically declassified."[55] Guideline K specifically makes "inappropriate efforts to obtain or view classified or other protected information outside one's need to know" a potentially disqualifying condition. However, because of the unusual circumstances involved, it's questionable whether viewing classified information at WikiLeaks or any other public website will actually result in a security clearance denial or revocation, particularly for people who were not subject to government security regulations at the time. The most likely response will be an admonishment regarding future violations.

A literal interpretation of Guideline K suggests that it only applies to violation of security rules directly related to accessing, handling, and storing protected information. However, adjudicators use a broader interpretation of Guideline K that includes violation of rules regarding the duty to self-report potentially disqualifying conditions

---

[55] Paragraph 4-106, National Industrial Security Program Operating Manual, DoD 5220.22-M, February 28, 2006.

and comply with other security requirements. An Administrative Judge's decision to revoke a clearance in DOHA ISCR Case No. 06-26489 is particularly instructive. This decision was affirmed on appeal.

"Applicant's failure to comply with rules and regulations for protecting classified and other sensitive information occurred in April 2005, and is not therefore recent. However, at his hearing, Applicant maintained that he was confused by the reporting requirement and, therefore, his failure to follow the instructions given to him should be excused. Applicant's continuing refusal to acknowledge his responsibility to comply with a reporting requirement was intentional and has not been mitigated by the passage of time. He knew that he should report the [foreign] relationship and deliberately chose not to do so. He failed to demonstrate a positive attitude toward the discharge of his security responsibilities."

Under DoD Regulation 5200.2-R (*Personnel Security Program*) personnel who possess security clearances must report all potentially disqualifying information listed under Guidelines A through M of the *Adjudicative Guidelines*, plus:

- Change in name, marital status, and citizenship.

- Change in job assignment that eliminates the need for access to classified information.

- Any situation related to actual, probable, or possible espionage, sabotage, or subversive activities directed at the United States.

- Any known or suspected security violation or vulnerability.

- Efforts by any person, regardless of nationality, to obtain illegal or unauthorized access to classified information.

In most instances supervisors and coworkers have an equal obligation to advise appropriate security officials when they become aware of information with potentially serious security significance regarding someone with access to classified information.

Individuals with Sensitive Compartmented Information or other Special Access Program authorizations have additional reporting requirements, such as impending unofficial foreign travel and any close and/or continuing contact with a foreign national where ties of kinship, affection, influence, or obligation exist, even if the contact does not create a heightened risk of foreign exploitation.

Like all security issues, security violations can be mitigated, if they are unlikely to recur because they happened long ago or under unusual circumstances. Security violations can also be mitigated, if the applicant received improper or inadequate training and subsequently obtained the needed training.

If you commit a security violation or fail to comply with some other security requirement, report the matter to your security officer immediately and request remedial or additional training. The training can be as informal as reading security manuals under the supervision and direction of a security officer. The DSS Academy offers a variety of security education courses for federal employees and contractors. Complete the training in a timely manner, obtain documentation that the training was completed, and insure that a copy of the documentation is placed in your security file.

CHAPTER 20

OUTSIDE ACTIVITIES

ADJUDICATIVE CRITERIA

HSPD-12 Credentialing: No applicable criteria.

Employment Suitability/Fitness: No applicable criteria.

Security Clearance (Guideline L):
36   *The Concern*. *Involvement in certain types of outside employment or activities is of security concern if it poses a conflict of interest with an individual's security responsibilities and could create an increased risk of unauthorized disclosure of classified information.*

37   *Conditions that could raise a security concern and may be disqualifying include:*

(a) any employment or service, whether compensated or volunteer, with:

   (1) the government of a foreign country;

   (2) any foreign national, organization, or other entity;

   (3) a representative of any foreign interest;

   (4) any foreign, domestic, or international organization or person engaged in analysis, discussion, or publication of material on intelligence, defense, foreign affairs, or protected technology;

(b) failure to report or fully disclose an outside activity when this is required.

38. Conditions that could mitigate security concerns include:

(a) evaluation of the outside employment or activity by the appropriate security or counterintelligence office indicates that it does not pose a conflict with an individual's security responsibilities or with the national security interests of the United States;

(b) the individual terminates the employment or discontinued the activity upon being notified that it was in conflict with his or her security responsibilities.

DISCUSSION

Although not addressed in the suitability criteria for federal employment, there are job-specific "outside activity" restrictions. Generally a federal employee cannot engage in outside employment or activity directly related to his/her federal employment. For example a federal investigator would not be allowed to work in a compensated or uncompensated role for a private company involved in security or investigative work. Similar restrictions apply to the involvement of IRS employees in outside activities related to income tax preparation or representation. Some federal employees are required to obtain permission to engage in any outside activities remotely related to their federal jobs.

Although merely being a member of an organization of the type described above in paragraph 37(a)(4) of the *Adjudicative Guidelines* wouldn't be considered a disqualifying condition for a security clearance; employment with or service to such an organization could be. "Service" could encompass such things as holding a leadership position or contributing written material including blogging. For federal employees, requesting permission from their security office to assume a leadership position in organizations like the World Affairs Council or the Association of Former Intelligence Officers shouldn't present any problems. Obtaining permission would depend on the exact nature of the organization and the services to be performed. For federal contractor personnel, just requesting permission from the appropriate federal security office can be somewhat daunting, especially if their company has classified contracts with more than one government agency.

Outside activities that present a security concern are usually those involving a foreign business, organization, or government. Without a favorable security evaluation of the outside activity by the appropriate federal agency, the applicant is left with the problem of deciding whether to preemptively eliminate the potential security concern by terminating the activity and suffer a loss of income or other personal benefit before being told if the activity actually represents a disqualifying condition.

If the importance of receiving a clearance as quickly as possible outweighs the importance of the activity, the applicant should sever all ties with the activity before submitting his/her SF86 and provide detailed information about this in the appropriate "Optional Comment" field of the SF86. The applicant can also include a "statement of intent" in the "Optional Comment" field, promising:

1) Not to travel to the foreign country,

2) To discontinue any contact with representatives of the former outside activity, and/or

3) To report all future contact by anyone associated with the former activity and/or citizens of the foreign country.

If the personal benefit from the activity is significant, the applicant can wait to see whether the adjudicative authority determines that the activity is a disqualifying condition. If the applicant receives a "Statement of Reasons" (SOR) stating intent to deny/revoke security clearance because the activity is a disqualifying condition, there should be enough time to sever the relationship with the activity and document this action in time to submit it with a rebuttal to the SOR. If there isn't enough time to do this:

- Applicants, whose cases are adjudicated by the Defense Office of Hearings and Appeals (DOHA) or the Department of Energy (DOE), can state their intentions in the SOR rebuttal, sever the relationship, document it, and present it to an Administrative Judge or hearing officer before a final clearance determination is made. This presentation can be made either at the hearing or in response to a "File Of Relevant Materials" (FORM) when a hearing is not requested.

- Applicants, whose cases are adjudicated by a federal agency other than DOHA or DOE, can state their intentions in the SOR rebuttal and complete the necessary actions before they appeal their clearance denial.

In either of these 2 situations, it is possible that a clearance could be granted with a "condition" following a review of the SOR rebuttal and eliminate the need for a hearing or an appeal. The "condition" would probably require the applicant to sever all involvement with the activity by a certain date and refrain from any future activity of a similar nature.

There were 2 DOHA cases involving "Outside Activities" in 2010. In one case (ISCR Case No. 09-05655) the "Outside Activities" issue was based on the applicant's intentional omission of information on his SF86 regarding part-time involvement as an officer of a subchapter "S" corporation. "Outside Activities" should never have been cited as an issue in this case, because no foreign or other entity of the type described at Guideline L was involved, there was no conflict of interest, and the applicant's omission was adequately covered by the "Personal Conduct" issue that was also cited in the case. The other case (DOHA ISCR Case No. 09-02708) involved multiple issues and the applicant was denied a clearance on the basis of the Foreign Influence and Personal Conduct issues, but not for the Outside Activities issue. This case was appealed and the DOHA PSAB affirmed the clearance denial. Regarding the Outside Activities issue the DOHA Administrative Judge found that:

> Applicant has a long-standing relationship with the government of Egypt as a result of his important position with the Egyptian security forces prior to immigrating to the United States, his brothers' work in important positions of the Egyptian government, his services to Middle Eastern country newspaper, and his pro bono legal services to Egyptian embassy personnel in the United States. Additionally, through the years, he had sporadic business with one of his Egyptian law professors. I find Applicant's contacts and behavior trigger the applicability of AG [Adjudicative Guidelines] ¶¶ 37(a)(1), (2), and (3).

> Applicant has not practiced law since 2005, and he credibly testified he has no intention of practicing law again. He has not traveled to Egypt since 2007, he does not intend to work for the Middle East newspaper in the future, and has not hosted Egyptian government officials visiting the United States. The evidence supports a conclusion that Applicant has discontinued his activities of concern.

There were also 2 DOHA cases involving Outside Activities in 2009. In one case (DOHA ISCR Case No. 08-00312) the applicant was granted a security clearance because he severed all relationship with the foreign company sometime after receiving a "written interrogatory" from DOHA but before his DOHA hearing. The salient facts and rationale for granting the security clearance are shown in this extract from the written DOHA case decision.

> *Applicant has now resigned from the Chinese company, terminated his interests in the company, and pledged not to travel to China, Hong Kong, and Taiwan, and he has advised the defense-contractor company of his actions. First, he notified the CEO of the Chinese company that he was resigning, effective July 16, 2009, as an employee, officer, and director of the company. Second, the three-page separation agreement between Applicant and the Chinese company sets forth the terms of the separation. It specifies, among other things, that Applicant will not receive any form of severance or separation payment, and that he irrevocably surrendered all outstanding stock, stock options, and warrants. Third, Applicant agreed in writing not to travel for whatever purpose to China, Hong Kong, and Taiwan, and he agreed to report any contact by a Chinese national.*

> *The record contains substantial evidence of Applicant's connections to China through his business activities with the Chinese company. This evidence raises security concerns under both guidelines [B and L]. The concerns are now resolved, however, by Applicant's affirmative actions. He wholly mitigated the concerns by resigning from the Chinese company and terminating his interests in it. At this point, Applicant has no connections to the Chinese company, and he has no other connections to China that are of concern. His actions were probably to his financial detriment given the potential future value of his equity interest in the Chinese company. But his actions demonstrate his true sense of loyalty or obligation is in favor of U.S. interests. And there is no [longer any] conflict of interest between Applicant's business activities and his security responsibilities. Applicant has done everything he could do to mitigate the security concerns.*

In the other case (DOHA ISCR Case No. 07-06767) decided in 2009 the applicant's security clearance was denied. The applicant owned or had substantial interest in a number of companies in Israel and had extensive business dealings with the government of Israel. The applicant did not sever any of his relationships with the Israeli government or companies, and there was no evaluation by a security or counterintelligence office indicating that Applicant's activities did not pose a conflict with his anticipated security responsibilities or with the national interests of the United States. This case was appealed and the DOHA PSAB affirmed the clearance denial.

The July 2008 version of the SF86 required that "all full-time and part-time work, paid or unpaid" be listed at Section 13 (Employment Activities). The new March 2010 version of the SF86 has eliminated the requirement to list unpaid work. It asks only to "List all of your employment activities, including unemployment and self-employ-

ment." This doesn't mean that unpaid work for a domestic organization defined at paragraph 37(a)(4) of the *Adjudicative Guidelines* will
no longer be a security concern. It only means there will be less likelihood that this type of outside activity will surface during a security
clearance investigation. It will probably also result in some people
using a narrower interpretation of the word "employment."

Because of the numerous and broadly worded questions at section
20b (*Foreign Business, Professional Activities, and Foreign Government Contacts*) of the SF86, any outside activity involving a foreign
entity will still have to be listed.

CHAPTER 21

USE OF INFORMATION TECHNOLOGY SYSTEMS

ADJUDICATIVE CRITERIA

HSPD-12 Credentialing:.
A PIV card will not be issued to a person if:

There is a reasonable basis to believe the individual will use Federally-controlled information systems unlawfully, make unauthorized modifications to such systems, corrupt or destroy such systems, or engage in inappropriate uses of such systems

Most disqualifying acts will be covered by the above criteria. See also criminal or dishonest conduct [under the Criminal Conduct criterion] *and misconduct or negligence in employment considerations* [under the Personal Conduct criterion].

Employment Suitability/Fitness:
While there is no specific suitability factor related to use of information technology, issues involving criminal acts should be evaluated under the criminal or dishonest conduct factor [under the Criminal Conduct criterion]. *Incidents on the job should be evaluated under the misconduct or negligence in employment factor* [under the Personal Conduct criterion].

Security Clearance (Guideline M):
39. *The Concern. Noncompliance with rules, procedures, guidelines or regulations pertaining to information technology systems may raise security concerns about an individual's reliability and trustworthiness, calling into question the willingness or ability to properly*

protect sensitive systems, networks, and information. Information Technology Systems include all related computer hardware, software, firmware, and data used for the communication, transmission, processing, manipulation, storage, or protection of information.

40. Conditions that could raise a security concern and may be disqualifying include:

(a) illegal or unauthorized entry into any information technology system or component thereof;

(b) illegal or unauthorized modification, destruction, manipulation or denial of access to information, software, firmware, or hardware in an information technology system;

(c) use of any information technology system to gain unauthorized access to another system or to a compartmented area within the same system;

(d) downloading, storing, or transmitting classified information on or to any unauthorized software, hardware, or information technology system;

(e) unauthorized use of a government or other information technology system;

(f) introduction, removal, or duplication of hardware, firmware, software, or media to or from any information technology system without authorization, when prohibited by rules, procedures, guidelines or regulations.

(g) negligence or lax security habits in handling information technology that persist despite counseling by management;

(h) any misuse of information technology, whether deliberate or negligent, that results in damage to the national security.

41. Conditions that could mitigate security concerns include:

(a) so much time has elapsed since the behavior happened, or it happened under such unusual circumstances, that it is unlikely to recur or does not cast doubt on the individual's reliability, trustworthiness, or good judgment;

(b) the misuse was minor and done only in the interest of organizational efficiency and effectiveness, such as letting another person use

one's password or computer when no other timely alternative was readily available;

(c) the conduct was unintentional or inadvertent and was followed by a prompt, good-faith effort to correct the situation and by notification of supervisor.

DISCUSSION

The "*Use of Information Technology Systems*" criterion can potentially affect the clearance eligibility of many applicants. Over the past few years DOHA Administrative Judges have reviewed numerous cases involving Guideline M issues. Most of these cases involved only 1 of the 8 potentially disqualifying conditions"—the "*unauthorized use of a government or other information technology system.*" These cases have almost always involved the viewing of pornographic material on a government- or company-owned computer in violation of the employers' rules. Most of the other cases also involved workplace misconduct such as: sending inappropriate email, unauthorized viewing of other peoples' email, intentionally deleting files from a server, and preventing access to computer programs.

In 2001 "the Ninth U.S. Circuit Court affirmed a trial court's decision that about 75 million users were infringing copyright by exchanging music files via a peer-to-peer network."[56] Because of this, perhaps the greatest Guideline M concern to many clearance applicants will be the potentially disqualifying condition of "*introduction, removal, or duplication of hardware, firmware, software, or media to or from any information technology system without authorization, when prohibited by rules, procedures, guidelines or regulations.*" In the July 2008 version of the SF86, 3 questions specifically addressing "Use of Information Technology Systems" (questions 27a, b, & c) were added to the form. This change could significantly increase the number of cases involving Guideline M issues in the future. The March 2010 version of the SF86 included a minor change to these 3 questions by adding the word, "attempted." The questions now read:

- *In the last **seven (7) years** have you illegally or without proper authorization accessed or attempted to access any information technology system?*

---

[56] Quoted from DOHA Case No. 03-17291, referring to A&M Records, Inc. v. Napster, Inc.

- *In the last **seven (7) years** have you illegally or without authorization, modified, destroyed, manipulated, or denied others access to information residing on an information technology system or attempted any of the above?*

- *In the last **seven (7) years** have you introduced, removed, or used hardware, software, or media in connection with any information technology system without authorization, when specifically prohibited by rules, procedures, guidelines, or regulations or attempted any of the above?*

Guideline M uses broad language in defining the security concern regarding the use of information technology systems:

Noncompliance with rules, procedures, guidelines or regulations pertaining to information technology systems may raise security concerns about an individual's reliability and trustworthiness, calling into question the willingness or ability to properly protect sensitive systems, networks, and information. . . .

It goes on to list 8 specific examples of potentially disqualifying conditions that could result in a clearance denial or revocation. Three of these potentially disqualifying conditions duplicate disqualifying conditions under Guideline K (*Handling Protected Information*).

EVALUATING IT SYSTEMS MISUSE

The following factors are evaluated in determining the security significance of IT systems misuse:

- Knowing and willful rule violation.

- Frequency and extent of rule violation.

- Amount of potential or actual harm.

- Intent of the conduct and degree of malice.

For applicants who have duplicated copyrighted material on the internet without authorization, a 2008 DOHA decision (ISCR Case No. 03-17291) is instructive. In this case potentially disqualifying conditions 40(a), 40(c), and 40(f) under Guideline M were alleged. Also alleged were disqualifying conditions 16(c) and 16(e) of Guideline E (Personal Conduct). The Administrative Judge determined that the applicant only accessed systems available to the public when he downloaded programs and files without paying for them. Therefore the applicant's conduct was not illegal or unauthorized under 40(a) or 40(c). The only unresolved matter under Guideline M was whether the applicant's actions were *"prohibited by rules, procedures, guidelines or regulations"* as specified by 40(f).

From 1993 to 2007 applicant downloaded from $750 to $1,000 worth of files or programs without paying for them. He did it for private financial gain in that he avoided payment for the downloaded materials, but he never sold or profited from anything he downloaded. On at least one occasion "he downloaded a serial number for a multimedia program and used it to unlock the program and view a movie trailer. The serial number would have cost $29.99 if purchased, but applicant was able to download it without paying for it." The Administrative Judge considered the applicant's conduct in light of:

- Sony Corporation of America v. Universal City Studios (US Supreme Court, 464 U.S. 417 [1984])

- AHR—Audio Home Recording Act of 1992 (17 U.S.C. 1008)

- NET—No Electronic Theft Act of 1997 (17 U.S.C. 506)

- DMC—Digital Millennium Copyright Act of 1999 (17 U.S.C. 1201)

In Sony v. Universal the Supreme Court ruled that recording movies for personal, noncommercial use is not a violation of The Copyright Act (17 U.S.C. 106, et seq). The AHR extended that exception to recording music for personal, noncommercial use.

The NET makes electronic copyright infringement a crime when it is committed for private financial gain by reproducing or distributing, during any 180-day period, copyrighted works having a total retail value of more than $1,000 or by the distributing of a work being prepared for commercial distribution by making it available on a computer network accessible to members of the public knowing that the work was intended for commercial distribution. The applicant did not violate the NET because the total value of the items he downloaded was not more than $1,000.

But the DMC states, *"No person shall circumvent a technological measure that effectively controls access to a work protected under this title."* By downloading the serial number for a multimedia program and using it to unlock the program, the applicant circumvented the access control to a protected work and violated the DMC. Based on this, the Administrative Judge decided the applicant's conduct was *"prohibited by rules, procedures, guidelines or regulations."* The Administrative Judge found no applicable mitigating condition under

Guideline M and ruled against the applicant. The Administrative Judge also ruled against the applicant under Guideline E (*Personal Conduct*) for his 15 years of downloading copyrighted material without paying for it. This conduct by itself constituted:

> *16(c) credible adverse information in several adjudicative issue areas that is not sufficient for an adverse determination under any other single guideline, but which, when considered as a whole, supports a whole-person assessment of questionable judgment, untrustworthiness, unreliability, lack of candor, unwillingness to comply with rules and regulations, or other characteristics indicating that the person may not properly safeguard protected information*

For most people who use their own computer to download publicly accessible copyrighted files from the internet without paying for them or to participate in file sharing on a peer-to-peer network, their activity doesn't amount to criminal conduct, which is probably necessary to support a security clearance denial or revocation under disqualifying condition 40(f) of Guideline M. For this type of conduct applicants only risk security clearance denial under Guideline M when they download and/or share more than $1,000 worth of copyrighted files in any 180-day period without paying for them or when they try to circumvent a security measure used to protect copyrighted material. However, as shown in this case, this type of conduct can result in a clearance denial under Guideline E independent of whether disqualifying conduct is established under Guideline M.

MITIGATING SECURITY CONCERNS

As with most other security/suitability issues, when an applicant's past misconduct was intentional and serious, the most common and successful mitigating condition is *"(a) so much time has elapsed since the behavior happened, or it happened under such unusual circumstances, that it is unlikely to recur or does not cast doubt on the individual's [current] reliability, trustworthiness, or good judgment."* This is because the basic purpose of the security clearance process is to attempt to predict future conduct based on past and current conduct. Rehabilitation as evidenced by passage of time without recurrence is one of the strongest predictors of future conduct.

In the past the most prevalent disqualifying conduct under Guideline M has been viewing pornographic material on government- or employer- owned computers. When there are rules against accessing pornography using employer-owned computers, attempts to minimize culpability by claiming ignorance of the rules (because of failure to read the rules as required) only highlights an applicant's disregard for work rules. This occurred in a 2010 DOHA case (ISCR Case No. 08-11135), and the applicant was denied a clearance even though 2 years had gone by without recurrence of the conduct. In 2 other DOHA cases (ISCR Case Nos. 07-02238 and 08-06538) passage of 3 years without recurrence, acknowledgment of knowingly violating a company rule, plus otherwise positive work records were sufficient to mitigate accessing pornography on employer-owned computers. In all three cases none of the applicants self-reported their violation of company rules and only admitted to the misconduct when confronted about it. In cases with strong positive whole-person factors related to work and complying with other work rules, self-reporting and seeking professional counseling could result in the granting of a clearance in less than 3 years after discontinuing the conduct.

In cases where the viewing of pornography occurred over a short period of time and/or under unusual circumstances, the possibility of being granted a clearance after a shorter period of rehabilitation may be possible. Since viewing of pornography per se is not the issue under Guideline M, many temporary situations where access to one's own personal computer is not available could qualify as an unusual circumstance (e.g. temporary work assignment at a remote location). Likewise, temporary emotional stress caused by serious illness, separation, divorce, death of a spouse, or similar events could also viewed as unusual circumstances of the type that makes recurrence unlikely. Acknowledging the behavior, accepting responsibility, obtaining professional counseling, and following the advice of the counselor to change the behavior always increases the possibility of fully mitigating conduct-related security/suitability issues, as does other positive steps to alleviate the stressors, circumstances, or factors that caused the behavior.

Appendix A – Glossary of Terms

Active Clearance
Security clearance status where the individual granted a clearance currently occupies a position for which the clearance is required.

Adjudicative Guidelines
Document containing 13 criteria used by security clearance adjudicators to determine an applicant's eligibility for access to classified national security information.

ANACI
Access National Agency Check with Inquiries—Type of personnel security investigation required for initial-hire federal employees who need a Confidential or Secret clearance or a DOE "L" Access Authorization.

ARC
Automated Record Check—Basic investigative component for all future federal personnel security investigations. The ARC will collect data from numerous government and commercial databases and will replace the NAC. (The ARC will be implemented as part of the security/suitability process reform.)

BI
Background Investigation—Type of personnel security investigation conducted for High-Risk Public Trust Positions. BI is also used as a generic term for any personnel security investigation. DoD used the term BI to describe the type of investigation previously required for critical sensitive positions and collateral Top Secret clearances. The DoD BI was replaced by the SSBI in December 1991.

CAF
Central Adjudication Facility—The office of a federal agency that adjudicates all security clearances for that agency. Within the Department of Defense there are 10 CAFs (Army, Navy, Air Force, DISCO, JCS, WHS, DIA, NSA, NGA, and NRO).

CATS
Case Adjudication Tracking System—A DoD computer program that allows electronic receipt of investigative case files from OPM and electronic screening and adjudication.

CE
Continuous Evaluation—will replace what is now known as a Periodic Reinvestigation (PR). CE (although not actually continuous) will be conducted annually for critical sensitive and special sensitive positions and once every 5 years on moderate-risk, high-risk, and non-critical sensitive positions. (To be implemented as a component of the reformed security/suitability process.)

Classified Information
The 3 levels of classified national security information are: Confidential, Secret, and Top Secret. There are categories of classified information, such as SCI, SAP, and

COMSEC, within these 3 levels requiring special safeguarding and access controls that exceed those normally required for information at the same classification level.

CNWDI
Critical Nuclear Weapons Design Information—A category of DoD Secret and Top Secret Restricted Data that reveals the theory of operation or design of the components of a thermonuclear or fission weapon or test device. Special access controls and briefings are required for CNWDI.

COMSEC
Communications Security—Protective measures taken to deny unauthorized persons information derived from telecommunications of the U.S. Government relating to national security and to ensure the authenticity of such communications. COMSEC is also a category of classified information that requires special safeguarding, access restrictions, and briefings.

COSMIC Top Secret
COSMIC stands for "Control Of Secret Material in an International Command." COSMIC Top Secret is the term used for NATO Top Secret information.

CRYPTO
Cryptographic—A category of classified information at the Secret and Top Secret levels related to cryptographic logic, keys, and authenticators that require special access controls and briefings.

Current Clearance
Commonly used term to describe the status of an individual's security clearance where the clearance has terminated but is eligible for reinstatement.

CUI
Controlled Unclassified Information—Unclassified information pertinent to the national interest of the United States. Other unclassified information protected by law from unauthorized disclosure is also designated CUI. (See also FOUO and SBU.)

CVS
Central Verification System—OPM's online computer database of investigations and clearances. CVS will eventually replace OPM's older SII database. CVS has linkage to DoD's JPAS database. CVS maintains data on security clearances, HSPD-12 credentialing, and suitability/fitness for federal employment.

DCII
Defense Central Index of Investigations—Computer database containing records of criminal and security investigations conducted by Department of Defense investigative agencies. Since July 2005 the DCII has not been updated with new clearance data, which is now being entered into the Joint Personnel Adjudication System (JPAS).

DISCO
Defense Industrial Security Clearance Office—Component of DSS that processes, adjudicates and grants security clearances for industrial (contractor) personnel under the National Industrial Security Program (NISP).

DOHA
Defense Office of Hearings and Appeals—Component of the Defense Legal Services Agency that issues decisions in security clearance cases for contractor personnel doing work for DoD components and 20 other Federal agencies. It also conducts personal appearances for federal employee and military personnel security clearance appeals.

DISS
Defense Information Systems for Security—New system being designed to replace DSS legacy systems (JPAS, ISFD, DCII, iIRR, and ENROL) and integrate new programs like SWFT and CATS.

DSS
Defense Security Service—DSS is responsible for administering the National Industrial Security Program (NISP) and providing security education and training to DoD and other federal personnel and contractors.

eApplication
New terminology for the enhanced version of e-QIP.

eAdjudication
The use of a computer program to screen and adjudicate investigations and make favorable Secret clearance, employment suitability, and employment fitness determinations on cases containing very little or no derogatory information.

EFI
Expandable Focused Investigation—New field investigative component to be used as needed to resolve identified issues in any type of security/suitability investigation. (To be implemented as a component of the reformed security/suitability process.)

Eligibility for Access
The term used in most government documents and by government personnel security specialist for a security clearance.

e-QIP
Electronic Questionnaires for Investigations Processing—Web-based versions of OPM Standard Forms 85, 85P, 85PS and 86 used for initiating federal personnel security investigations. The e-QIP version of the SF86 replaced DoD's Electronic Personnel Security Questionnaire (EPSQ).

ESI
Enhanced Subject Interview—New in-depth interview of a clearance applicant to ensure a full understanding of the applicant's personal history, potential issues, and mitigating factors. The ESI is a standard component of OPM MBIs, BIs, SSBIs, SSBI-PRs, PPRs and PRIs. OPM replaced the PRSI with the ESI and also began using the ESI as a replacement for the SPIN in October 2010.

Expired Clearance
Commonly used term to describe the status of an individual's security clearance where the clearance has terminated and is no longer eligible for reinstatement because time limits for reinstatement have been exceeded.

FISD
Federal Investigative Services Division—A division of OPM that conducts personnel security investigations for most executive branch agencies of the Federal Government.

FORM
File Of Relevant Materials—The FORM consists of all material submitted by the DOHA Department Counsel to the DOHA Administrative Judge for a clearance decision based solely on the written record.

FOUO
For Official Use Only—Protective marking used to identify unclassified sensitive government information requiring special handling and access controls. FOUO is being replaced by the term Control Unclassified Information. (See also CUI and SBU)

FRD
Formerly Restricted Data—Classified information which has been removed from the Restricted Data category after DoE and DoD have jointly determined that it relates primarily to the military utilization of atomic weapons and can be adequately safeguarded as national security information.

FSO
Facility Security Officer—The security manager for a cleared federal contractor facility under the National Industrial Security Program (NISP).

HSPD-12
Homeland Security Presidential Directive Number 12—Mandated a standard for secure and reliable forms of identification for personnel requiring physical or logical access to federal facilities or computer systems. Sponsorship plus a favorable NACI are needed to obtain a Personal Identity Verification (PIV) card required by this directive.

Interim Security Clearance
Temporary security clearance based on the favorable completion of minimum investigative requirements, pending the completion of the full investigative requirements for the final clearance determination.

JPAS
Joint Personnel Adjudication System—Web-based system that connects DoD security personnel with a database used to initiate, manage, and maintain a record of personnel security clearances.

LAA
Limited Access Authorization—Permission granted by the Government to non-U.S. citizens for access to classified national security information where the non-U.S. citizen possesses unique or unusual skill or expertise that is urgently needed to support a specific government project involving access to specified classified information and a clearable U.S. citizen is not readily available.

"L" Access Authorization
Department of Energy clearance that authorizes access up to Secret Formerly Restricted Data and Secret National Security Information.

LBI
Limited Background Investigation—Type of personnel security investigations previously used for Moderate-Risk or High-Risk Public Trust positions. OPM stopped using this investigation in October 2010.

LOD
Letter of Denial—Letter issued by an adjudication facility informing an applicant of a final decision to deny the applicant a security clearance and of the applicant's right to appeal the decision to the agency's Personnel Security Appeals Board.

LOI
Letter of Intent or Letter of Instruction—Letter that accompanies a "Statement of Reasons" explaining why a tentative decision to deny a security clearance was made and offering the applicant an opportunity to rebut or mitigate the reasons.

Loss of Jurisdiction
Status of an individual's security clearance when employment for the required clearance terminates after a clearance action is initiated but before a final determination is made to grant, continue, deny, or revoke the clearance. This status is also applied when a previously granted interim clearance is withdrawn before a final clearance determination is made.

MBI
Moderate Risk Background Investigation—Type of personnel security investigation used for Moderate-Risk Public Trust positions. Prior to October 2010 this investigation was known as a Minimum Background Investigation.

NAC
National Agency Check—Basic component of all federal personnel security investigations. As a minimum all NACs include a check of FBI Headquarters records, an FBI technical fingerprint search, and a check of OPM and DoD investigative databases.

NACI
National Agency Check with Inquiries—Type of personnel security investigation used for determining federal employment suitability or for the issuance of a Personal Identity Verification (PIV) card required by HSPD-12. An NACI plus credit check can be used as the basis for contractor Moderate-Risk Public Trust positions.

NACLC
National Agency Check with Local Agency Checks and Credit Check—Type of personnel security investigation used for Confidential and Secret clearances or for DOE "L" access authorizations. This investigation is not authorized for initial-hire federal employees requiring a Secret clearance or a DOE "L" Access Authorization.

National Security Position
Positions designated "non-critical sensitive," "critical sensitive," and "special sensitive." Almost all positions are designated as national security positions because of the need to access certain levels of classified information. Exceptions to this rule include ADP-I (IT1), ADP-II (IT2), and federal investigators positions.

NISP
National Industrial Security Program—Program established by E.O. 12829 and implemented by the NISP Operating Manual (NISPOM—DoD 5220.22M) for the safeguarding of classified national security information by federal contractors.

OHA
Office of Hearings and Appeals—Component of the Department of Energy (DOE) responsible for conducting hearings and issuing decisions involving personnel security clearance cases of DOE employees and contractors.

OPM
Office of Personnel Management—Government agency responsible for regulating federal employment practices. One of its major components, FISD, is the principal supplier of personnel security investigations to the Federal Government.

Period of Coverage
Also known as the "Period of Investigation"—Standard period of time covered by a Personnel Security Investigation (PSI). Each type of PSI has an overall period of coverage and specific periods of coverage for individual components (e.g. employment, police records, education, etc.) of a PSI.

Polygraph
Device that measures and records physiological responses while a subject answers a series of questions. It relies on the belief that false answers will produce distinctive measurements. Polygraph screening examinations are used as an adjunct to an SSBI for some Special Access Programs and can be either Counterintelligence-Scope or Full-Scope (lifestyle and counterintelligence questions).

PPR
Phased Periodic Reinvestigation—A periodic reinvestigation of limited scope used in lieu of a Single Scope Background Investigation—Periodic Reinvestigation (SSBI-PR). The PPR is an optional form of the SSBI-PR reserved for personnel with no unfavorable information listed in their SF86.

PR
Periodic Reinvestigation—Reinvestigations required at specific intervals to maintain a security clearance or a designated public trust position.

PRI
Periodic Reinvestigation—Type of reinvestigation used for Public Trust positions.

PRIR
Periodic Reinvestigation and Residence Coverage—Type of reinvestigation previously used for Public Trust position. This reinvestigation was eliminated in October 2010.

PRSI
Personal Subject Interview—OPM renamed the PRSI an Enhanced Subject Interview (ESI) in October 2010. It is an in depth interview of the subject of a personnel security investigation by a security investigator. The ESI is a standard component of the SSBI, SSBI-PR, PPR, BI, MBI and PRI and it can be added to an NACLC or ANACI.

PSAB
Personnel Security Appeal Board—A three member board created by a federal agency to review appeals to security clearance denials and revocations.

PSI
Personal Security Investigation—Term that encompasses all types of background investigations used for employment suitability, HSPD-12 credentialing, and security clearance determinations.

Public Trust (PT) Position
Designated federal employee and contractor positions involving sensitive unclassified duties. PT positions are designated as Moderate Risk or High Risk. These positions may involve "policy making, major program responsibility, public safety and health, law enforcement duties, fiduciary responsibilities or other duties demanding a significant degree of public trust. . . ."

PT-SBI
Public Trust-Special Background Investigation—Type of personnel security investigation previously conducted for selected High Risk Public Trust positions. This investigation was eliminated in October 2010.

"Q" Access Authorization
Department of Energy clearance that authorizes access up to Top Secret Restricted Data and Top Secret National Security Information.

RD
Restricted Data—Classified information defined by the Atomic Energy Act as concerning: 1) design, manufacture, or utilization of atomic weapons; 2) production of special nuclear material; or 3) use of special nuclear material in the production of energy. RD is considered a special access program.

ROI
Report of Investigation—A report documenting the results of a personnel security investigation by a federal or federal contract investigator.

RRU
Request for Research/Recertify/Upgrade Eligibility—Direct notification by an authorized requestor to the appropriate CAF through JPAS of any personnel security clearance status changes a JPAS user cannot make himself/herself within the system.

RSI
Reimbursable Suitability/Security Investigation—A customized investigation composed of specific investigative action(s) to gather information to resolve issues that surfaced during or after a standard OPM personnel security investigation.

SAP
Special Access Program—Certain programs established for a specific categories of classified information that impose safeguarding and access requirements that exceed those required for information at the same classification level.

SBI
Special Background Investigation—Type of personnel security investigation previously required for special-sensitive positions/Sensitive Compartmented information (SCI) eligibility. The SBI was replaced by the SSBI in December 1991.

SBPR
Single Scope Background Investigation-Periodic Reinvestigation—A shorter acronym for an SSBI-PR

SBU
Sensitive But Unclassified—Term that is being replaced by "Controlled Unclassified Information." (See also CUI and FOUO).

Scattered Castles
Consolidated personnel security investigation and clearance database of U.S. Intelligence Community personnel. The database is operated and maintained by the Director of National Intelligence.

SCI
Sensitive Compartmented Information—Category of classified information with many separate subcategories or compartments that imposes safeguarding and access restrictions that exceed those normally required for collateral classified information at the same classification level. SCI is a Special Access Program (SAP) involving intelligence sources, methods, or analytical processes.

Scope of Investigation
Standard components of an investigation, such as character references, employment records, credit report, police record checks, educational records, etc. The term "scope" is often misused to describe an investigation's "Period of Coverage."

Security Clearance
Determination made by a government personnel security adjudicator that an individual's access to classified information is clearly consistent with the interests of national security. Among adjudicators the term "Security Clearance" is being replaced by the term "Eligibility for Access."

SF85
Standard Form 85—Questionnaire for Non-Sensitive Positions. Form used for a NACI to determine an individual's suitability for federal employment or to hold certain non-sensitive, low risk federal contractor positions or for HSPD-12 credentialing.

SF85P
Standard Form 85P—Questionnaire for Public Trust Positions. Form used as the basis for an investigation to determine an individual's suitability to hold a Public Trust position and in some cases for HSPD-12 credentialing.

SF85P-S
Standard Form 85P-S—Supplemental Questionnaire for Selected Positions. Form used in addition to the SF85P as the basis for an investigation to determine an individual's suitability to hold selected High Risk Public Trust positions.

SF86
Standard Form 86—Questionnaire for National Security Positions. Form used as the basis for an investigation to determine an individual's eligibility for a security clearance or for continuation of an existing security clearance.

SII
Security/Suitability Investigations Index—OPM's online computer database of personnel security investigations accessible to federal security personnel.

SOR
Statement of Reason—Document from a security clearance adjudication facility advising an applicant of the specific reason(s) why the adjudication facility intents to deny or revoke a security clearance. The SOR also advises the applicant of his/her right to submit a written rebuttal and/or mitigating information regarding the allegations. In the contractor cases it also advises of the right to a hearing before an administrative judge.

SPIN
Special Interview—Subject interview to address unresolved issues present in a clearance application form or developed during an OPM personnel security investigation.

SPR
Secret Periodic Reinvestigation—An NACLC used as the periodic reinvestigation for a Secret clearance.

SSBI
Single Scope Background Investigation—Type of personnel security investigation used for Top Secret clearances, DOE "Q" access authorizations, Sensitive Compartmented Information (SCI), and other designated Special Access Programs (SAP).

SSBI-PR
Single Scope Background Investigation-Periodic Reinvestigation—Type of reinvestigation used when the initial clearance investigation was an SSBI and the individuals access is unchanged.

SWFT
Secure Web Fingerprint Transmission—a web-enabled biometric system to transmit electronic fingerprints to DSS and OPM.

Appendix B – HSPD-12 Credentialing Standards

UNITED STATES OFFICE OF PERSONNEL MANAGEMENT
Washington, DC 20415

The Director

July 31, 2008

MEMORANDUMFOR HEADS OF DEPARTMENTS AND AGENCIES

FROM: LINDA M. SPRINGER
               DIRECTOR

SUBJECT: Final Credentialing Standards for Issuing Personal Identity Verification Cards under HSPD-12

This memorandum provides final government-wide credentialing standards to be used by all Federal departments and agencies in determining whether to issue or revoke personal identity verification (PIV) cards to their employees and contractor personnel, including those who are non-United States citizens. These standards replace the interim standards issued in December 2007. The authority is section 2.3(b) of Executive Order 13467 of June 30, 2008.[1]

In addition to the requirements in this memorandum, credentialing determinations are also subject to the requirements of Homeland Security Presidential Directive (HSPD) 12 and issuances developed by the National Institute of Standards and Technology (NIST) and OMB.[2]

HSPD-12 Credentialing Standards

The purpose of this section is to provide minimum standards for initial eligibility for a PIV card. If an individual who otherwise meets these standards is found: 1) unsuitable for the competitive civil service under 5 CFR part 731,2) ineligible for access to classified information under E.O. 12968, or 3) disqualified from appointment in the excepted service or from

---

[1] The authority for the interim guidance was a June I, 2007 delegation by OMB for OPM to develop adjudication policy for PIV cards under a framework jointly established by OPM and the National Security Council. In the June 30, 2008 Executive Order, however, the President conferred upon OPM the continuing responsibility "for developing and implementing uniform and consistent policies and procedures to ensure the effective, efficient and timely completion of investigations and adjudications relating to . . . eligibility for logical and physical access" to federally controlled facilities or information systems (other than occasional or intermittent access). Accordingly, OPM's authority to issue these standards is now a direct delegation from the President.

[2] NIST FIPS 20 I-I, March 2006; OMB Memorandum M-05-24, August 2005.

working on a contract, the unfavorable decision is a sufficient basis for non-issuance or revocation of a PIV card.

A PIV card will not be issued[3] to a person if:

1. The individual is known to be or reasonably suspected of being a terrorist;[4]

2. The employer is unable to verify the individual's claimed identity;

3. There is a reasonable basis to believe[5] the individual has submitted fraudulent information concerning his or her identity;

4. There is a reasonable basis to believe the individual will attempt to gain unauthorized access to classified documents, information protected by the Privacy Act, information that is proprietary in nature, or other sensitive or protected information;

5. There is a reasonable basis to believe the individual will use an identity credential outside the workplace unlawfully or inappropriately; or

6. There is a reasonable basis to believe the individual will use Federally-controlled information systems unlawfully, make unauthorized modifications to such systems, corrupt or destroy such systems, or engage in inappropriate uses of such systems.

Supplemental Credentialing Standards

Many departments and agencies work with individuals who do not require a suitability determination or a security clearance. In such cases, agencies have the flexibility to apply supplemental credentialing standards in addition to the six basic standards above.[6] The supplemental standards are intended to ensure that the grant of a PIV card to an individual does not create unacceptable risk, when the individual is not subject to an adjudication of suitability for employment in the competitive service under 5 CFR part 731, of qualification for employment in the excepted service under 5 CFR part 302 or under a similar authority, or of eligibility for access to classified information under E.O. 12968. These standards may be applied based on the risk associated with the position or work on the contract.

A department or agency may consider denying or revoking a PIV card to an individual based on one of these supplemental credentialing standards.[7] In the following standards, an "unacceptable risk" refers to an unacceptable risk to the life, safety, or health of employees, contractors, vendors, or visitors; to the Government's physical assets or information systems; to personal property; to records, including classified, privileged, proprietary, financial, or medical records; or to the privacy of data subjects.

---

[3] Refer to section 2.1 of FIPS 201-1 for additional instructions on the issuance of PIV cards.

[4] OPM's background investigation includes checking names against the FBI's investigation files.

[5] A reasonable basis to believe occurs when a disinterested observer, with knowledge of the same facts and circumstances, would reasonably reach the same conclusion. Departments and agencies should consult with their legal counsel about any legal questions concerning the standards.

[6] Agencies may have unique specific categories of individuals such as guest researchers, volunteers, or intermittent, temporary, or seasonal employees. OMB Memorandum M-05-24, August 2005 directs that these credentialing standards generally apply to such categories unless they are short-term (i.e. less than 6 months) employees, in which case the agency has discretion based on risk and other factors.

[7] Although some of these factors may be similar to factors considered in making suitability determinations for competitive service employment, see 5 CFR Part 731, the determinations being made are not suitability determinations and the procedures to be applied are the procedures laid out in HSPD-12 and guidance issued thereunder, not procedures that apply to suitability determinations or suitability actions.

1. There is a reasonable basis to believe, based on the individual's misconduct or negligence in employment, that issuance of a PIV card poses an unacceptable risk;

2. There is a reasonable basis to believe, based on the individual's criminal or dishonest conduct, that issuance of a PIV card poses an unacceptable risk;

3. There is a reasonable basis to believe, based on the individual's material, intentional false statement, deception, or fraud in connection with Federal or contract employment, that issuance of a PIV card poses an unacceptable risk;

4. There is a reasonable basis to believe, based on the nature or duration of the individual's alcohol abuse without evidence of substantial rehabilitation, that issuance of a PIV card poses an unacceptable risk;

5. There is a reasonable basis to believe, based on the nature or duration of the individual's illegal use of narcotics, drugs, or other controlled substances without evidence of substantial rehabilitation, that issuance of a PIV card poses an unacceptable risk;

6. A statutory or regulatory bar prevents the individual's contract employment; or would prevent Federal employment under circumstances that furnish a reasonable basis to believe that issuance of a PIV card poses an unacceptable risk; or

7. The individual has knowingly and willfully engaged in acts or activities designed to overthrow the U.S. Government by force.

Credentialing Process

OMB's guidance and FIPS 201-1 require that departments and agencies initiate a background investigation (NACI or at least equivalent) and ensure the FBI fingerprint check is completed before issuing an identity credential. Consequently, departments and agencies should begin the credentialing process at least as soon as a person accepts an offer of employment. This may be done by authorizing the person to complete the appropriate investigation forms online through OPM's e-QIP application site. Departments and agencies are to apply the HSPD-12 credentialing standards set forth above to determine whether the results of a person's background investigation support the grant, denial or revocation of a PIV card. The PIV credentialing process does not interfere with department or agency discretion to make suitability or national security (security clearance) determinations either before or after a person has entered on duty.

Please note that Departments and agencies must verify employment authorization of all new Federal hires with the Department of Homeland Security (DHS) in accordance with OMB Memorandum 07-21, *Verifying the Employment Eligibility of Federal Employees*.[8] When credentialing for new Federal hires, departments and agencies should confirm that a query was conducted through the E-Verify system operated by the U.S. Citizenship and Immigration Services (USCIS).[9]

Departments and agencies may issue credentials using one of the following options:

Option 1 — Interim credentialing determination followed by a final credentialing determination:

---

[8] For additional information on USCIS' E-Verify program, please call 1-888-464-4218 or visit www.uscis.gov/E-Verify.

[9] If the PIV process identifies that an E-Verify query has not been conducted on a Federal employee hired after the hiring agency's enrollment in the program, that omission in the hiring process should be corrected by the agency by initiating the query as soon as possible.

When a department or agency wishes to bring a new employee or contract employee[10] on board pending completion of a background investigation or any applicable suitability and/or national security decision under 5 CFR part 731 and EO 12968 respectively, or any decision as to whether an individual is qualified for an excepted service appointment or to work on a contract, the department or agency may first make an interim credentialing determination. The interim credentialing determination must be based on:

A. The person presenting two identity source documents, at least one of which is a valid Federal or State government-issued picture identification, and

B. A National Agency Check (NAC) or an FBI National Criminal History Check (fingerprint check).

Upon completion of a background investigation, and at the time of a determination of suitability for an appointment in the competitive service under 5 CFR part 731, eligibility for access to classified information under E.O. 12968, or qualification for an appointment in the excepted service or to work on a contract, a department or agency should simultaneously make a final credentialing determination.

Option 2 – Single and final credentialing determination before employment:

A department or agency may decide to issue a PIV card only after a single and final credentialing determination is made based on a completed background investigation, or after any applicable determination of suitability for an appointment in the competitive service under 5 CFR part 731, eligibility for access to classified information under E.O. 12968, or qualification for an appointment in the excepted service or to work on a contract, is made on the same person.

Reconsideration (Appeal) Process

FIPS 201-1 requires that each department and agency establish a reconsideration (appeal) process to review requests by persons who have been denied a PIV card or have had their PIV cards revoked by that agency. The precise content of such reconsideration processes is left to the discretion of each agency or department. However, no reconsideration is required when the department or agency denies a PIV card based on the results of a negative suitability determination under 5 CFR part 731 or a decision to deny or revoke a security clearance. In those situations, the reconsideration process does not apply because the person is already entitled to seek review under applicable suitability or national security procedures. Likewise, there is no right to reconsideration in those situations where the department or agency denies a PIV card based on the results of a determination to disqualify the person from an appointment in the excepted service or from working on a contract. The reconsideration process is final and there is no further right of review.

Reciprocity of Credentialing Determinations

OMB guidance requires agencies to accept PIV card credentialing determinations for a person transferring from another department or agency when the possession of a valid Federal identity credential can be verified by the person's former department or agency and the individual has undergone the required NACI or other suitability or National Security

---

[10] Credentialing requirements also apply to other categories of individuals being brought on board and identified by agencies as requiring PIV credentials.

investigation at the person's former department or agency.[11] Beginning in 2009, agencies will record in CVS whether the person received a PIV card and its investigative basis (e.g. NACI).[12]

At a department or agency's discretion, a person may be ineligible for a PIV card when the former employing department or agency (1) determined he or she is unsuitable for employment in the competitive service under 5 CFR part 731, (2) denied (or revoked) his or her security clearance under E.O. 12968, or (3) disqualified him or her from an appointment in the excepted service or from working on a Federal contract. Credentialing determinations are maintained by the granting agency in its Identity Management System (IDMS) and the agency also provides the data to CVS for reciprocity purposes. This will allow agencies to certify to each other the HSPD-12 credentialing of employees and contractor personnel.

If a person's eligibility for a PIV card is unfavorably adjudicated for reasons other than standards 1-6 of the basic HSPD-12 Credentialing Standards, and the person is subsequently determined to be suitable, granted a clearance, qualified for appointment in the excepted service or qualified to work on a Federal contract, the department or agency should simultaneously make a new credentialing determination.

Privacy Protection/Records Management

FIPS 201-1 requires that departments and agencies ensure the privacy of applicants for identity credentials and ensure that PIV cards are used solely "to enhance security, increase government efficiency, reduce identity fraud, and protect personal privacy."

The credentialing process used by departments and agencies must follow Federal privacy laws and policies as well as the requirements for privacy protection and records management outlined in the NIST issuances concerning credentialing (e.g., FIPS 201-1).

Credentialing of non-United States Nationals

Departments and agencies are required to apply the above credentialing process and standards to non-U.S. nationals[13] who work as employees or contractor employees for Federal departments or agencies and may include others who require long-term logical or physical access to Federal government facilities whether overseas or in the United States. However, special considerations apply to non-U.S. nationals.

At U.S.-Based Locations and in U.S. Territories (Other than American Samoa and Commonwealth of the Northern Mariana Islands (CNMI):[14]

Departments and agencies must verify employment authorization of new Federal employees with the Department of Homeland Security (DHS) in accordance with OMB Memorandum 07-21, *Verifying the Employment Eligibility of Federal Employees.*

---

[12] This capacity for CVS is currently in the final development phase and is slated for introduction by October 1, 2008. OPM will provide information to agencies on utilizing this capability.

[13] The term "United States national" includes both U.S. citizens and U.S. non-citizen nationals (i.e., American Samoans).

[14] The U.S. territories of American Samoa and CNMI are not included in the "United States" as defined by the Immigration and Nationality Act, and therefore the DHS E-Verify and SAVE verification programs are unable to verify work authorization or immigration status of individuals in those locations. Agencies should conduct such background investigation as may be possible and appropriate under the circumstances in these territories. Recent legislation (Public Law 110-229) will phase-in U.S. immigration law to the CNMI in the future but this has not yet occurred.

For individuals who are non-U.S. nationals in the United States or U.S. territory for 3 years or more a background investigation (i.e. NACI or equivalent) must be initiated after employment authorization is appropriately verified through E-Verify (or immigration status is appropriately verified for those individuals not working for the Federal Government through the USCIS' Systematic Alien Verification for Entitlements (SAVE) system).[15]

For non-U.S. nationals in the U.S. or U.S. territory for less than three years, agencies may delay the background investigation until the individual has been in the U.S. or U.S. territory for three years. In such cases, an alternative facility access identity credential may be issued at the discretion of the relevant agency official as appropriate based on a risk determination. Before an alternative identity credential may be issued, the individual's employment authorization must be verified and an FBI fingerprint based criminal history must be completed if the agency decides to delay the background investigation, the agency must request an FBI Investigations Files (name check search), a name check against the Terrorist Screening Database, and a USCIS Check against SAVE.

Agencies may also choose to include additional checks as appropriate. Furthermore, agencies may establish a Special Agreement Check (SAC) with OPM for the purpose of conducting the FBI fingerprint based criminal history check and other national agency checks on non-U.S. nationals. Please contact the Agency Liaison Group (ALG) with OPM's Federal Investigative Services Division (FISD) at (703) 603-0442.

At Foreign Locations:

Departments and agencies must initiate and ensure the completion of a background investigation before applying the credentialing standards. However, the type of background investigation may vary based on standing reciprocity treaties concerning identity assurance and information exchange that exist between the United States and its Allies or agency agreements with the host country. In most cases OPM will not be able to conduct a NACI, unless the non-U.S. national is or has been residing in the United States.

The background investigation must be consistent with a NACI to the extent possible and include a fingerprint check against the FBI criminal history database, an FBI Investigations Files (name check search), and a name check against the Terrorist Screening Database. Agencies may also choose to include additional checks as appropriate.

As in the United States, for those non-U.S. nationals where a NACI or equivalent cannot be performed, an alternative facility access identity credential may be issued at the discretion of the Department of State Chief of Mission Authority, Department of Defense Installation Commander, and/or other agency official as appropriate based on a risk determination.

Further Information

For additional information or if you have questions about the HSPD-12 credentialing standards or the credentialing process, please contact the Operational Policy Group, Federal Investigative Services Division, OPM at 202-606-1042.

Whether at a U.S.-based or foreign location, reciprocity between agencies is not mandatory in the case of alternative identity credentials issued to non-U.S. nationals. Agencies may choose to honor such credentials from other agencies, but that is at their discretion.

---

[15] for additional information about USCIS's SAVE program, please call 1-888-464-4218.

Appendix C – 5 CFR 731.202

TITLE 5--Administrative Personnel, CHAPTER I--OFFICE OF PERSONNEL MANAGEMENT SUBCHAPTER B--CIVIL SERVICE REGULATIONS, PART 731--SUITABILITY

§731.202 Criteria for making suitability determinations.

(a) *General.* OPM, or an agency to which OPM has delegated authority, must base its suitability determination on the presence or absence of one or more of the specific factors (charges) in paragraph (b) of this section.

(b) *Specific factors.* In determining whether a person is suitable for Federal employment, only the following factors will be considered a basis for finding a person unsuitable and taking a suitability action:

(1) Misconduct or negligence in employment;

(2) Criminal or dishonest conduct;

(3) Material, intentional false statement, or deception or fraud in examination or appointment;

(4) Refusal to furnish testimony as required by §5.4 of this chapter;

(5) Alcohol abuse, without evidence of substantial rehabilitation, of a nature and duration that suggests that the applicant or appointee would be prevented from performing the duties of the position in question, or would constitute a direct threat to the property or safety of the applicant or appointee or others;

(6) Illegal use of narcotics, drugs, or other controlled substances without evidence of substantial rehabilitation;

(7) Knowing and willful engagement in acts or activities designed to overthrow the U.S. Government by force; and

(8) Any statutory or regulatory bar which prevents the lawful employment of the person involved in the position in question.

(c) *Additional considerations.* OPM and agencies must consider any of the following additional considerations to the extent OPM or the relevant agency, in its sole discretion, deems any of them pertinent to the individual case:

(1) The nature of the position for which the person is applying or in which the person is employed;

(2) The nature and seriousness of the conduct;

(3) The circumstances surrounding the conduct;

(4) The recency of the conduct;

(5) The age of the person involved at the time of the conduct;

(6) Contributing societal conditions; and

(7) The absence or presence of rehabilitation or efforts toward rehabilitation.

(d) *Reciprocity.* An agency cannot make a new determination under this section for a person who has already been determined suitable or fit based on character or conduct unless a new investigation is required under §731.104 or §731.106, or no new investigation is required but the investigative record on file for the person shows conduct that is incompatible with the core duties of the relevant covered position.

Appendix D – OPM Suitability Adjudication Guidance

(Extracted from Attachment 2 to NASA Desk Guide for Suitability and Security Clearance Processing—Version 2, January 2008)

ADDITIONAL CONSIDERATIONS
[5 CFR 731.202(c)]

ADDITIONAL CONSIDERATIONS	DISCUSSION
(1) The Nature of the Position for Which the Person is Applying or in Which the Person is Employed.	The more authority, responsibility, sensitivity and public trust associated with the position, the higher the risks involved and the more potential adverse impact there is to the efficiency and integrity of the service; thus the misconduct becomes more serious as a potentially disqualifying issue. However, certain kinds of conduct may result in disqualification regardless of the position.
(2) The Nature and Seriousness of the Conduct.	The more serious the conduct, the greater the potential for disqualification.
(3) The Circumstances Surrounding the Conduct.	Full facts and circumstances are essential to ensure justice to the person and to protect the interests of the Government.
(4) The Recency of the Conduct.	The more recent the conduct, the greater the potential for disqualification.
(5) The Age of the Person at the Time of the Conduct.	Offenses committed as a minor are treated as less serious than those committed as an adult, unless the offense is very recent, part of pattern, or particularly heinous.
(6) Contributing Social Conditions.	Economic and cultural conditions might be a mitigating factor if the conditions are now removed. This is generally considered in cases with relatively minor issues.
(7) The Absence or Presence of Rehabilitation or Efforts toward Rehabilitation.	Clear, affirmative evidence of rehabilitation is required for a favorable adjudication. Rehabilitation is a consideration in all cases, not just those involving alcohol and drug abuse. While formal counseling or treatment may be a consideration, other factors such as the individual's employment record, etc., may also be indications of rehabilitation.

Issue Characterization Chart

1. Intoxicants

A	B	C	D
Drunk Drunk and disorderly Liquor law violation (use or possession by minor)	Drinking and driving Driving under influence Driving while intoxicated	Illegal manufacturing Illegal sale	Pattern of excessive use as reflected in: - convictions - job performance - employment gaps - inability to function responsibly - medical treatment or poor health

2. Drug Use

A	B	C	D
Infrequent use or pos- session of marijuana Posssession of mari- juana paraphernalia Arrested or charged with possession of marijuana	Regular use or posses- sion of marijuana Infrequent use or pos- session of other con- trolled substance Possession of drug paraphernalia Cultivating marijuana for personal use	Transfer of controlled substance Possession for sale or resale Prescription fraud or forgery Sale of controlled substance Unlawful dispensing of prescription drugs Smuggling contraband drugs into prison Regular use of con- trolled substances other than marijuana	Pattern of use or exces- sive use as reflected in 1D above. manufacturing addiction importing trafficking cultivating for sale

3. Financial Responsibility

A	B	C	D
Bad check Infrequent, irregular, but deliberate delinquency in meeting financial obligations	Non-support Judgment, tax lien or other default with no attempt at restitution	Pattern of irresponsibil- ity reflected in . . . - credit history - disregard for debts - abuse of fiduciary trust	Pattern of irresponsibility in 3C, plus . . . - continuing, major, valid liabilities

4. Criminal and Immoral Conduct

A	B	C	D
	Indecent exposure Solicitation Voyeurism, peeping tom Mailing, selling, or dis- playing obscene ma- terial Obscene phone call Indecent proposal	Carnal knowledge Sodomy Prostitution Bigamy or polygamy Pimping or pandering Keeping house of ill repute Contributing to delin- quency of or corrupt- ing morals of minor Sexual harassment Other sexual miscon- duct with impact on job	Pattern of misconduct as reflected in conviction records Child molestation Sexual assault Statutory rape Incest Bestiality

5. Honesty

A	B	C	D
Non-material intentional false statement or deception or fraud in	Altering Breaking & entering Forgery	Bribery Embezzlement Grand larceny	Pattern of dishonesty as reflected in . . . - disregard for truth

examination or appointment	Fraud
	Possession of stolen
	  property
	Black market activities
	  (non-profit)
	Petty larceny
	Minor stealing or petty
	  theft
	Shoplifting
	Abuse of property
	False instrument
	Filing false statement
	Failure to file income tax
	  return
		Grand theft
		Mail theft
		Burglary
		Robbery (unarmed)
		Perjury
		False impersonation
		  (e.g., impersonating a
		  law enforcement officer)
		Interstate transportation
		  of stolen goods
		Black market activities
		  (with intent to profit)
		Income tax evasion
		Receiving stolen property
			- conviction records
			- abuse of trust, or
			- employment records
			Blackmail
			Counterfeiting
			Extortion
			Armed robbery
			Material, intentional
			  false statement or
			  deception or fraud in
			  examination or
			  appointment *
			Deliberate misrepre-
			  sentation, falsification
			  or omission of
			  material fact **

* 731.202(b)(3) applies – Use solely for falsification in the competitive examination/appointment process
** 731.202(b)(2) applies – Use for falsification outside the competitive examining process

6. Disruptive or Violent Behavior

A	B	C	D

Disorderly conduct
Disturbing the peace
Making a threat
Resisting arrest
Abusive language
Unlawful assembly
	Assault
	Damaging property
	Destroying property
	Hit & run
	Vandalism
	Criminal or malicious
	  mischief
	Harassment
	Cruelty to animals
	Hindering prosecution
	Eluding police
		Assault & battery
		Battery
		Manslaughter
		  (involuntary)
			Pattern of violence as
			  reflected in . . .
			- conviction record
			- disregard for life or
			  property
			- civil actions
			- employment record
			- medical record
			Aggravated assault
			Assault with deadly
			  weapon
			Assault with intent to
			  commit rape
			Kidnapping or abduction
			Murder
			Rape
			Arson
			Threat or assault upon
			  public official
			Manslaughter (voluntary)
			Child abuse

7. Employment Misconduct, Negligence*

A	B	C	D

Attitude
Personality Conflict
	Insubordination
	Absenteeism or attend-
	  ance problem
	Rules or regulation
	  violation
			Pattern of unemploy-
			  ability based on mis-
			  conduct or negligence
			  as reflected in employ-
			  ment history

* Other issues (use or possession of intoxicants, controlled substances and marijuana, financial responsibility, criminal immoral conduct, honesty, disruptive or violent behavior, etc.) which lead to termination or forced resignation are raised one level for adjudication purposes. For example, petty theft, a "B" issue by itself, becomes a "C" issue if it is determined to be the reason for termination or forced resignation from employment.

8. Firearms and Weapons

A	B	C	D
Possession of an unregistered firearm	Possession of a prohibited weapon Possession of illegal ammunition Carrying deadly weapon Unlawful discharge of firearms	Carrying concealed weapon or firearm Brandishing firearm Possession of firearm by felon Possession of loaded firearm Possession of explosive	Improper or illegal sale or transportation of firearms or explosives Illegal manufacture of firearms or explosives

9. Miscellaneous

A	B	C	D
Vagrancy Loitering Trespassing Minor traffic violation (traffic violations not required to be admitted on OF306 or other application material/QSP will not be considered issues)	Traffic violations greater than "A," but less than "C" Contempt of court Driving motor vehicle without owner's consent Possession of instrument of crime	Vehicular homicide Refusal to furnish testimony by 5 CFR 5.4 Tampering with witness Harboring a fugitive	Hatch Act violation Mutilation or destruction of public records Engaging in riots or civil disorder Striking against the Government Desertion

NOTE:

For conduct not listed in this chart, attempt to find a like or related issue, and use the characterization of the listed issue. If unlisted conduct does not equate with a listed issue, but seems to relate more appropriately to a level where no issues are identified (such as level A for issue 4), identify the issue at that level. Criminal offenses shown as "attempted" or "accessory to" are characterized by the base charge (e.g., Attempted Burglary equals Burglary). Characterize the seriousness of the issue by the conduct itself rather than its outcome (e.g., "assault" may warrant actual characterization as a "D" issue rather than a "B" if the details show serious injury inflicted on the victim, etc). Any uncertainty about an issue should be resolved by an experienced Adjudicator.

The ranking of probation/parole violations is determined by the nature of the issue leading to the violation. For example, a probation/parole violation for driving while intoxicated is adjudicated at level "B" while a violation for assault with a deadly weapon is adjudicated at level "D."

10. Statutory Debarment

The following issues require AUTOMATIC debarment from Federal employment for the period specified below. The legal authority for debarment must be consulted prior to taking action.

Issue	Debarment Period	Legal Authority
Illegally receiving, seeking, promising or offering compensation for services in matters affecting the Government	Indefinite	18 U.S.C 203
Current, habitual use of intoxicating beverages to excess	NTE 3 years	5 U.S.C. 7352
Evidence of disloyalty: advocates or is a knowing member of an organization that advocates the overthrow of our constitutional form of government	Indefinite	5 U.S.C. 7311; 18 U.S.C. 1918
Participation in a strike against the Government	Indefinite	5 U.S.C. 7311; 18 U.S.C. 1918
Willful and unlawful concealment, removal, muti-	Indefinite	18 U.S.C. 2071(b)

lation or destruction (or attempts) of public records and materials

Inciting, organizing, promoting, encouraging, engaging or aiding others to engage in riots or civil disorders	5 years from date the conviction becomes final	5 U.S.C. 7313
Interference by an officer or member of the armed forces with elections	Indefinite	5 U.S.C. 593
Unlawful approval of bond or sureties by a post-master	Indefinite (from employ-ment as postmaster only)	18 U.S.C. 1732
Theft or unlawful concealment of money or other property of value from a bank or safe in, or adjacent to, a bank which is a Federal Reserve member or is insured by the Federal Deposit Insurance Corporation (FDIC)	Indefinite (from positions of national bank examiner only)	18 U.S.C. 655
Unlawful trading in public property by collections or disbursing officer	Indefinite	18 U.S.C. 1901
Unauthorized disclosure of information by a farm credit examiner	Indefinite (from employ-ment as a farm credit examiner only)	18 U.S.C. 1907
Unauthorized disclosure of information by a National Agricultural Credit Corporation (NACC) examiner	Indefinite (from employ-ment as an NACC exam-iner only)	18 U.S.C. 1908
Committing treason against the United States	Indefinite	18 U.S.C. 2381
Inciting, assisting or participating in any rebellion or insurrection against the United States	Indefinite	18 U.S.C. 2383
Knowingly and willfully advocating, abetting, advising or teaching the overthrow of the United States Government or any political subdivision of the United States	5 years from the date of the conviction	18 U.S.C. 2385
Activities intended to impair the loyalty, morale and discipline of the United States Armed Forces	5 years from the date of the conviction	18 U.S.C. 2387
Conviction for misdemeanor crime (under Federal or State law) of domestic violence (use or attempted use of physical force, or the threatened use of deadly weapon, committed by current or former spouse, parent, or guardian of the victim, by a person who is cohabiting or who has cohab-ited with the victim as a spouse, parent, or guard-ian, or by a person similarly situated to a spouse, parent, or guardian of the victim).	Indefinite from any position requiring the individual to ship, transport, possess, or receive firearms or am-munition	PL 104-208 Omnibus Consoli-dated Appropria-tions Act of 1997 (amended the Gun Control Act of 1968)
Any individual who has been found guilty of, or has entered a plea of nolo contendere or guilty to any offense under Federal, State, or tribal law involv-ing crimes of violence, sexual assault, molestation, exploitation, contact or prostitution; or crimes against persons.	Indefinite from any posi-tion involving regular con-tact with or control over, Indian children	PL 101-630, Indian Child Protection and Family Vio-lence Act, dated November 28, 1990, contains minimum stan-dards. Refer also to Department of Interior or Health and Human Ser-

		vices agency regulations, as appropriate.
Knowing and willful failure to register under Section 3 of the Military Selective Service Act (50 U.S.C. App. 453)	Indefinite (only from positions in executive agencies)	5 U.S.C. 3328

- Applies to men born after December 31, 1959, who are or were required to register and who are not registered, or did not register before the requirement terminated or became inapplicable to the individual. Processing guidance can be found at 5 CFR 300.

11. Loyalty and Security

- Any *SUITABILITY* issue indicating evidence of disloyalty or terrorism that does *NOT* require statutory debarment will be adjudicated at level D.
- Homosexuality, in and of itself, while not a suitability issue, may be a security issue and must be addressed completely, when indications are present of possible susceptibility to coercion or blackmail.
- Cohabitation, adultery, illegitimate children, etc. are rarely suitability issues but, in certain circumstances, may be security issues.
- Previous instances of security violations, clearance denials or revocation are included.
- Any other issue not listed elsewhere may be a suitability issue considered in security adjudication. (Examples are judgment, reliability, and dependability issues)

12. Qualifications (including health)

- Lack of required knowledge, skills, and abilities;
- Inability to perform or poor performance which is not due to negligence or misconduct;
- Physical health issues; and
- Mental, emotional, psychological, or psychiatric issues which do not include other issues in this Appendix.

13. Issues Relating to Associates

- Issues listed in this chart that relate to an associate of the person under investigation.

14. Issues Relating to Relatives

- Issues listed in this chart that relate to a relative of the person under investigation.
- Use issue codes 13 or 14 only when the issue has a bearing on the suitability or security determination of the person under investigation.

Bribery of public officials and witnesses, and graft in connection with public service matters may also serve as a basis for debarment. Some misconduct requires removal from Federal employment, but no automatic debarment. *(See 5 CFR 735)*

- **SUITABILITY UPGRADE** – considers that multiple issues raise more serious questions about suitability

FREQUENCY	UPGRADE ACTION
2 ISSUES IN 0-36 MONTHS	RAISE BOTH ISSUES ONCE (e.g., "A" to "B")
3 OR MORE ISSUES IN 0-36 MONTHS	RAISE ALL ISSUES TWICE (e.g., "A" to "C")

- **DOWNGRADE (CONVERSION) OF ISSUES** – considers issues over 36 months old to be less serious

ISSUE		RECENCY		
		0-36 MO	37-72 MO	73-108 MO
B	CONVERTS TO	B	A	NON-ISSUE
C		C	B	A
D		D	C	B

- **DEBARMENT ACTION** (only OPM may impose the maximum 3 year period of debarment. Agencies may impose up to one year and may use the chart to determine if referral to OPM for a longer bar is warranted)

ISSUE	RECENCY		
	0-12 MO	13-24 MO	25-36 MO
C	24 MO DEBAR	18 MO DEBAR	12 MO DEBAR*
D	36 MO DEBAR	24 MO DEBAR	18 MO DEBAR*

* OPM would rarely take action on a case in which less than a 24 month bar remains. Debarment action will only be taken on C issue cases when careful assessment of the job-relatedness of the specific issue(s) involved warrants such action. The disqualifying nature of the conduct in D issue cases usually warrants debarment action.

The debarment period begins on the date of the final decision letter or 120 days after the control date, whichever is closer to the control date. **IN REMOVAL DECISION, CONSIDER IMPOSING MAXIMUM DEBARMENT RATHER THAN RELYING ON THE DEBARMENT PERIODS STATED IN THE CHART.**

- **DETERMINING RECENCY OF ISSUE(S)** – The following control dates by type of case are used in determining the recency of issue(s) for issue conversion or upgrade purposes:

TYPE OF CASE	CONTROL DATE
Civil Service Register or Outside Register Applicant Filing Directly with Agency	Date document (i.e., OF 306, etc.) containing conduct information was first considered by Personnel Office. (If referred to OPM-FIPC-SAS, use the date of referral or objection/passover)
Investigated Applicant	Date subject signed investigative data form.

Appointee or Employee	Date subject signed investigative date form. (However, if falsification/fraud of a material fact is discovered, use date conduct first identified as an issue. In addition, when determining debarment length at the final decision stage, consider imposing the maximum debarment rather than relying on the debarment periods calculated with the control date.)

When new actionable issues arise subsequent to the original control date, the control date becomes the date of occurrence of the most recent actionable conduct.

The control date for cases involving an applicant whose previous application was canceled because of pending charges is the date of referral of the current or most recent application. If two or more applications are received for suitability determination, the control date for the case is the earliest referral date.

Appendix E – 5 CFR 302.203

TITLE 5--Administrative Personnel, CHAPTER I--OFFICE OF PERSONNEL MANAGEMENT
SUBCHAPTER B--CIVIL SERVICE REGULATIONS, PART 302--EMPLOYMENT IN THE EXCEPTED SERVICE

§302.203 Disqualifying factors.
(a) The qualification standards established by an agency or by an administrative level or subdivision of an agency may provide that certain reasons disqualify an applicant for appointment. The following, among others, may be included as disqualifying reasons:

(1) Dismissal from employment for delinquency or misconduct;

(2) Criminal, infamous, dishonest, immoral, or notoriously disgraceful conduct;

(3) Intentional false statement or deception or fraud in examination or appointment;

(4) Habitual use of intoxicating beverages to excess;

(5) Reasonable doubt as to the loyalty of the person involved to the Government of the United States;

(6) Any legal or other disqualification which makes the individual unfit for service; or

(7) Lack of United States citizenship.

Appendix F – ICPG 704.3

INTELLIGENCE COMMUNITY POLICY GUIDANCE
NUMBER 704.3

DENIAL OR REVOCATION OF ACCESS TO SENSITIVE COMPARTMENTED INFORMATION, OTHER CONTROLLED ACCESS PROGRAM INFORMATION, AND APPEALS PROCESSES
(EFFECTIVE: 02 OCTOBER 2008)

A. AUTHORITY: The National Security Act of 1947, as amended; the Counterintelligence Enhancement Act of 2002, as amended; Executive Order (EO) 12333, as amended; EO 13355; EO 12968; and other applicable provisions of law.

B. APPLICABILITY: This directive applies to the Intelligence Community (IC), as defined by the National Security Act of 1947, as amended, and other departments or agencies that may be designated by the President, or designated jointly by the Director of National Intelligence (DNI), and the head of the department or agency concerned, as an element of the IC or those government entities designated to determine eligibility for Sensitive Compartmented Information (SCI) access.

C. SCOPE: Determinations regarding eligibility for initial or continued access shall be made in accordance with Intelligence Community Directive (ICD) 704, Personnel Security Standards and Procedures Governing Eligibility for Access to Sensitive Compartmented Information and other Controlled Access Program Information. Subjects who have been considered for and denied initial or continued access to SCI and other controlled access programs pursuant to the provisions of ICD 704 shall, to the extent provided herein, be afforded an opportunity to appeal the denial or revocation of such access .

D. PROCESS

　　1. Subjects whose access has been denied or revoked shall be provided with the following:

　　　　a. A comprehensive written explanation of the basis for the denial or revocation as the national security interests of the United States and other applicable laws permit;

b. An explanation of the right to be represented by counsel or other representative at their own expense; to request any documents, records or reports upon which the denial or revocation is based; and to request the entire investigative file as permitted by the national security and applicable law;

c. Any documents, records and reports upon which a denial or revocation is based to be provided within thirty (30) days of request and to the extent they would be provided if requested under applicable law, to include the Freedom of Information Act (5 U .S.C. 552) or the Privacy Act (5 U.S.C . 552a);

d. An opportunity to respond, in writing, within forty-five (45) days of receipt of relevant documentation to request a review of the determination;

e. Written notice of and reasons for the results of the review, the identity of the deciding authority in accordance with operational requirements, and written notice of the right to appeal;

f. An opportunity to appeal to the Head of their IC Element, who may either make a final determination himself, or appoint a high-level panel which shall be comprised of at least three members, two of whom shall be selected from outside the security arena. Recommendations of the panel shall be complete and in writing. Nothing in this document shall prohibit a Head of an IC Element from personally exercising the appeal authority based upon recommendations from an appeals panel. In such case, the decision of the Head of an IC Element shall be final; and

g. An opportunity to appear personally before an adjudicative or other authority, other than the investigating entity, as determined by the Head of an IC Element, to present relevant documents, materials, and information. A written summary or recording of such an appearance shall be made a permanent part of the subject's security record. The decision of any appeal panel shall be made a permanent part of the subject's security record.

2. When the Head of an IC Element, or designee, personally certifies that a procedure set forth herein cannot be made available without damaging national security interests, the particular procedure shall not be made available. This certification shall be conclusive. Should it be determined that the appeal procedures prescribed in this Policy Guidance cannot be invoked in a manner that is consistent with the national security, the individual may be denied an appeal.

3. The DNI or Principal Deputy DNI, in consultation with the relevant agency head, may take any lawful action(s) regarding a subject's access to SCI or other controlled access program information without regard to the provisions of this or any other regulation or directive.

5. This document does not create or confer on any person or entity any right to administrative or judicial review of these procedures, their implementation, or decisions or actions rendered there under. Nor does it create or confer any right, benefit, or privilege, whether substantive or procedural, for access to classified national intelligence or create or confer any substantive or procedural right, benefit, or privilege enforceable by any party against the United States or any agency, department, or instrumentality of the executive branch, its officers or employees, for any other person.

E. EFFECTIVE DATE: This ICPG is effective on the date of signature.

/s/ David R. Shedd _____   October 2, 2008 _____

Deputy Director of National Intelligence for   Date

  Policy, Plans and Requirements

ICPG 704.3

APPENDIX A – ACRONYMS

ICPG 704.3 -- DENIAL OR REVOCATION OF ACCESS TO SENSITIVE COMPARTMENTED INFORMATION, OTHER CONTROLLED ACCESS PROGRAM INFORMATION, AND APPEALS PROCESSES

DNI	Director of National Intelligence
EO	Executive Order
IC	Intelligence Community
ICD	Intelligence Community Directive
SCI	Sensitive Compartmented Information
ICPG	Intelligence Community Policy Guidance

FEDERAL SECURITY/SUITABILITY CLEARANCE CHART

This chart identifies sensitivity levels applied to all federal jobs and most federal contractor jobs. It shows the related application forms, investigation, security/suitability clearance determinations, and reinvestigations. Some jobs are designated as both Public Trust and National Security positions. When this occurs the Public Trust consideration for the job will demand a more thorough security investigation than is required for National Security Clearance at the Confidential or Secret levels.

SENSITIVITY LEVEL[1]	CATEGORY	APPLICATION FORM	TYPE OF INITIAL INVESTIGATION	SECURITY/SUITABILITY CLEARANCE DETERMINATION	REINVESTIGATION
Level 1	Non-Sensitive	SF85	None or NACI[2]	None, HSPD-12 PIV Card	None
Level 2	National Security Non-Critical Sensitive	SF86	NACLC or ANACI[3]	Secret[4] or DOE "L"	NACLC every 10 yrs
Level 3	National Security Critical Sensitive	SF86	SSBI	Top Secret	SSBI-PR every 5 yrs
Level 4	National Security Special Sensitive	SF86	SSBI[5]	Top Secret w/SCI eligibility or DOE "Q"	SSBI-PR or PPR[6] every 5 yrs
Level 5	Public Trust (PT)[7]	SF85P[8]	NACI + Credit	Moderate Risk (for contractors only)	NAC+Credit (recommended)[9]
Level 5	Public Trust	SF85P	MBI or LBI	Moderate Risk	NAC+Credit (recommended)
Level 5	National Security & PT	SF86	MBI or LBI	Secret & Moderate Risk	NACLC every 10 years
Level 6	Public Trust	SF85P	LBI or BI	High Risk	PRI (recommended)
Level 6	Public Trust	SF85P-S	LBI or BI	High Risk involving designated duties[10]	PRI (recommended)
Level 6	National Security & PT	SF86	LBI or BI	Secret & High Risk	PRI or NACLC

Footnotes:

1. Degree of sensitivity is not related to the numerical values of Sensitivity Levels (i.e. Sensitivity Level 4 is more sensitive than Sensitivity Level 6 and Level 2.
2. NACI is the minimum investigation required for federal employment. If a "Personal Identity Verification" Card is required by Homeland Security Presidential Directive 12, a minimum an NACI may be required for contractor non-sensitive, positions.
3. ANACI investigation is a combination of an NACI and NACLC and is only used for federal employment applicants.
4. Applicants for Confidential clearances are subject to the same requirements as a Secret clearance, but their reinvestigation are conducted every 15 years.
5. Some Sensitivity Level 4 positions require a polygraph examination.
6. PPR (Phased Periodic Reinvestigation) may be requested as in lieu of an SSBI-PR, when no security/suitability issues are listed on the applicant's SF86.
7. Regulations require certain federal "competitive service" jobs be designate as Public Trust positions. OPM recommends that equivalent federal excepted service and contractor positions be similarly designated and subject to appropriate investigations. Most federal agencies follow OPM's recommendation.
8. People granted Public Trust positions based on an SF85P or SF85P-S are not eligible for Confidential or Secret clearanced regardless of the investigation conducted.
9. Reinvestigations for PT positions are permitted, but not required; however, regulations are currently being revised.
10. Designated duties generally involve public safety and fiduciary responsibilities.

Appendix H – Sample Reference Affidavit

AFFIDAVIT
(SAMPLE)

<u>State of California</u>   }
                          } SS.
<u>County of Monterey</u>   }

BEFORE ME, the undersigned Notary, <u>Mary L. Jones</u>, on this <u>31</u>st day of <u>December</u>, 2010, personally appeared <u>James T. Wilson</u>, known to me to be a credible person and of lawful age, who being by me first duly sworn, on *his* oath, deposes and says:

I, James T. Wilson, reside at 795 Oak Street, Apartment 7, Anytown, California.

I met John X. Doe in about February 2007 at a party in a dormitory room at Anytown College, Anytown, CA. We became acquainted during the party and learned that we were both majoring in electrical engineering. From February 2007 to May 2010 we saw each other 2 or 3 times a week in class and about twice a week for lunch. From fall 2009 to May 2010 we saw each other at monthly meetings of the Anytown College Science and Technology Club and we were involved in a couple of computer projects together.

From February 2007 to May 2008 we also saw each other at small student parties in and around Anytown College about once every month or two. I quit going to these parties in May 2008, because students there almost always smoked marijuana. I tried it a few times and decided that I didn't want to be involved in that type of activity. When I declined to smoke marijuana with the other students, my presence at the parties became awkward and uncomfortable, so I quit going. John told me that he had started attending the parties and smoking marijuana shortly after he first arrived at Anytown College in fall 2006. I saw him smoke marijuana several times at these parties. I never saw him use marijuana at any other time, and I am not aware of him having any other involvement with illegal drugs. It was my impression that his use of marijuana was limited to these parties where others provided the marijuana.

In fall 2009 John told me that he quit smoking marijuana and stopped attending parties where marijuana was present, because it was illegal and because he was concerned about his future career and the negative impact it could have. I believe he has made a sincere commitment to abstain from any future involvement with illegal drugs. He has not disclosed his past use of marijuana to many people, but he hasn't made any special effort to conceal it either. I know that his wife is aware of it, and I believe his parents, whom I have met on 3 occasions, also know about it.

I met Alice Smith in spring 2010. Alice is a very responsible, reliable, spiritual person with strong moral convictions. She and John both graduated with honors from Anytown College in May 2010. Alice began dating John in fall 2009. Shortly after that, John joined Alice's church and became an active member of the church. I attended John and Alice's wedding in July 2010, and since then I have had dinner with them once a month either at their apartment or at local restaurants. They are happily married, expecting their first child next summer, and in the process of buying a house. John had a very good reputation in the Electrical Engineering Department of Anytown College. He was well regarded by his professors and classmates. He was rarely absent from class, always punctual and respectful of the rights of others, and consistently completed his class assignments on time.

John and I were both hired by Anytown Aerospace Corporation in June 2010, and although we are not assigned to the same department, we carpool to work and usually have lunch together every day in the company cafeteria. I have heard other engineers in his department, including his supervisor, praise his work. I have always known John to be an honest, loyal, trustworthy, responsible, dependable person. He does not drink alcohol. He is financially solvent and responsible and lives within his means. Other than his past use of marijuana, I don't believe he has ever been involved in any criminal activity. He is mentally sound and exercises good judgment and common sense. He told me he has never been outside the United States, and he has never mentioned any foreign friends, relatives, or financial interests. I believe he has the strength of character to do what is right, regardless of how unpopular or distasteful it might be and regardless of whether his actions are observed or unobserved by others. He is completely loyal to the United States and would never do anything contrary to the security interests of the United States. In October 2009 after I had knee surgery, John came to my apartment every day after school, did my grocery shopping, walked my dog, and helped me during my convalescence. In January 2010 while I was gone on vacation for two weeks, he stayed at and took good care of my apartment and my dog. In May 2010 I lent him $3,000, and he repaid me exactly as agreed in August 2010.

I have sought John's advice on a number of occasions and in doing so I disclosed some very personal information about myself to him. I have always felt comfortable talking to John about personal matters, because I am confident that he would never repeat what I told him to anyone else.

I recommend him without reservation for any position of trust and responsibility with the U.S. Government, including positions requiring access to highly classified national security information.

I swear/affirm under penalty of perjury that the foregoing is true and complete to the best of my knowledge and belief.

James T. Wilson   December 31, 2010
James T. Wilson   *[date]*

State of California   }
                       } SS.
County of Monterey   }

Subscribed and sworn to (or affirmed) before me, on this ___31st___ day of December___, 2010, by ___James T. Wilson___, proved to me on the basis of satisfactory evidence to be the person who appeared before me.

WITNESS my hand and official seal.

Mary L. Jones
Notary Public

(SEAL)

Continuation of Affidavit   Page 3 of 3 pages. Initials *JTW*

Appendix I – Sample Subject Affidavit

AFFIDAVIT
(SAMPLE)

State of California   }
                } SS.
County of Monterey   }

BEFORE ME, the undersigned Notary, _Mary L. Jones_, on this _31st_ day of _December_, 2010, personally appeared _John X. Doe_, known to me to be a credible person and of lawful age, who being by me first duly sworn, on *his* oath, deposes and says:

I, John X. Doe, reside at 123 Elm Street, Apartment 23, Anytown, California.

I first smoked marijuana at a social gathering in a dormitory room at Anytown College, Anytown, California in October 2006 at the age of 18. I was in a room with a group of about 8 people. A marijuana cigarette was passed around. I initially declined the marijuana. The others encouraged me to try it, insisting that I was being close-minded by rejecting marijuana without ever having tried it. That evening I smoked the equivalent of one-half of one marijuana cigarette. It made me feel relaxed and slightly euphoric. I smoked marijuana about once a month for the next 3 years while attending Anytown College. This always occurred at small social gatherings in dormitory rooms and private residences of other students. I never directly purchased any marijuana, but on about 15 occasions a few others and I each gave $5.00 to the student who brought the marijuana to the gathering. I first tried marijuana due to curiosity and peer pressure. I continued to smoke marijuana because I enjoyed it and because it was a normal part of the social gatherings I attended. I never smoked more than a portion of one marijuana cigarette on any one occasion. I last smoked marijuana in October 2009, shortly before I attended a career seminar at Anytown College and became aware of the Federal Drug-Free Workplace Program and the Drug-Free Workplace Act. At that time I began seriously thinking about potential employment after graduation from college. I understood that smoking marijuana was not good for my health, it would not be compatible with any professional career, particularly one in the federal government or with a federal contractor, and most importantly, it is against the law. I had been deceiving myself about the criminal nature of my activity, the possibility of being arrested, and its negative future consequences. In October 2009 I stopped going to social gatherings where marijuana was present and stopped associating with people who smoked marijuana. I redirected to interest and free time to participating in the Anytown College Science and Technology Club (ACSTC). James Wilson, the former President of ACSTC and a personal reference listed on my Standard Form 86, can attest to my constructive involvement with the club from October 2009 to May 2010. I originally met James Wilson at a social gathering in February 2007. He decided to stop attending these gatherings about a year before I did, and he later suggested that I join ACSTC. He can corroborate my past use of marijuana and my extra-curricular activities at Anytown College from February 2007 to May 2009.

My use of marijuana from October 2006 to October 2009 did not negatively affect my academic performance, my finances, my personal or academic relationships, or any other aspect of my life. Except for possession incidental to smoking marijuana and occasionally giving money to a person who brought marijuana to a social gathering, I have never possessed, bought, sold, manufactured, cultivated or trafficked any illegal drugs. I have never used any illegal drug other than marijuana. I have never misused any prescription medication. I have never received any counseling or treatment for substance abuse. I have no intention of ever illegally using any drugs in the future. If I am granted a security clearance and I have any future illegal involvement with drugs, I agree to the automatic revocation of my clearance.

I sincerely regret the poor choice I made regarding the use of marijuana. I believe I have matured significantly since then. I applied myself diligently to my studied and graduated with honors. Shortly after graduation I was hired as an electrical engineering at Anytown Aerospace Corporation, and in September 2010 at the end of my probationary period I received a superior performance appraisal. In July 2010 I married. My wife is also a recent Anytown College graduate and employed as an electrical engineer. She has never illegally used any drugs. My wife and I are expecting our first child next summer. In the last six months we saved enough money (with a little help from our parents) for the down payment on a house, and we are in the final stages of purchasing our first home. In August 2010 I began assisting the youth pastor, Michael Jones, at my church in organizing and supervising youth group activities. He is aware of my past involvement with marijuana, as are my parents, wife, and closest friends. I cannot be pressured, coerced, or blackmailed by anyone who might threaten to disclose my past use of marijuana.

I swear/affirm under penalty of perjury that the foregoing is true and complete to the best of my knowledge and belief.

John X. Doe   December 31, 2010
John X. Doe   [date]

State of California   }
                       } SS.
County of Monterey   }

Subscribed and sworn to (or affirmed) before me, on this ___31st___ day of __December__, 2010, by __John X. Doe__, proved to me on the basis of satisfactory evidence to be the person who appeared before me.

WITNESS my hand and official seal.

Mary L. Jones
Notary Public

```
┌─────────────────────────────┐
│                             │
│         (SEAL)              │
│                             │
└─────────────────────────────┘
```

Appendix J –Sample DoD SOR & Instructions

(*Sample—Extracted from Appendix 11, DoD 5200.2-R*)

Statement of Reasons (SOR)

From: Director, [Component] Central Adjudication Facility
Through: Director, Service Graphics Facility, Washington, DC
To: Mr. John Doe, SSN 000-00-0000

Subject: INTENT TO (DENY/REVOKE) ELIGIBILITY FOR ACCESS TO CLASSIFIED
            INFORMATION OR ASSIGNMENT IN SENSITIVE DUTIES

Reference: (a) Component Personnel Security Regulation

Enclosure: 1. Security Concerns and Supporting Adverse Information
            2. Instructions for Responding to a Statement of Reasons
            3. Applicable Personnel Security Guidelines [removed]

1. A preliminary decision has been made to (deny/revoke) your eligibility for access to classified information or employment in sensitive duties. Adverse information from an investigation of your personal history has led to the security concerns listed in enclosure (1) and has raised questions about your trustworthiness, reliability, and judgment. If this preliminary decision becomes final, you will not be eligible for access to classified information or employment in sensitive duties as defined by reference (a).

2. You may challenge this preliminary decision by responding, in writing, with any information or explanation which you think should be considered in reaching a final decision. Enclosure (2) is provided to assist you if you choose to respond. Enclosure (3) provides an extract from the reference (a) of the specific personnel security guidelines used in the preliminary decision to (deny/revoke) your eligibility for access to classified information or employment in sensitive duties. The preliminary decision will become final if you fail to respond to this letter. You may obtain legal counsel or other assistance; however, you must do so at your own expense.

3. You must notify your (Component) Central Adjudication Facility (CAF) via the head of your organization within 10 calendar days as to whether or not you intend to respond. If you choose not to respond, you will forfeit an opportunity to contest this unfavorable personnel security determination. Should you choose to respond, your response must be submitted via the head of your organization within 30 calendar days from the date you received this letter. Your organization may grant up to 30 additional calendar days if you submit a written request to your security office. Additional time extensions may only be granted by the CAF. Contact the point of contact with the CAF for help in preparing and forwarding your notice of an intent to respond and your response and if you wish to obtain releasable investigative records used in your case.

4. If you currently have access to classified information, this access (is/may be) suspended pending the final decision. Please direct questions regarding this letter to your security officer or the point of contact with the CAF.

Enclosure 1

Security Concerns and Supporting Adverse Information

Subject of Investigation: (Mr. John Doe, 000-00-0000)

Statement of Reasons

1. Available information tends to show criminal or dishonest conduct on your part:

    a. You were arrested on 28 March 1985 in Arlington, VA, for assault on a police officer. You were found guilty and fined $4,000.

    b. You were arrested on 10 January 1993 in Fairfax, VA, and charged with interfering with an arrest. You were released on $300 bail which you forfeited for failure to appear.

    c. You were arrested on 22 June 1994 in Fairfax, VA, on a bench warrant and charged with failure to appear (as set forth above). You were found guilty of interfering with an arrest on 10 January 1993 (as set forth above) and fined $400. The charge of failure to appear was dismissed.

2. Available information tends to show financial irresponsibility on your part:

    a. You filed for Bankruptcy under Chapter 7 in the U.S. District Court, Washington, DC on 10 August 1987. You were discharged from debts.

    b. A judgment was entered against you for $2,500 on 20 July 1992, in the Superior Court, Washington, DC. As of 30 January 1995, the judgment had not been paid.

    c. As of 20 July 1994, your credit account with the Hecht Company, Washington, DC was $350 overdue and referred for collection.

    d. As of 20 July 1994, your credit account with J.C. Penney Co., Arlington, VA, was $500 overdue and referred for collection.

Enclosure 2

Instructions for Responding to a Statement of Reasons (SOR)

A preliminary decision has been made to deny or revoke your eligibility for access to classified information or employment in sensitive duties. This preliminary decision will automatically become final if you fail to notify the Central Adjudication Facility (CAF) within 10 days that you intend to respond to the SOR. You will also lose your right to appeal that final decision if you do not submit a timely response. If this decision becomes final, you will not be eligible to handle classified information or perform sensitive duties. This could prevent you from continuing in you present position or pursuing your current career.

The SOR is based on adverse information revealed by an investigation into your personal history. Specific security concerns about your conduct or background, along with supporting adverse information, are listed in enclosure (1) to the Statement of Reasons.

These instructions are intended to help you provide the most accurate and relevant information as to why the preliminary decision should be overturned. However, it is only a guide. You should provide whatever information you think ought to be considered in reaching the final decision.

It is in your best interest to provide the most complete and accurate information possible at this stage in the decision-making process. Therefore, if you decide to challenge the preliminary decision, you must respond to the statement of reasons as completely as possible.

A. Before Responding

(1) Follow the instructions. The SOR and these instructions provide specific requirements and deadlines for compliance. You will forfeit your right to appeal if you fail to follow these instructions. You must notify the CAF via the point of contact (POC) within 10 calendar days as to whether or not you intend to respond. Should you choose to respond, your response must be submitted via the head of your organization within 30 calendar days from the date you received the SOR, unless you requested and were granted an extension of time.

(2) Review adverse information. You should carefully read the security concerns and supporting adverse information (enclosure 1) to the SOR to determine if the findings are accurate and whether there are circumstances that were not included and which might have a favorable bearing in your case. You may obtain relevant investigative or other information pertinent to the adverse information listed in enclosure (1) to the SOR. In addition, you may obtain a complete copy of releasable investigative records concerning your personal history under the provisions of the Privacy Act. Your security officer or point of contact with the CAF can help you obtain copies of these records. If you do submit a request for your investigative records, make sure to ask the POC for a time extension to the deadline for responding to the SOR since it may take up to 30 calendar days to receive these records.

(3) Obtain and organize supporting documents. Gather any documentation that supports your case. Documentation should be organized according to security concerns presented in enclosure (1). The most useful documents will be those that refute, correct, explain, extenuate, mitigate, or update the adverse information presented in enclosure (1). Examples of useful documentation include copies of correspondence; court records with details or dispositions of arrests and status of probation; receipts; copies of canceled checks or letter from creditors verifying the status of delinquent accounts; certificates of completion for rehabilitation programs; releases from judgment or attachment; transcripts of court testimony taken under oath; probation reports; copies of negotiated plea bargains; etc. Mere statements, such as "I paid those bills," "I didn't do it," or "It wasn't my fault," will not carry as much weight as supporting documentation. You may provide statements from co-workers, supervisors, your commander, friends, neighbors and others concerning your judgment, reliability and trustworthiness, and any other information that you think ought to be considered before a final decision is made.

(4) Seek assistance. An individual at your organization has been designated as a point of contact with the CAF on this matter. If this person cannot answer your questions, he or she can request assistance from higher authority. The process is designed so that individuals can represent themselves. Nonetheless, you may obtain legal counsel or other assistance in preparing your response. However, if you obtain assistance, it must be at your own expense.

Remember—it is up to you to decide whether to respond. You are responsible for the substance of your response and it must be signed by you.

B. Writing a Response

(1) Your response should be in the form of a letter from you to the CAF. You should address each security concern separately. You should admit or deny each security concern and admit or deny each item of supporting adverse information.

(2) It is essential that you address each security concern and the adverse information cited to support it. Provide any information that explains, refutes, corrects, extenuates,

mitigates or updates each security concern. Include, wherever possible, copies of the types of documents described above. Organize supporting documents in the order that they are referred to in your letter and enclose copies with your letter. Finally, be sure to sign and date your letter.

(3)   The impact of your response will depend on the extent to which you can specifically refute, correct, extenuate, mitigate, or update security concerns and adverse information presented in enclosure (1). Information that is untrue should be specifically refuted. If you believe that the adverse information, though true, does not support the security concern or presents an incomplete picture, you should provide information that explains your case. This additional information could help you disprove or lessen the security concern.

(4)   Personnel security guidelines are used by decision-makers to determine whether certain adverse information is of security concern. The guidelines pertinent to security concerns in your case are listed in enclosure (3) to the SOR. These guidelines are general rules used by decision-makers in determining whether an individual should be granted eligibility for access to classified information or permitted to perform sensitive duties. The guidelines provide a framework for weighing all available information, both favorable information, as well as adverse information that is of security concern. The guidelines help decision-makers make a common-sense determination concerning an individual's eligibility for access to classified information and performance of sensitive duties based upon all that is known about the an individual's personal history.

(5)   Place your written response and supporting documents in a single envelope or package and forward it to the CAF via the head of your organization. You organization will add its comments at that time. An endorsement by your organization that does not include substantive comments and a recommendation will be interpreted to mean that your organization concurs with the SOR. Be sure to meet the time deadlines. You will be notified in writing of the final decision. In most cases this decision will be made within 60 days. If the decision is in your favor, your access eligibility will be granted or restored. If not, you may appeal the decision to a higher authority.

Appendix K – Sample DOHA SOR and Response

DEPARTMENT OF DEFENSE
DEFENSE LEGAL SERVICES AGENCY
DEFENSE OFFICE OF HEARINGS AND APPEALS
PERSONNEL SECURITY DIVISION
POST OFFICE BOX 3990
COLUMBUS OHIO 43218 -3990

January 31, 2011

Mr. John James Jones
C/o XYZ Corporation
123 Oak Street
Anytown, CA 93000

Dear Mr. Jones:

The matter of your eligibility for security clearance has been referred to this office in accordance with DoD Directive 5220.6 (copy enclosed).

The enclosed Statement of Reasons recommends that it is not clearly consistent with the national interest to grant the security clearance requested for you and that any security clearance you currently hold should be revoked.

YOU MUST do the following:

1. Answer the Statement of Reasons by stating **"I admit"** or **"I deny"** for *each* paragraph and subparagraph. Every paragraph and subparagraph *must* be identified clearly and answered in this manner.

2. **State whether or not you wish to have a hearing or a decision without a hearing.**

3. Provide a telephone number where you can be reached during the daytime.

4. Sign your completed answer under *oath* or *affirmation* before a *Notary Public*.

5. Return your completed, *signed, notarized answer within twenty (20) days of receipt* of this letter to DOHA, P.O. Box 3990, Columbus, OH 43218-3990.

YOU MAY do the following:

Provide additional information that explains, refutes, extenuates or mitigates the information set forth in each paragraph and subparagraph of the Statement of Reasons together with documentation supporting you explanation. Doing this may provide a basis for favorable resolution of your case without the need for further proceedings.

IF YOU REQUEST A HEARING, it will be held in the United States near where you live or work before an Administrative Judge who will decide your case. An attorney employed as a Department Counsel by the Government will present evidence and argument supporting the allegations made against you in the Statement of Reasons. You may appear without counsel or with an attorney or personal representative. You may cross examine government witnesses, and introduce witnesses and other evidence in your own behalf. Further guidance about the hearing process is contained in the DoD Directive 5220.6. You may, or Department Counsel may, request a hearing.

IF YOU DO NOT WISH TO HAVE A HEARING, documentary information supporting the Statement of Reasons will be given to an Administrative Judge. You will be given a copy of this information and will have thirty (30) days to submit your written response to the Administrative Judge who will then make a decision in your case on the basis of the written materials provided to him. *If you do not submit a written response, your case will be decided on the basis of the material submitted to the Administrative Judge by Department Counsel.*

If your employer does not require that you have a security clearance for access to classified information *at any level*, your employer's security officer must provide a JCAVS (Joint Clearance And Verification System) print-out showing your separation date to the Defense Office of Hearings and Appeals (DOHA). If your company does not access JCAVS, your employer may submit notice to terminate the need for your security clearance on company letterhead, signed by the facility security officer (FSO). Upon receipt of either a JCAVS separation notification or company letter, this office will cancel any further processing of this matter and any existing security clearance you have will be terminated.

IF YOU DO NOT TIMELY ANSWER THE STATEMENT OF REASONS COMPLETELY AND PROPERLY, as instructed in subparagraphs 1 through 5 of this letter, or notify this office of termination of need for *any security clearance* within *twenty (20) days* of receipt of this letter, processing of your case will be terminated and any pending security clearance requested for you will be denied. *These actions could possibly result in loss of your present employment and have an adverse affect on any future employment requiring access to classified information.*

It is imperative you keep DOHA advised of any changes in your mailing address. Direct any questions you may have on procedures for answering the Statement of Reasons to Security Specialist xxx-xxx-xxxx.

Before submitting your notarized answer, make and keep a copy of it in case your mailed copy is lost or delayed in the mail.

DOHA Department Counsel will provide you with a copy of records he or she will use to support the allegations set forth in the Statement of Reasons whether you request a hearing or wish to have your case resolved without a hearing.

If you wish a copy of your investigative file, you may request it from the Office of Personnel Management (OPM) by writing to:

FOIP
OPM-FIPC
1137 Branchton Road
Boyers, PA 16018-0618

You should provide your full name, social security number, date and place of birth, and an address where you wish the copy of your investigative file to be sent. You must sign your request. Additionally, you should provide a copy of this cover letter so that the OPM knows that the Defense Office of Hearings and Appeals (DOHA) has no objection to the release of the investigative file directly to you.

Sincerely,

Chief, Personnel Security Division

3 Enclosures
1. Statement of Reasons
2. Privacy Act Notification [removed]
3. DoD Directive 5220.6 [removed]

DEPARTMENT OF DEFENSE
DEFENSE LEGAL SERVICES AGENCY
DEFENSE OFFICE OF HEARINGS AND APPEALS
PERSONNEL SECURITY DIVISION
POST OFFICE BOX 3990
COLUMBUS OHIO 43218 -3990

Date: <u>January 31, 2011</u>

In re:)
)
    JONES, John James   )
    SSN: 123-45-6789   )   ISCR Case: 10-00000
)
Applicant for Security Clearance   )
)

STATEMENT OF REASONS

A review of your eligibility for security clearance has been made pursuant to Executive Order 10865 (as amended) and as implemented by DoD Directive 5220.6, dated, January 2, 1992, (as amended), and this office is unable to find that it is clearly consistent with the national interest to grant you access to classified information and recommends that your case be submitted to an Administrative Judge for a determination whether to deny or revoke your security clearance. This recommendation is based on the following reasons:

    1. Guideline G: Excessive alcohol consumption often leads to the exercise of question-able judgment or the failure to control impulses, and can raise questions about an individual's reliability and trustworthiness. Available information raising this concern shows that:

    a. You consumed alcohol, at times to excess and to the point of intoxication, from at least October 2005 to at least May 2009.

    b. You were arrested on February 5, 2008 in Monterey, CA for being drunk in public. You were held in jail overnight. When released the next morning your arrest was reclassified as a "detention not amounting to an arrest."

    c. You were arrested on May 16, 2009 in Seaside, CA for driving while under the influence of alcohol. You were found guilty and placed on one year unsupervised probation, served five days in jail, fined $1,000, performed 100 hours of community service, and completed a 3-month first offender alcohol program.

    d. You received treatment from about September 2009 to December 2009 at the Sun Street Center, Salinas, CA, for your use of alcohol, as set forth in subparagraph 1.c, above.

    2. Guideline E: Conduct involving questionable judgment, lack of candor, dishonesty, or unwillingness to comply with rules and regulations can raise questions about an individu-al's reliability, trustworthiness and ability to protect classified information. Of special interest is any failure to provide truthful and candid answers during the security clearance process or any other failure to cooperate with the security clearance process. Available information raising this concern shows that:

    a. You falsified material facts on a security clearance application, dated September 3, 2010, on which you were required to reply to the following question: 24a Has your use of alcohol had a negative impact on your work performance, your professional or personal relationships, your finances, or resulted in intervention by law enforcement/public safety personnel? You failed to list that you were detained by police on February 5, 2008 in Monterey, CA for being drunk in public, as set forth in subparagraph 1.b., above.

The guidelines cited above were implemented for the Department of Defense by the Under-secretary of Defense for Intelligence on August 30, 2006 and made effective for any State-ment of Reasons issued on or after September 1, 2006 and are provided to you along with this Statement of Reasons as Enclosure 2 to the copy of DoD Directive 5220.6, dated January 2, 1992 contained in this package.

Chief, Personnel Security Division

DEPARTMENT OF DEFENSE
DEFENSE LEGAL SERVICES AGENCY
DEFENSE OFFICE OF HEARINGS AND APPEALS

In Re:)
)
    JONES, John James   )
    SSN: 123-45-6789   )   ISCR Case No. 10-00000
)
Applicant for Security Clearance   )
)

APPLICANT'S ANSWER TO STATEMENT OF REASONS

I, John James Jones, being duly sworn, hereby answer the Statement of Reasons as follows:

1.a.   You consumed alcohol, at times to excess and to the point of intoxication, from at least October 2005 to at least May 2009.

    ANSWER: I admit in part and deny in part. I consumed alcohol from October 2007 to May 29, 2009. On three occasions I consumed more alcohol than I personally feel I should have consumed. On one of those three occasions I consumed enough alcohol to meet the legal definition of driving while under the influence of alcohol. Please see my additional statement in mitigation, below.

1b.   You were arrested on February 5, 2008 in Monterey, CA for being drunk in public. You were held in jail overnight. When released the next morning your arrest was reclassi-fied as a "detention not amounting to an arrest."

    ANSWER: I admit. Please see my additional statement in mitigation, below.

1c.   You were arrested on May 16, 2009 in Seaside, CA for driving while under the influence of alcohol. You were found guilty and placed on one year unsupervised proba-tion, served five days in jail, fined $1,000, performed 100 hours of community service, and completed a three-month first offender alcohol program.

    ANSWER: I admit. Please see my additional statement in mitigation, below.

1d.   You received treatment from about September 2009 to December 2009 at the Sun Street Center, Salinas, CA, for your use of alcohol, as set forth in subparagraph 1.c, above.

    ANSWER: I admit. Please see my additional statement in mitigation, below.

2a.   You falsified material facts on a security clearance application, dated September 3, 2010, on which you were required to reply to the following question: 24a Has your use of alcohol had a negative impact on your work performance, your professional or personal relationships, your finances, or resulted in intervention by law enforcement/public safety personnel? You failed to list that you were detained by police on April 1, 2008 in Monte-rey, CA for being drunk in public, as set forth in subparagraph 1.b., above.

ANSWER: I deny. I did not intend to provide any inaccurate information on my security clearance application (SF86) of September 3, 2010. Please see my additional statement, below.

I request a hearing before a DOHA Administrative Judge. My daytime telephone number is (831) 555-0000.

Additional Statement

I am providing this additional information about myself in response to the Statement of Reasons for consideration of the Defense Office of Hearings and Appeals.

I was raised by my parents, neither of whom drinks alcohol. I left home in September 2005 to attend California State University Anytown (CSUA). Except for summers, I lived in a dormitory on CSUA campus from then until I graduated in May 2009. I did not consume any alcohol until October 2007 shortly after my 21st birthday and the beginning of my junior year at CSUA. My dormitory roommate, George Thompson, regularly drank beer in the evenings with his friends in our dormitory room. I was often present when this happened, and I began drinking beer with them. I usually drank no more than one or two 12-ounce servings, about once a week from October 2007 to May 2009.

On one occasion in fall 2007 I drank four beers over a two hour period while watching a football game on television in our dormitory room. Because I was not accustomed to drinking more than one or two beers, I believe I fell asleep while drinking the fourth beer but the others present may have thought that I passed out. After that I tried to limited myself to only one or two beers at a time and to be safe I tried to only drink beer in my dormitory room. On two subsequent occasions I failed to do this.

On February 5, 2008 I went with my roommate and a few friends to Cannery Row in Monterey, CA where there was a Mardi Gras celebration. I got caught up in the festivities and did not pay attention to how much I was drinking. I drank four beers over a four hour period. I became separated from the others, one of whom was the designated driver. While I was searching for the others, a police officer saw me walking unsteadily on the sidewalk. He stopped an asked me if I had a way to get home. I told him what happened and that I didn't have enough money for taxi fare back to CSUA. He offered to take me to the police station where I could sober up and telephone my friends later. I accepted the offer. I did not realize that I had been arrested since I was not handcuffed, nor was I fingerprinted or photographed at the police station. I did not take a field sobriety test or any other test to determine whether I was drunk. Everyone was very pleasant at the police station. I slept on a cot in an unlock jail cell until the next morning, and then telephoned my roommate who came and picked me up. No one at the police station said anything to me about being arrested or detained. I was not asked to sign anything, so I thought that the police were just providing a type of public service. It was not until my interview with a government background investigator that I became aware there was even a record of this matter. After discussing my DUI with the investigator, he asked me if I had had "any other contact with police or public safety personnel as a result of drinking alcohol?" I immediate thought of the night I spent in the jail cell in February 2008. Without hesitation I told the investigator about what happened during the Mardi Gras celebration. When answering question 24a on a security clearance application, I did not think of this incident as being an "intervention" by law enforcement personnel. I thought of it as a police community relations type of service, because I honestly believed that if I had a way to get home that night I would have been allowed to do so.

On May 16, 2009 I was with my roommate and friends celebrating our graduation from CSUA. We were at a nightclub in Monterey. My roommate was the designated driver that night.

Continuation of Affidavit   Page 2 of 3 pages. Initials *JJJ*

My roommate and I shared ownership of a car during our senior year, and we both had keys to the car. Near the end of the evening my roommate and another friend disappeared. I later learned that they met two girls and left the nightclub with them. The remaining friend and I unwisely decided to drive back to CSUA. I had four beers over a four hour period—much less than my friend—but I had two of the beers within an hour and a half of leaving the nightclub. At about 11:30 PM I was stopped by a Seaside police officer for driving too slow. He smelled alcohol on my breath; I failed a field sobriety test; and I registered 0.08% BAC on a breathalyzer test. I was arrested for DUI and held for about 6 hours before being released on my own recognizance on my promise to appear in court. At court in August 2009 I represented my, and I told the Assistant District Attorney that I wanted to plead guilty. I was ashamed of myself for risking the safety of my friend and the safety of others. I completed all requirements the judge ordered as part of my suspended sentence, including my one-year unsupervised probation which ended in August 2010 without any problems.

After my arrest on May 16, I completely quit drinking alcohol and have not consumed any alcohol since then. I left CSUA at the end of May 2009 and have not had any contact with my former roommate and college friends. I fully participated in the First Offender Alcohol Program and successfully completed the program in December 2009. My counselor advised me that I was neither an alcoholic nor an alcohol abuser, but that I had to be cautious about my drinking if I should choose to resume drinking in the future. I am sorry for having consumed more alcohol than I should have in the past. It is my intention not to consume any alcohol in the future. It has been more than a year and a half since I last consumed alcohol. I feel comfortable with the fact that I am a non-drinker, and I feel comfortable declining alcohol when it is offered to me by others.

I swear/affirm under penalty of perjury that the foregoing is true and complete to the best of my knowledge and belief.

John J. Jones _____   _February 18, 2011_____
First Middle Last Name   Date

State of California   }
                      } SS.
County of Monterey }

Subscribed and sworn to (or affirmed) before me, on this __18th__ day of __February__, 2011, by __John James Jones__, proved to me on the basis of satisfactory evidence to be the person who appeared before me.

WITNESS my hand and official seal.

_Mary L. Jones_____   ┌─────────────────┐
Notary Public   │   (SEAL)   │
                                         └─────────────────┘

Appendix L – DOHA Prehearing Guidance

Prehearing Guidance

MEMORANDUM FOR ALL APPLICANTS AND THEIR RESPECTIVE ATTORNEYS OR PERSONAL REPRESENTATIVES, AND DEPARTMENT COUNSEL

SUBJECT: Prehearing Guidance for DOHA Industrial Security Clearance (ISCR) Hearings and Trustworthiness (ADP) Hearings

In an effort to expedite the hearing in DOHA industrial security clearance cases and trustworthiness cases, the following guidance is provided to Applicants and their respective attorneys or Personal Representatives, and Department Counsel (the parties) to assist them in preparing for the hearing. This guidance is not exhaustive, and the parties should also refer to Department of Defense Directive 5220.6, *Defense Industrial Personnel Security Clearance Review Program*, for guidance on hearing matters. In the event of any conflict between this guidance and the provisions of DoD Directive 5220.6, the provisions of the Directive control. For your information, the January 2, 1992 edition of the Directive has been officially changed on four occasions: Change 1 became effective on November 22, 1993; Change 2 became effective on May 20, 1994; Change 3 became effective on February 16, 1996; and Change 4 became effective on April 20, 1999. Enclosure 2 of the Directive was amended on September 1, 2006, with the implementation of *Revised Adjudicative Guidelines For Determining Eligibility For Access To Classified Information.*

1. The hearing is an adversarial proceeding in which the parties have the responsibility to present their respective cases. The Government is normally represented by an attorney known as a Department Counsel. The Applicant has the option of appearing by himself or herself without an attorney, or being represented by an attorney selected and paid for by the Applicant, or by being represented by a Personal Representative such as a friend, family member, or union representative.

2. Your hearing may be conducted in a federal, state, county, or local hearing room, conference room, court room, or video tele-conference center, depending on the availability of suitable facilities. **Applicants employed within the United States can expect the hearing to be held at a facility within 150 miles of their residence or place of employment, or at DOHA facilities in the Washington D.C.; Los Angeles, California; Chicago, Illinois; or Boston, Massachusetts, metropolitan areas.** An effort has been made to find a location that provides an appropriate degree of privacy and that is consistent with the seriousness of the proceeding.

3. Each party is expected to be prepared to present at the hearing whatever evidence (testimonial or documentary, or both) that party intends to offer. In this regard, it should be noted that the Administrative Judge is not empowered by law to issue a subpoena. Thus, the appearance of witnesses or production of documents is purely voluntary, and is the sole responsibility of the person intending to offer that evidence. The cost associated with the attendance of witnesses is also the sole responsibility of the party calling that witness.

4. To facilitate the exchange of correspondence, proposed evidence, the handling of preliminary matters, and the scheduling of hearings, any person representing an Applicant

should file a written Entry or Notice of Appearance with both Department Counsel and the Hearing Office Docket Clerk. The facsimile number and mailing address for the particular office handing the matter appears at the top of this memorandum. No special form or format is required.

5. A party requesting a continuance of a scheduled hearing date must make a **timely showing of good cause, in writing**, to the Administrative Judge assigned the case, for any such continuance. Among the factors to be considered are the requester's diligence in readying his or her case prior to the date set for the hearing, and inconvenience to the opposing party, witnesses, and the Administrative Judge. Failure of an Applicant to appear for the scheduled hearing or to comply with an order of the Administrative Judge may result in the case being returned to the Director, DOHA for discontinuance of processing and revocation of any security clearance or assignment to sensitive duties or position the Applicant currently possesses.

6. Neither party should attempt to furnish the Administrative Judge any information relating to the case without giving the other party the opportunity to be present. Such actions constitute what are known as prohibited *ex parte* communications. Also, copies of any proposed exhibits must not be submitted to the Administrative Judge prior to any hearing, except those conducted by video tele-conference. For all other hearings, any documents to be offered as evidence should be presented at the hearing itself during the presentation of that party's case. In some instances, when an Applicant has appended documents to the response to the Statement of Reasons, the documents have been returned with an explanation that such materials are inappropriate to a pleading and that they should be resubmitted as proposed exhibits during the hearing. If such action has occurred, an Applicant should inform the Administrative Judge during the hearing, and be prepared to again offer the material previously rejected.

7. The order of proceeding is as follows: Department Counsel may make an opening statement. Then, Applicant may make an opening statement, waive opening statement, or wait until the Government has concluded calling witnesses and submitting evidence before making or waiving his or her opening statement. An opening statement is not evidence. It is merely a summary of the theory of the case and a brief explanation as to the nature of the expected testimony of witnesses and the nature of documents, which serves to provide the Administrative Judge with some general idea of the case to be better able to understand the evidence. The Government presents its case (testimony of witnesses or presentation of documents, or both) first, followed by the Applicant's case. The parties will have the opportunity to present rebuttal evidence as appropriate.

8. The parties have a wide degree of discretion in deciding what order to present the evidence in their respective cases. The Federal Rules of Evidence are used as a guide.

9. The parties should *not* mark any proposed exhibits. At the hearing, the Administrative Judge will mark the exhibits. Exhibits offered as evidence, but not admitted as such, will be retained by the Administrative Judge. As a general rule, photocopies of documents may be offered in lieu of the original, *provided* that the copies are legible. In the case of public records or business records, it is **not** required that the copies being offered be certified copies. However, nothing in this paragraph relieves a party from the responsibility of laying a proper foundation for a document when necessary. It is generally good practice to make sufficient photocopies of each proposed exhibit so that separate complete copies can be offered to the Administrative Judge and the opposing party. Preparation of such additional copies should take place before the scheduled hearing date, because there may not be any photocopying facilities available at the hearing location.

10. Witnesses will be sequestered (kept out of the hearing room while other witnesses are testifying) during the hearing, with the exception of the Applicant and any expert witness-

es. The parties may have the assistance of any expert witness, selected and paid for by the party wishing to call the witness, during the course of the hearing.

11. The Administrative Judge does not swear in Applicants or other witnesses who testify. Instead the Administrative Judge will direct their attention to, and advise them that Section 1001 of Title 18 of the United States Code applies to the proceedings. Section 1001 of Title 18 of the United States Code makes it a criminal offense, punishable by a substantial fine and period of imprisonment, to knowingly and willfully make a false or misleading statement or representation to any department or agency of the United States.

12. All witnesses are subject to cross examination, or questioning, by the other party. The scope of cross examination is not limited to the scope of the witness's direct examination. However, any cross examination must cover issues that are material and relevant to the issues in the case or the witness's credibility. As a general rule, the parties will be allowed an opportunity to conduct one redirect examination and one recross examination of a witness. The Administrative Judge may, in his or her discretion, question any witness.

13. Each party has the right to raise appropriate objections to any evidence, or portion thereof, being offered by the other party. Objections must be made in a timely fashion. Failure to raise an objection, at the time the objectionable evidence or testimony is offered, will be construed as acquiescence. When raising an objection, the objecting party should address the objection to the Administrative Judge, stating the basis for the objection. An Applicant, not represented by an attorney, need only state the objection as clearly as he or she can, in plain English. "Legalese" is not necessary. The non objecting party will be given an opportunity to respond to the objection, if he or she wishes. The Administrative Judge will rule on any objection raised. In the event an objection is overruled, the objecting party has an automatic exception to the Administrative Judge's ruling.

14. After completion of the presentation of evidence by the parties, they will have an opportunity to make closing arguments. A closing statement is not evidence. It is merely a review of the significant evidence and commentary regarding the applicability or non-applicability, as appropriate, of adjudication policy factors, both disqualifying and mitigating, as set forth in the Directive, which serves to provide the Administrative Judge with a better or "guided" understanding of the evidence. Department Counsel will go first. Applicant follows, with Department Counsel having a right to rebuttal. Applicant does not have a right to respond to Department Counsel's rebuttal argument.

15. A court reporter will be present to make an official transcript of the hearing. The court reporter will send the original transcript to the Administrative Judge, and a copy of the transcript, free of charge, to the Applicant or Applicant's attorney, as appropriate.

16. The Administrative Judge will **not** announce his or her decision to the parties at the end of the hearing. A copy of the Administrative Judge's written decision will be sent to the parties by letter explaining the provisions for appeal.

17. The Administrative Judge has the discretion to vary the provisions of this guidance upon a showing of good cause, or whenever necessary to provide for the fair and efficient administration of the proceeding under the Directive.

Robert Robinson Gales
Chief Administrative Judge
This page was last updated on:
July 12, 2007

Appendix M – DOHA Appeal Instructions

OSDGC - Defense Office of Hearings and Appeals

APPEALS OF INDUSTRIAL SECURITY
CLEARANCE CASES
UNDER DoD DIRECTIVE 5220.6

A copy of Department of Defense (DoD) Directive 5220.6 can be found on-line at
http://www.defenselink.mil/dodgc/doha/directive.html

or

http://www.dtic.mil/whs/directives/current.htm

1. Authority of Appeal Board.

    (a) The Appeal Board has authority over appeals from decisions issued by Defense Office of Hearings and Appeals Administrative Judges in industrial security clearance cases adjudicated under Executive Order 10865, as implemented by Department of Defense Directive 5220.6 ("Directive"). The Appeal Board does not have authority to handle interlocutory appeals (*i.e.*, appeals challenging actions or rulings that occur before the Administrative Judge issues a decision). The Appeal Board does not have authority over security clearance cases involving members of the U.S. military or civilian employees of the Department of Defense, which are adjudicated under Executive Order 12968, as implemented by Department of Defense Regulation 5200.2-R.

    (b) The appeal process in industrial security clearance cases is governed by the Directive, Additional Procedural Guidance, Items E3.1.28 through E3.1.35. The provisions of this document supplement, but do not supersede, the provisions of the Directive. If there is any conflict between the provisions of this document and the provisions of the Directive, then the provisions of the Directive control.

2. Communicating with Appeal Board.

    (a) Written communications about an appeal should be addressed to the Chairman, Appeal Board, P.O. Box 3656, Arlington, Virginia 22203. Written communications can be submitted to the Appeal Board by fax (703-696-1832), but the party also should send the original (without additional copies) to the Appeal Board by regular mail. Any communication should identify the applicant's full name, the case number, and the current mailing address of the applicant (or personal representative or applicant's counsel, if applicant is represented).

    (b) **Parties are advised NOT to send written communications to the Appeal Board by certified or registered mail.** Certified or registered mail tends to slow delivery. Any party who uses certified or registered mail assumes the risk of losing important appeal rights if any delay in delivery results in failure to meet an appeal deadline.

(c) Experience shows that fax submission of documents is generally reliable and significantly less costly than overnight mail delivery. Furthermore, there is no one present to accept overnight delivery that arrives on a Saturday, Sunday, or federal holiday. If a document is submitted by fax, the party should send the original of the document to the Appeal Board by regular mail.

(d) Attorneys are presumed to be authorized to act on behalf of their clients with respect to communicating with the Appeal Board on any matter pertaining to an appeal.

(e) The Appeal Board is not bound by any communication or agreement about an appeal matter that a party has with the Hearing Office, the other party, or counsel representing the other party.

3. Meaning of "days."

All references to "days" mean calendar days, not business days. If a due date falls on a Saturday, Sunday, or federal holiday, the due date will be considered to fall on the next business day.

4. Appeal deadlines.

To meet an appeal deadline, a document must be **received** by the Appeal Board on or before the due date. **An appeal deadline is not satisfied just by sending or post-marking a document on or before the due date.** Whenever a party submits a document to the Appeal Board, the party has the obligation and responsibility to take reasonable steps to ensure that the document is **received** by the Appeal Board on time.

5. Consequence of failing to meet appeal deadlines.

Failure to meet an appeal deadline could result in rejection of a late notice of appeal, default of an appeal, denial of a request for extension of time, or rejection of an appeal brief.

6. Extensions of time.

Because the timely filing of a notice of appeal is mandatory and jurisdictional, **no extensions of time to file a notice of appeal will be granted**. Except for filing notices of appeal, any party can request an extension of time to meet an appeal deadline. Any request for an extension of time must be **received** by the Appeal Board **before the deadline passes**. Absent unforeseen emergencies or unusual circumstances, last minute requests for an extension of time are strongly discouraged. The party asking for more time must take reasonable steps to inform the other party of the request when it is submitted. The request for additional time must state how much additional time is being requested, and must give specific reasons for why the request is being made. **Submitting a request for more time will not automatically result in it being granted.** The Chairman, Appeal Board may grant reasonable extensions of time upon a showing of good cause.

7. Submitting notice of appeal.

To appeal an Administrative Judge's security clearance decision, a written notice of appeal must be **received** by the Appeal Board of Defense Office of Hearings and Appeals within 15 days of the date of the Administrative Judge's decision. **Failure to meet that 15-day deadline can result in the loss of appeal rights and the Administrative Judge's decision becoming the final decision in this case.** To meet the 15-day deadline for submitting a notice of appeal, the appealing party can submit the notice appeal to the Appeal Board by fax. If the notice of appeal is submitted by fax, the original notice of appeal should be sent to the Appeal Board by regular mail.

8. Contents of notice of appeal.

The notice of appeal should contain the following:

(a) applicant's full name;

(b) applicant's Social Security number;

(c) the ISCR case number;

(d) applicant's current mailing address (preferably a home mailing address) if applicant is not represented by a lawyer or a personal representative;

(e) the mailing address of applicant's lawyer or personal representative, if applicant is represented; and

(f) a one-sentence statement that the party submitting the notice is appealing the Administrative Judge's decision.

The notice of appeal should not contain:

(a) any statements, reasons, or explanations about why the party is submitting the notice of appeal; or

(b) any arguments about the merits of the Administrative Judge's decision or the case.

9. Late notice of appeal.

Timely filing of a notice of appeal is mandatory and jurisdictional. A late notice of appeal cannot be accepted unless there has been a showing of good cause to accept a late filing. The party submitting a late notice of appeal has the burden of showing that there is good cause for accepting it late.

10. Notice of cross-appeal.

Within 10 days of receiving a notice of appeal, the nonappealing party may submit a notice of cross-appeal. The contents of a notice of cross-appeal are the same as the contents of a notice of appeal.

11. Late notice of cross-appeal.

Timely filing of a notice of cross-appeal is mandatory and jurisdictional. A late notice of cross-appeal cannot be accepted unless there has been a showing of good cause to accept a late filing. The party submitting a late notice of cross-appeal has the burden of showing that there is good cause for accepting it late.

12. Withdrawal of appeal.

A party can withdraw its appeal if it decides to not continue with the appeal. Withdrawal of an appeal will result in the Administrative Judge's decision becoming the final decision in the case. If the appealing party decides to withdraw the appeal, the appealing party should notify the Appeal Board in writing as soon as possible. The appealing party does not have to explain or justify its decision to withdraw an appeal.

13. Request or motion for stay pending appeal.

The Appeal Board does not have authority to stay or suspend an Administrative Judge's decision pending appeal. The Appeal Board does not have authority to stay or suspend actions taken pursuant to Directive, Additional Procedural Guidance, Item E3.1.27 (involving notification of applicant's employer in the event of an adverse decision being issued by an Administrative Judge).

14. Record on appeal.

Once an appeal has been timely filed, or a late appeal has been accepted upon a showing of good cause, the Appeal Board will receive the case file that was before the Administrative Judge, and the Administrative Judge's written decision. The parties do not need to supply the Appeal Board with copies of the Administrative Judge's decision or documents that are in the case file.

15. Prohibition on new evidence.

No new evidence (documentary or testimonial) can be considered by the Appeal Board on appeal. The prohibition on new evidence is mandated by the Directive. Neither party has the right to submit new evidence, nor the right to ask other persons to submit new evidence, for consideration by the Appeal Board. New evidence includes: (a) evidence about matters that occurred after the record below closed; and (b) evidence that could have been presented for the Administrative Judge's consideration during the proceedings below but was not offered by a party. Any evidence that was presented or offered by a party during the proceedings below, but which was rejected or excluded, is not new evidence. However, such rejected or excluded evidence will be considered by the Appeal Board only for the limited purpose of addressing a claim that such evidence was wrongfully or improperly rejected or excluded.

16. Format of briefs.

Whenever possible, briefs should be produced by typewriter or word processor. Each page of the brief should have at least one-inch margins on top, bottom, and both sides of each page. Each page of the brief should have text only on one side of the page. Typed or printed briefs should be submitted on regular, unlined, white paper (8 1/2 x 11). Hand-written briefs should be submitted on lined paper, preferably white paper (8 1/2 x 11). Pages of briefs should be fastened by staple or binder clip whenever possible. Do not submit briefs in binders, notebooks, plastic folders, or similar devices.

17. Contents of appeal brief.

There is no presumption of error below and the appealing party has the burden of raising claims of error with specificity and demonstrating factual or legal error that prejudiced the substantial rights of the appealing party. Failure to raise claims of error with specificity could result in the Appeal Board deciding that the appealing party has failed to meet its burden on appeal. An appeal brief should include the following:

    (a) The applicant's full name and Social Security number;

    (b) The case number;

    (c) If the applicant is the appealing party, the brief should contain the applicant's mailing address (if the applicant is not represented by a lawyer or a personal representative), or the mailing address of applicant's lawyer or personal representative (if the applicant is represented);

    (d) Specific claims of factual error, legal error, or both that are being raised by the appealing party;

    (e) Reasons, arguments, legal citations, and references to the record evidence that support each of the appealing party's claims of error; and

(f) The form of relief the appealing party is seeking (*i.e.*, remand or reversal).

The appealing party should raise appeal issues and make appeal arguments only when the party has a good-faith basis for doing so, based on the record evidence, applicable law, or a combination of the two.

18. Submission of appeal brief.

The appealing party must submit an appeal brief (original and one copy) and ensure that it is **received** by the Appeal Board within 45 days after the date of the Administrative Judge's written decision.

19. Failure to submit an appeal brief on time.

The Chairman, Appeal Board will decide whether there is good cause to accept a late appeal brief. **If the appealing party fails to submit a timely appeal brief, the Chairman, Appeal Board may enter an order affirming the Administrative Judge's decision by default**. The Chairman, Appeal Board has the authority to vacate a default order if the appealing party makes a showing of good cause for such action.

20. Submission of reply brief.

Upon receipt of a timely appeal brief, the Chairman, Appeal Board will provide a copy of the appeal brief to the nonappealing party and advise the nonappealing party of the right to submit a reply brief. The nonappealing party has the option of submitting a reply brief or deciding not to submit one. If the nonappealing party decides to submit a reply brief, the nonappealing party must ensure that the reply brief (original and one copy) is **received** by the Appeal Board within 20 days from the nonappealing party's receipt of the appeal brief. If the nonappealing party decides to not submit a reply brief, the nonappealing party should notify the Chairman, Appeal Board in writing of its decision as soon as practical.

21. Contents of reply brief.

If submitted, a reply brief should include the following:

(a) The applicant's full name and Social Security number;

(b) The case number;

(c) If the applicant is the nonappealing party, the brief should contain the applicant's mailing address (if the applicant is not represented by a lawyer or a personal representative), or the mailing address of applicant's lawyer or personal representative (if the applicant is represented);

(d) Reasons, arguments, legal citations, and references to the record evidence that:

(i) support the nonappealing party's responses to the claims of error made by the appealing party;

(ii) support a claim that the Administrative Judge's decision should be affirmed on alternate grounds; or

(iii) both.

The nonappealing party should make appeal arguments only when the party has a good-faith basis for doing so, based on the record evidence, applicable law, or a combination of the two. Upon receipt of a reply brief, the Chairman, Appeal Board will provide a copy to the appealing party.

22. <u>Absence of a reply brief</u>.

The Chairman, Appeal Board will decide whether there is good cause to accept a late reply brief. If no reply brief is received within the specified time, or if the nonappealing party states in writing that no reply brief will be submitted, the Chairman, Appeal Board will so inform the appealing party. In either situation, the appeal will be deemed ready for consideration by the Appeal Board based on the issue(s) raised by the appealing party.

23. <u>Cross-appeal briefs</u>.

If a timely cross-appeal has been filed, or a late notice of cross-appeal accepted upon a showing of good cause, the cross-appealing party will be allowed to submit written arguments in support of its cross-appeal, and the appealing party will be allowed to submit written arguments in response to the cross-appeal. To expedite the appeal process and to avoid undue delay, the Chairman, Appeal Board may, in his sole discretion, allow separate appeal and cross-appeal briefs or direct the parties to consolidate their appeal and cross-appeal arguments in a single brief from each party. The Chairman will notify the parties in writing of his decision on whether separate or consolidated briefs will be required.

24. <u>Additional briefs</u>.

No further briefs will be allowed except upon a showing of good cause. The Chairman, Appeal Board will decide whether there is good cause to accept any further briefs.

25. <u>Appeal Board decision</u>.

The Appeal Board will issue a written decision in appeal cases that are decided on the merits. A copy of the Appeal Board decision will be sent to each party. The original copy of the Appeal Board decision will be kept in the case file. The Director, DOHA shall notify the Defense Industrial Security Clearance Office (DISCO) of the Appeal Board's decision as appropriate.

26. <u>Further administrative appeals</u>.

Except for cases covered by Item E3.1.23 of the Directive's Additional Procedural Guidance, there is no further appeal from an Appeal Board decision within the Department of Defense. If the Appeal Board remands a case, the Director, DOHA will forward the case file to an Administrative Judge for further processing as appropriate.

27. <u>Researching DOHA decisions</u>.

Redacted copies of DOHA decisions issued after 1992 can be researched online at Westlaw. Redacted copies of DOHA decisions issued since November 1, 1996 are available online at http://www.defenselink.mil/dodgc/doha. Hearing Office Administrative Judge decisions may be cited as persuasive authority. However, a decision by a Hearing Office Administrative Judge is not legally binding precedent on an Administrative Judge in another case or on the Appeal Board in any case. Do not cite or rely on a decision by a Hearing Office Administrative Judge to support an appeal argument if there are Appeal Board decisions on point.

28. <u>Duties of Chairman, Appeal Board</u>.

Another member of the Appeal Board may be designated to act in the absence of the Chairman, Appeal Board. When an Appeal Board member is acting in that capacity, the Appeal Board member's actions shall have the same legal effect as actions taken by the Chairman, Appeal Board.

29. Variances from appeal procedures.

The Chairman, Appeal Board may, in his sole discretion, vary the application of the provisions of this document in a given appeal: (a) upon a showing of good cause, or (b) whenever he deems it necessary to provide for the fair and efficient handling of appeals under the Directive. **Neither the Chairman nor the Appeal Board has the authority to vary the provisions of the Directive.**

Appendix N – Sample DoD LOD and Appeal Instructions

(Sample—Extracted from Appendix 11, DoD 5200.2-R)

Letter of Denial/Revocation (LOD)

From: Director (Component) Central Adjudication Facility
Through: Director, Service Graphic Facility, Washington, D.C.
To: Mr. John Doe, SSN 000-00-0000

Subject: FINAL (DENIAL/REVOCATION) OF ELIGIBILITY FOR ACCESS TO
              CLASSIFIED INFORMATION (OR EMPLOYMENT IN SENSITIVE DUTIES)

Reference: (a) Our ltr (Ser XXX) of (date)
              (b) Personnel Security Regulation
              (c) Your ltr of (date)

Enclosure: 1. Notice of Intent to Appeal Instructions for Appealing a Letter of
                   (Denial/Revocation)

1.   Reference (a) informed you of our intent to [deny/revoke] your eligibility for access to classified information (or employment in sensitive duties). An enclosure of this reference listed security concerns and supporting adverse information supporting this preliminary decision. The contents of your response have been carefully considered. Our final assessment of the security concerns presented in reference (a) is as follows:

    a.   Criminal conduct – The information you provided successfully mitigated the security concerns related to your arrest on 28 March 1985. However, you did not sufficiently address or provide any new information to explain or mitigate the other adverse information (items 1b and 1c). Your criminal conduct is still of security concern.

    b.   Financial irresponsibility – While you provided an explanation for the Superior Court Judgment, you did not sufficiently address or provide any new information to explain the other adverse information (items 2a, 2c and 2d). Your financial irresponsibility is still of security concern.

2.   Given the remaining security concerns, effective this date, we have (denied/revoked) your eligibility for access to classified information and for assignment to a sensitive position using the provisions of reference (b).

3.   You may appeal this letter of denial (LOD) in one of two ways: (1) by notifying the Personnel Security Appeal Board (PSAB) within 10 calendar days after you receive this LOD of your intent to appeal directly to the PSAB and by providing the PSAB within the next 30 calendar days with any supporting material not already provided as to why the LOD should be overturned; or (2) by requesting a personal appearance before an Administrative Judge to present your case. If you request a personal appearance, it must be sent to the Director, Defense Office of Hearings and Appeals (DOHA), Post Office Box 3656, Arlington, Virginia, 22203 (FAX No. 703-696-6865) within 10 calendar days of your receipt of the LOD. A form

(enclosure 1) for requesting a personal appearance is appended. In either case, inform the head of your employing organization that you are submitting an appeal. Instructions for preparing and executing an appeal are provided at enclosure 1.

4. If you appeal, the case file including all of the information you supplied in accordance with reference (c) will be forwarded to either the PSAB or the DOHA for consideration. If you require an extension to a deadline, you must make your request in writing to the PSAB or the DOHA and notify the head of your organization.

5. Questions regarding this LOD should be directed to POC designated by your organization.

Use The Following If The Individual Did Not Respond to SOR:

1. Reference (a) informed you of our intent to (deny/revoke) your eligibility for access to classified information and for assignment to sensitive duties.

2. Reference (a) further informed you that the unfavorable personnel security decision would become automatically final if you failed to submit a timely response.

3. Because we have received no timely response, your eligibility for access to classified information or performance of sensitive duties is hereby (denied/revoked). This decision is final and is not subject to further appeal.

Enclosure 1

Instructions for Appealing a Letter of Denial/Revocation (LOD)

A decision has been made to deny or revoke your eligibility for access to classified information or performance of sensitive duties. This means that you are not eligible to handle classified information or perform sensitive duties. This could prevent you from continuing in your present position or pursuing your current career. The letter of denial or revocation (LOD) explains this decision. It is based on adverse information which raises security concerns about your trustworthiness, reliability or judgment.

A. How to Appeal

1. You may request a personal appearance before an administrative judge (AJ) from the Defense Office of Hearings and Appeals (DOHA). This appearance is intended to provide you with an additional opportunity to present a full picture of your situation. You will have an opportunity to orally respond to the security concerns noted in the LOD and submit supporting documentation to the AJ who will make a recommendation to the Personnel Security Appeal Board (PSAB). The PSAB will consider both your written record and the results of the personal appearance in the making of its final decision.

2. You may, however, prefer to submit a written appeal to the PSAB and forego the personal appearance. If you submit a written appeal, you may also provide supporting documentation. Having or not having a personal appearance will not bias the PSAB in making a fair determination in your case.

You must elect either (1) or (2); you may not do both.

B. Appealing Without a Personal Appearance

If you choose to appeal without a personal appearance, your written response should provide whatever information you think ought to be considered in the final decision. You should try to specifically explain, refute, extenuate, mitigate or update the security concerns presented in the LOD.

You should review enclosure (2) to the SOR, "Instructions for Responding to a Statement of Reasons (SOR)" to make sure that your appeal follows the guidelines outlined in that document. It will help you understand how to develop and write your appeal so that it can best address the security concerns in your case. Supporting documents should be provided in the order referred to in your written response.

Place your written appeal and supporting documents in a single envelope or package and forward it to the PSAB via the head of your organization. Be sure to sign and date your appeal and submit it within 30 days of your notice of appeal.

C. Appealing with a Personal Appearance

If you choose to have a personal appearance, you must provide DOHA with your request within 10 calendar days of receipt of the LOD. You will receive a notice designating the time, date and place for the personal appearance, which generally will be held within 30 calendar days after your request. The personal appearance generally will be conducted at or near your duty station if it is in the lower 48 states. For people stationed elsewhere, it will be held at or near your duty station or at a DOHA facility in the Washington, D.C. or Los Angeles, California metropolitan area.

At the appearance you will have an opportunity to present oral and documentary information on you own behalf. While the personal appearance is designed so that you can represent yourself, you may obtain legal counsel or other assistance at your own expense to be present at the appearance. If you desire counsel, arrange for it now. Postponement of the personal appearance can be granted only for good cause.

In getting ready for the personal appearance, make sure that you are prepared to address all of the security concerns and supporting adverse information. Also, make sure that your supporting documents are organized and readily accessible for presentation to the AJ presiding at the appearance and for use in answering questions.

The AJ presiding at the appearance will have already reviewed your case file. Therefore, your goal should be to clarify you reasons for overturning the LOD and adding additional information and documentation when appropriate rather than merely repeat material that you previously submitted. You will not have the opportunity to present or cross-examine witnesses. If you want the views of others presented, make sure that you obtain these views in writing (e.g., letter of reference, letters from medical authorities, etc.) and that you present these documents to the AJ. [see note below.]

During the appearance, you will be allowed to make an oral presentation and submit documentation. You may be asked questions. Answer clearly, completely, and honestly. The AJ is not there to present the government's security concerns but rather to listen to any explanations that you may have concerning your case. This individual did not make the unfavorable personnel security determination set forth in the LOD, and is there to give you an opportunity to present your case as fully as possible.

At the end of the personal appearance, you will be given an opportunity to make a closing statement. You should stress the highlights rather than review your entire case. Try to show how the weight of all available information supports overturning the unfavorable personnel security determination in your cases.

The AJ will review the case file, listen to your comments and review any additional documentation that you submit, and then make a recommendation to the PSAB as to whether the clearance, access, or employment in sensitive duties should be denied, revoked or reinstated. The PSAB is not bound by the recommendation of the AJ but will consider it, as well as any additional information you present at your appearance.

[Note: Under Secretary of Defense for Intelligence, Memorandum of 19 November 2007, "Amendment to DoD Regulation 5200.2-R to Delete Bar on Witnesses," changed the rules regarding the presentation of witnesses. Applicants are now permitted to present witnesses at personal appearances.]

Appendix O – DOHA Personal Appearance Guidance

DEPARTMENT OF DEFENSE
DEFENSE LEGAL SERVICES AGENCY
DEFENSE OFFICE OF HEARINGS AND APPEALS
WASHINGTON HEARING OFFICE
POST OFFICE BOX 3627
ARLINGTON, VIRGINIA 22203-1995
FAX (703) 696-1831

MEMORANDUM FOR ALL APPELLANTS AND THEIR RESPECTIVE ATTORNEYS OR
PERSONAL REPRESENTATIVES IN PERSONAL APPEARANCES

SUBJECT: Prehearing Guidance for Your Personal Appearance

This set of questions and answers is provided to help Appellants and their Attorneys or Personal Representatives to prepare for the Personal Appearance which was requested before a Defense Office of Hearings and Appeals (DOHA) Administrative Judge. The guidance is not exhaustive, and merely implements Department of Defense Regulation 5200.2-R, Personnel Security Program Regulation, as amended by Change 3, dated November 1, 1995. Appendix 8 of the Regulation was replaced by the Revised Adjudicative Guidelines For Determining Eligibility For Access To Classified Information, effective for all Statements of Reasons issued on or after September 1, 2006.

For those individuals whose eligibility for access to Sensitive Compartmented Information (SCI) is in issue, the following Intelligence Community Directive (ICD) and Intelligence Community Policy Guidance (ICPG) apply: ICD 704, Personnel Security Standards and Procedures Governing Eligibility for Access to Sensitive Compartmented Information and Other Controlled Access Program Information, effective October 1, 2008; ICPG 704.2, Personnel Security Adjudicative Guidelines for Determining Eligibility for Access to Sensitive Compartmented Information and Other Controlled Access Program Information, effective October 2, 2008; and ICPG 704.3, Denial or Revocation of Access to Sensitive Compartmented Information, Other Controlled Access Program Information and Appeals Processes, effective October 2, 2008.

1. **What are the steps of the proceeding?** An Administrative Judge will preside at your personal appearance and will follow the standard order of procedure described below. The proceeding will be conducted so that it can be understood by a person with no legal training. It will begin with the Administrative Judge introducing him or, herself and then asking the person who asked for the personal appearance, referred to as the Appellant, to identify himself or herself. The Government's attorney, who is called a Department Counsel, will be asked to introduce him or herself; if one is present. The Administrative Judge will then ask if there are any procedural questions that need to be answered.

The Administrative Judge has already been provided with the case file containing the documents that the Central Adjudication Facility (CAF) considered in making its adverse decision. You will then be asked to submit documents one at a time for the Administrative Judge to identify and consider which were not already provided to the CAF.

You or your representative will be asked to question any witness whom you asked to come to the proceeding on your behalf who may then be questioned by Department Counsel, if one is present, or the Administrative Judge. You will be asked to give your own oral testimony relevant to resolution of the case or have your representative ask you questions to get this information on the record. The Administrative Judge and a Department Counsel, if one is present, may also ask you questions.

At the appropriate point in the proceeding, as determined by the Administrative Judge, the Administrative Judge will ask the Department Counsel, if one is present, to question any witness for the Government. The Department Counsel may have asked a witness to be present to provide testimony as to why you should be denied eligibility for access to classified information, SCI, or performance of sensitive duties. If such a witness testifies, you will then have an opportunity for you or your representative to question the witness.

At the end of the proceeding you or your representative will have an opportunity to sum up why it is clearly consistent with the national security for you to be eligible for access to classified information, SCI, or the performance of sensitive duties, and finally the Department Counsel, if one is present, will have the opportunity to summarize the opposite point of view.

2.   **Where will the proceeding be conducted?** The personal appearance may be conducted in a hearing room, conference room, court room, or video teleconference center, depending on the availability of suitable facilities. Appellants can expect the personal appearance to be held at a facility at or near their duty station, the nearest metropolitan area, or at DOHA facilities in the Washington D.C. or Los Angeles, California metropolitan areas. An effort has been made to find a location that provides an appropriate degree of privacy and that is consistent with the seriousness of the proceeding.

3.   **Will the Government be represented by an attorney at the proceeding?** Aside from the person you may invite to assist or represent you during your· personal appearance, the Administrative Judge assigned to your case generally will be the only other Government employee present. He or she will be impartial and objective in evaluating the facts set forth in the record of the case supplied to him or her by your CAF as supplemented by what you say at the proceeding, what other witnesses, if any, have to say, and whatever additional documentation is presented by you or other witnesses, if any.

However, the Government may elect to have a Department Counsel participate in the proceeding on its behalf. If a Department Counsel attends, it will be his or her responsibility to present the testimony of any witness asked by the Department Counsel to attend the proceeding in order to support any reasons set forth by the CAF supporting denial or revocation of your security clearance. It is also the Department Counsel's responsibility, if he or she elects to attend, to ask questions of you and any witness whom you may elect to bring to the proceeding.

4.   **Do I need to hire an attorney?** You can prepare for, and appear at, the personal appearance by yourself. The proceeding is designed so that it can be understood and used by all Department of Defense civilian employees and members of the Military Departments. Many appear personally and are successful without any assistance. However, any adult of your choosing such as a co-worker, supervisor, friend, spouse, colleague, union representative or member of the clergy may assist you if you arrange for it, or you may hire an attorney at your own expense. If you want to be represented by an attorney or anyone else, you must arrange for it immediately. Postponement of the personal appearance can be granted by the

Administrative Judge only for good cause, and delay in finding an attorney or other representative is generally not a good reason to delay a scheduled personal appearance.

5.   **What should I do to prepare for my personal appearance?** The personal appearance is your opportunity to provide oral comments and documents demonstrating that your eligibility for access to classified information, SCI, or performance of sensitive duties should be granted or reinstated. The Administrative Judge presiding at your personal appearance will have already reviewed your case file which was provided to him or her by the CAF that made the decision to deny or revoke your eligibility for access to classified information or performance of sensitive duties. Therefore, your goal should be to explain your reasons for having the CAF's decision reversed by providing additional information and documentation rather than only repeating information which you had previously submitted. You may also elect to bring a person or persons to the proceeding to provide testimony as to why you should be granted a security clearance but are not required to do so and may choose to submit a letter or affidavit from them as explained in paragraph 6 below.

Make sure that your documents are organized in the order that you want to present them and bring an extra copy of the documents so that you can refer to them if needed to answer questions that may be directed to you by your representative, the Department Counsel, if one elects to be present, or the Administrative Judge. If your personal appearance is conducted by video teleconference, copies of your new documents should be forwarded to the Administrative Judge at least 24 hours in advance of your personal appearance. The facsimile number and mailing address for the particular office handling the matter appears at the top of this memorandum.

6.   **Must I or the Government bring people to the proceeding so they can testify?** If you want the Administrative Judge to consider what other people, such as supervisors, co-workers, family, friends, neighbors, doctors or other experts, have to say about your eligibility for access to classified information, SCI, or performance of sensitive duties, you may bring them to the personal appearance so they can testify in person in response to questions you ask them and questions asked them by a Department counsel, if one is present, and the Administrative Judge; or you may obtain their comments in writing for submission to the Administrative Judge at the proceeding. Usually a signed and dated letter is sufficient, but more weight can be given to statements that are in the form of a notarized affidavit or otherwise attested to as being true.

If you elect to bring witnesses to the proceeding, it is your responsibility to have them there at the outset of the proceeding as generally it will not be delayed because of the absence of a witness. You should also expect that the Administrative Judge will limit testimony to comments that are relevant and material to resolution of your case and limit the number of people allowed to testify so that information presented is not cumulative or redundant. If you experience difficulty obtaining the timely presence of witnesses that you would like to be present, you may contact the Administrative Judge and ask for assistance. He or she may, in turn, ask a Department Counsel to assist you to obtain the witness. But the Government has no subpoena power in these proceedings and Department Counsel has no obligation to provide the requested assistance in obtaining witnesses. Any election by Department Counsel to assist with facilitating the appearance of a witness does not create a right to a witness or a right to any delay.

7.   **Will the proceeding be delayed or postponed if a witness cannot be present at the scheduled place, date and time for the proceeding?** If you have elected to have anyone appear on your behalf as a witness, it is your obligation to have that person present and ready to testify at the proceeding on the day and time it has been scheduled. The proceeding will generally not be delayed because of a missing witness, regardless of the reason. You will instead generally be given an opportunity to supplement the record with a written statement from the absent witness.

8. Will I be questioned at the personal appearance? You may be questioned by your representative. You also may be questioned by the Administrative Judge if he or she wants clarification of information that is part of the record. You may also be cross-examined by a Department Counsel, if one is present. It is Department Counsel's job to ask questions that test the truthfulness of your testimony and he or she may do this in part by asking you questions based on information in the records that you submit or that are part of the case record that the CAF considered which has already been provided to the Administrative Judge. You should be prepared to answer any question clearly, completely, and honestly. You will be advised by the Administrative Judge that Section 1001 of Title 18 of the United States Code is applicable which makes it a criminal offense, punishable by a substantial fine and period of imprisonment, to knowingly and willfully make a false or misleading statement or representation to any department or agency of the United States.

9. Will the personal appearance be transcribed? The proceeding will be recorded by a court reporter. He or she will provide the Administrative Judge with a verbatim transcript and you will be given a copy.

10. Will there be formal rules of evidence that I must understand and comply with? The only requirement to admit information into the record is that it must be relevant and material to the issues affecting your eligibility for a security clearance, SCI, or performance of sensitive duties and not unduly repetitive of information that is already part of the record.

11. What documents may I submit? You may submit any documents that you believe should be considered by the Administrative Judge and ultimately by your component's Personnel Security Appeal Board (PSAB). The information can involve refutation, explanation, extenuation, or mitigation of the reasons provided to you in the Letter of Denial issued by your CAF as to why your security clearance or eligibility to perform sensitive duties should be denied or revoked. The only limitation is that the materials must be relevant and material to the concerns as to why your eligibility for security clearance, SCI, or performance of sensitive duties should be denied or revoked, and should not be unduly repetitive of information that is already part of the record.

12. What is the function of the Administrative Judge who will preside at my personal appearance? The Administrative Judge did not participate in the CAF's decision to deny or revoke your eligibility for access to classified information, SCI, or performance of sensitive duties. He or she is at the personal appearance to give you a fair opportunity to present your case as fully as possible.

13. Will the Administrative Judge make the final decision as to whether my eligibility for a security clearance or performance of sensitive duties should be denied or revoked? The Administrative Judge will prepare a recommended decision and forward it along with the record of your case to your component's PSAB. The Administrative Judge will not announce his or her recommended decision to the Appellant at the end of the personal appearance. The PSAB may adopt the recommended decision, or reverse or otherwise modify the Administrative Judge's recommendation.

14. What is the "record" of my case? The record in your case will consist of all of the information already considered by the CAF when it determined to deny or revoke your eligibility for access to classified information, SCI, or performance of sensitive duties, plus the verbatim transcript of the personal appearance, and any additional documentation which you submit at the personal appearance.

15. What regulations will the Administrative Judge consider? The Administrative Judge will consider the adjudicative guidelines, as amended, found in Department of Defense Regulation 5200.2-R, Personnel Security Program Regulation, as amended by Change 3, dated November 1, 1995. Appendix 8 of the Regulation was replaced by the Revised Adjudicative Guidelines For Determining Eligibility For Access To Classified Information, in a Memorandum dated August 30, 2006, effective for all Statements of Reasons issued on or after September 1, 2006. In other words, the Administrative Judge will use the adjudicative guidelines which were in effect when the CAF issued the Statement of Reasons giving you notice that it determined that it should deny or revoke your eligibility for access to classified information, SCI, or performance of sensitive duties. Furthermore, as indicated above, if your eligibility for access SCI is in issue, the provisions of Intelligence Community Directive (ICD) 704, Personnel Security Standards and Procedures Governing Eligibility for Access to Sensitive Compartmented Information and Other Controlled Access Program Information, effective October 1, 2008; Intelligence Community Policy Guidance (ICPG) 704.2, Personnel Security Adjudicative Guidelines for Determining Eligibility for Access to Sensitive Compartmented Information and Other Controlled Access Program Information, effective October 2, 2008; and ICPG 704.3, Denial or Revocation of Access to Sensitive Compartmented Information, Other Controlled Access Program Information and Appeals Processes, effective October 2, 2008, apply. The Revised Adjudicative Guidelines For Determining Eligibility For Access To Classified Information can be found on the DOHA web page at www.dod.mil/dodgc/doha.

16. **What will happen if I do not come to my personal appearance?** It is your responsibility to attend the personal appearance at the agreed date and time and at the location designated in the notice sent to you with these questions and answers. It is also your responsibility to request the Administrative Judge for a postponement or change of location which may be granted by the Administrative Judge only if you present him or her with reasons sufficient to demonstrate that you have been diligent and that there are good reasons for your request. If you have not been granted a postponement and fail to appear on the day and time and at the place designated by the Administrative Judge, he or she will so advise your component's PSAB with a recommendation that it sustain the CAF's determination to deny or revoke your eligibility for access to classified information, SCI, or performance of sensitive duties.

Erin C. Hogan
Chief Administrative Judge

Appendix P – Sample NOPA and Decision Letter

(Extracted from Department of Army Civilian Resources Agency Guidance Memorandum No. 01-08, 22 August 2008, Subj: Employment Suitability Adjudication Procedures)

SAMPLE NOTICE/LETTER OF PROPOSED ACTION

LETTERHEAD

REPLY TO
ATTENTION OF

(Date)

PECP-XXX

Mr. John Doe
123 Maple Avenue
Anywhere, USA 12345

Dear Mr. Doe:

This is in reference to your application for the position of Ammunition Specialist, GS-1234-05 at Alpha Army Base (AAB), USA. Your application was submitted to the selecting official for employment consideration. The selecting official has requested that your name be removed from the certificate of eligibles based on suitability considerations cited in sections (list applicable sections(s) of Title 5, Code of Federal Regulations (CFR)).

Under the provisions of section 731.202(b) of Title 5, CFR, issues that an agency may consider individually or collectively as a basis for finding an applicant unsuitable for Federal employment are:

1. Misconduct or negligence in employment;

2. Criminal or dishonest conduct;

3. Alcohol abuse of a nature and duration which suggests that the applicant would be prevented from performing the duties of the position in question or would constitute a direct threat to the property or safety of others;

4. Illegal use of narcotics, drugs, or other controlled substances, without evidence of substantial rehabilitation;

5. Knowing and willful engagement in acts or activities designed to overthrow the U.S. Government by force;

6. Any statutory or regulatory bar, which prevents the lawful employment of the person, involved in the position in question.

Management requested that your name be removed from consideration based on your prior employment at AAB from 1 January 2002 through your resignation on 30 June 2004. During this period of employment, you were suspended from duty without pay for insubordination and absence without leave (AWOL). Based on information provided by management, this disciplinary action was a result of your walking off the job. Management also indicates that a second suspension action would have been imposed had you not resigned.

In addition, the Housing Office notified the AAB Civilian Personnel Advisory Center (CPAC) that you abandoned your assigned quarters after being notified that your quarters would be inspected. It was further reported that you departed while in arrears for your rent payment – an issue currently under investigation.

Because the position for which you applied is a position of trust, the purpose of which is to handle explosive materials, we must consider misconduct and/or negligence in employment when determining you suitability for this position. In consideration of the information provided by management and the impact it may have on your employment opportunities at AAB, you are hereby given an opportunity to provide any comments or explanation you deem appropriate. You may also provide any documentary evidence, including affidavits in support of your comments. We will consider any response you provide in reaching a decision as to your suitability for Federal employment.

You are not required to respond to this letter. If you do elect to submit a response, your response must be received in our office not later than 15 days from the date of the notice. If you do not reply within the 15-day period, a suitability determination will be made based on the information currently available. Your reply, if any should be addressed to:

West Processing Center
ATTN: XXX-XX-XXXX
P.O. Box 12345
Anytown, USA 12345

If you have any questions, you may contact me by telephone at (XXX) XXX-XXXX.

Jane Smith
Human Resources Specialist

SAMPLE DECISION LETTER

LETTERHEAD

REPLY TO
ATTENTION OF

(Date)

PECP-XXX

Mr. John Doe
123 Maple Avenue
Anywhere, USA 12345

Dear Mr. Doe:

This is in reference to our letter of proposed action dated _____, copy attached. This proposal advised you of your rights including your right to reply to our notice, the time limits for filing your reply, and the process for requesting additional time to submit your reply. We have carefully considered the results of the investigation conducted by the local employing office and additional consideration cited in section 731.202(c) of Title 5, Code of Federal Regulations, when deemed pertinent:

1. The nature of the position which you applied;
2. The nature and seriousness of the conduct;
3. The circumstances surrounding the conduct;
4. The recency of the conduct;
5. The age of the person involved at the time of the conduct;
6. Contributing societal conditions; and
7. The absence or presence of rehabilitation or efforts toward rehabilitation.

Although you were provided the opportunity to respond within ___ days to the issues raised in our proposal, as of this date we have not received any information from you. Accordingly, based on our review of all currently available information, we consider you ineligible for the position of Ammunition Specialist, GS-1234-05, located at Alpha Army Base (AAB), USA. We have withdrawn any eligibility you may have been afforded from your application for this position.

As previously explained to you, the issues forming the basis for management's request to remove your name from the certificate of eligible candidates stems from your prior employment at AAB from January 1, 2002 through your resignation on June 30, 2004. During this period of employment, you were suspended from duty without pay for two (2) days for insubordination and absence without leave (AWOL). Based on information provided by management, this disciplinary action was a result of your walking off the job without authorization.

Management also stated that a second suspension action would have been imposed had you not resigned. In addition, the Housing Office notified the AAB Civilian Personnel Advisory Center that you abandoned your assigned quarters after being notified that your quarters would be inspected. It was further reported that you departed while in arrears for your rent payment – an issue currently under investigation.

The authorities for the action we are taking regarding your employment application(s) are cited in sections 731.201, 731.202(a), 731.202(b)(1), 731.205, and 731.304, Title 5 CFR. This action is effected in accordance with the procedures set forth in section 731.401 – 501, Title 5, CFR.

You have the right to appeal this decision. If you elect to file an appeal, it must be addressed to: [PUT IN THE ADDRESS OF THE SERVICING REGIONAL OFFICE OF THE U.S. MERIT SYSTEMS PROTECTION BOARD].

Your appeal must be postmarked no later than 30 days after the effective date of the action being appealed or 30 days after the date of your receipt of this decision, whichever is later. If your appeal is filed outside the 30 day time limit, you must file a motion for a waiver of the time limit with your appeal. This motion must contain evidence and argument, which shows good cause for the untimely filing. Your appeal and any motion for waiver of the time limit must be filed in writing, in any format, but it must contain the information prescribed at Section 1201.24, Title 5, CFR, United States Merit Systems Protection Board (MSPB) Practices and Procedures (enclosure 1). A copy of Title 5 CFR 1201, Subpart B, Procedures for Appellate Cases is also attached for your use (enclosure 2). Additional information regarding the MSPB – to include procedures for filing an appeal electronically – may be obtained at their internet website: http://www.mspb.gov/index.html.

If you have any questions regarding this matter, you may contact me by telephone at (XXX) XXX-XXXX.

Sincerely,

West Regional Director

Appendix Q – References & Case Citations

REFERENCES

1. **Federal Information Security Management Act (Title III of E-Government Act)**
http://frwebgate.access.gpo.gov/cgi-bin/getdoc.cgi?dbname=107_cong_public_laws&docid=f:publ347.107.pdf
2. **The Bond Amendment—50 U.S.C. 435b, Section 3002**
http://www.hss.doe.gov/deppersonnelsec/guidance/Bond_Amendment(2).pdf
3. **Executive Order 10450**
http://www.archives.gov/federal-register/codification/executive-order/10450.html
4. **Executive Order 12968**
http://frwebgate.access.gpo.gov/cgi-bin/getdoc.cgi?dbname=1995_register&docid=fr07au95-150.pdf
5. **Executive Order 13467**
http://edocket.access.gpo.gov/2008/pdf/08-1409.pdf
6. **Executive Order 13488**
http://edocket.access.gpo.gov/2009/pdf/E9-1574.pdf
7. **Adjudicative Guidelines**
http://www.state.gov/m/ds/clearances/60321.htm
8. **Homeland Security Presidential Directive—12 (HSPD-12)**
http://www.dhs.gov/xabout/laws/gc_1217616624097.shtm#1
9. **Intelligence Community Directive Number 704**
http://www.dni.gov/electronic_reading_room/ICD_704.pdf
10. **Intelligence Community Policy Guidance Number 704.1**
http://www.dni.gov/electronic_reading_room/ICPG_704_1.pdf
11. **Intelligence Community Policy Guidance Number 704.2**
http://www.dni.gov/electronic_reading_room/ICPG_704_2.pdf
12. **Intelligence Community Policy Guidance Number 704.3**
http://www.dni.gov/electronic_reading_room/ICPG_704_3.pdf
13. **Code of Federal Regulations, Title 5, Part 731—Suitability**
http://ecfr.gpoaccess.gov/cgi/t/text/text-idx?c=ecfr&tpl=/ecfrbrowse/Title05/5cfr731_main_02.tpl
14. **Office of Management and Budget (OMB), Circular No. A–130**
http://www.whitehouse.gov/omb/circulars_a130_a130trans4/
15. **OMB, Memorandum M-05-24**
http://www.whitehouse.gov/sites/default/files/omb/memoranda/fy2005/m05-24.pdf
16. **OPM Guidance on Implementing Executive Order 13488**
http://www.chcoc.gov/Transmittals/TransmittalDetails.aspx?TransmittalId=2518
17. **Federal Information Processing Standards Publication (FIPS) 201-1**
http://csrc.nist.gov/publications/fips/fips201-1/FIPS-201-1-chng1.pdf
18. **DoD Regulation 5200.2-R, Personnel Security Program**
http://www.dtic.mil/whs/directives/corres/pdf/520002r.pdf

19. DoD Regulation 5210.48, Polygraph Program
    http://www.taonline.com/securityclearances/DoDPolygraphProgram.pdf
20. National Industrial Security Program Operating Manual (DoD 5220.22-M)
    http://www.dss.mil/isp/odaa/documents/nispom2006-5220.pdf
21. DoD Directive 5220.6, Defense Industrial Security Clearance Review Program
    http://www.dtic.mil/whs/directives/corres/pdf/522006p.pdf
22. Defense Office of Hearings and Appeals (DOHA)
    http://www.dod.mil/dodgc/doha/isp.html
23. Department of Energy Manual 470.4-5, Personnel Security
    http://www.hss.energy.gov/IndepOversight/SecEvaluations/directives/m4704-5.pdf
24. Department of Energy, Office of Hearing and Appeals
    http://www.oha.doe.gov/default.asp
25. Standard Form 85
    http://www.opm.gov/forms/pdf_fill/SF85.pdf
26. Standard Form 85P
    http://www.opm.gov/forms/pdf_fill/SF85P.pdf
27. Standard Form 85PS
    http://www.opm.gov/forms/pdf_fill/SF85PS.pdf
28. Standard Form 86
    http://www.opm.gov/forms/pdf_fill/SF86.pdf
29. Optional Form 306
    http://www.opm.gov/forms/pdf_fill/of0306.pdf
30. Defense Industrial Security Clearance Office (DISCO)
    http://www.dss.mil/psco/indus_psc.html
31. Merit System Protection Board (MSPB)
    http://www.mspb.gov/
32. Money Memorandum
    http://www.dod.mil/dodgc/doha/policyinterpmemo.pdf
33. Washington Headquarters Service Administrative Instruction Number 23
    http://www.dtic.mil/whs/directives/corres/pdf/a023p.pdf
34. Army Civilian Resources Agency Guidance Memorandum No. 01-08
    http://www.chra.army.mil/guidmemo/guidmemo2/FY08/GM%2001-08%20-%20Employment%20Suitability%20Adjudication%20Procedures.pdf
35. NASA Desk Guide for Suitability and Security Clearance Processing, Version 2
    http://hspd12jpl.org/files/SuitabilitySecurityDeskGuide.pdf
36. Government Accountability Office (GAO), reports on Personnel Security Clearance Program
    http://www.gao.gov/highrisk/risks/dod-management/security_clearance.php
37. Defense Personnel Security Researcher Center (PESEREC), selected reports
    http://www.dhra.mil/perserec/reports.html
38. PERSEREC Adjudicative Desk Reference (ADR)
    http://www.dhra.mil/perserec/adr/index.htm
39. OPM Federal Investigations Notices
    http://www.opm.gov/investigate/fins/2011.aspx
40. OPM Privacy Act requests
    http://www.opm.gov/efoia/html/foia_contacts.asp

41. DSS Privacy Act requests
http://www.dss.mil/foia/priv_act_office.html

42. State Department document entitled: "Dual Citizenship – Security Clearance Implications"
http://careers.state.gov/uploads/7a/3e/7a3e09941d0d9861c0906b45b2af86d2/DualCitizenship.pdf

43. OPM document entitled: "Citizenship Laws of the World"
http://www.opm.gov/EXTRA/INVESTIGATE/is-01.PDF

44. Report of the Commission on Protecting and Reducing Government Secrecy 1997
http://www.gpo.gov/congress/commissions/secrecy/index.html

45. Debt and Home Foreclosures: Their Effect on National Security Clearances, by Sheldon Cohen, 2010
http://www.sheldoncohen.com/publications/Article%20on%20Guideline%20F.pdf

46. OMB, Wikileaks Memo
http://www.talkingpointsmemo.com/documents/2010/12/ombs-email-to-government-agencies-about-wikileaks-access.php?page=1

47. DSS, Wikileaks Notice
http://www.dss.mil/documents/AccessingPostedClassifiedInfo_9-10-2010.pdf

48. National Foundation for Credit Counseling
http://www.nfcc.org/

49. The Copyright Act (17 U.S.C. 106, et seq)
http://www.copyright.gov/title17/92chap12.html

50. DMC—Digital Millennium Copyright Act of 1999 (17 U.S.C. 1201)
http://www.copyright.gov/title17/92chap12.html

51. NET—No Electronic Theft Act of 1997 (17 U.S.C. 506)
http://www.copyright.gov/title17/92chap5.html#506

52. AHR—Audio Home Recording Act of 1992 (17 U.S.C. 1008)
http://www.copyright.gov/title17/92chap10.html#1008

Note: Some of these documents are also posted at:
http://lastpostpublishing.com/resources.aspx

CASE CITATIONS

1. Sony Corporation of America v. Universal City Studios (US Supreme Court, 464 U.S. 417 [1984])
http://www.law.cornell.edu/copyright/cases/464_US_417.htm

2. ISCR Case No. 10-00503 (illegal immigrant spouse)
http://www.dod.gov/dodgc/doha/industrial/10-00503.h1.pdf

3. ISCR Case No. 04-10400 (drug involvement)
http://www.dod.mil/dodgc/doha/industrial/04-10404.h1.html

4. ISCR Case No. 09-00521 (drug involvement)
http://www.dod.mil/dodgc/doha/industrial/09-00521.h1.pdf

5. ISCR Case No. 04-12742 (security violation)
http://www.dod.gov/dodgc/doha/industrial/04-12742.h1.pdf

6. ISCR Case No. 06-26489 (failure to report relationship with foreign national)

http://www.dod.gov/dodgc/doha/industrial/06-26489.h1.pdf
http://www.dod.gov/dodgc/doha/industrial/06-26489.a1.pdf

7.　ISCR Case No. 09-02708 (Outside Activities)
http://www.dod.mil/dodgc/doha/industrial/09-02708.h1.pdf
http://www.dod.gov/dodgc/doha/industrial/09-02708.a1.pdf

8.　ISCR Case No. 09-05655 (Outside Activities)
http://www.dod.mil/dodgc/doha/industrial/09-05655.h1.pdf

9.　ISCR Case No. 07-06767 (Outside Activities)
http://www.dod.mil/dodgc/doha/industrial/07-06767.h1.pdf
http://www.dod.gov/dodgc/doha/industrial/07-06767.a1.pdf

10.　ISCR Case No. 08-00312 (Outside Activities)
http://www.dod.mil/dodgc/doha/industrial/08-00312.h1.pdf

11.　ISCR Case No. 03-17291 (Use of IT Systems)
http://www.dod.gov/dodgc/doha/industrial/03-17291.h1.pdf

12.　ISCR Case No. 08-06538 (Use of IT Systems-Pornography)
http://www.dod.gov/dodgc/doha/industrial/08-06538.h1.pdf

13.　ISCR Case No. 07-02238 (Use of IT Systems-Pornography)
http://www.dod.gov/dodgc/doha/industrial/07-02238.h1.pdf

14.　ISCR Case No. 08-11135 (Use of IT Systems-Pornography)
http://www.dod.mil/dodgc/doha/industrial/08-11135.h1.pdf

15.　ISCR Case No. 04-11414 (App. Bd., Whole Person Factors)
http://www.dod.gov/dodgc/doha/industrial/04-11414.a1.pdf

15807885R00135

Made in the USA
Charleston, SC
21 November 2012